Jim Eames has been involved in aviation since he began work as an aviation writer in the 1960s. He has been a ministerial press secretary and aviation adviser to governments and a senior executive with Qantas. He is the author of eight books including *Taking to the Skies: Daredevils, heroes and hijackers, Australian flying stories from the Catalina to the Jumbo* and *The Flying Kangaroo: Great untold stories of Qantas . . . the heroic, the hilarious and the sometimes plain strange.*

Other books by Jim Eames

The Country Undertaker
Six Feet Under or Up in Smoke
Taking to the Skies
The Flying Kangaroo

JIM EAMES

COURAGE IN THE SKIES

The untold story of Qantas, its brave men and women and their extraordinary role in World War II

ALLEN&UNWIN
SYDNEY • MELBOURNE • AUCKLAND • LONDON

First published in 2017
This edition published in 2019

Maps by MAPgraphics based on originals by Phil Vabre

Allen & Unwin
83 Alexander Street
Crows Nest NSW 2065
Australia
Phone: (61 2) 8425 0100
Email: info@allenandunwin.com
Web: www.allenandunwin.com

Cataloguing-in-Publication details are available
from the National Library of Australia
www.trove.nla.gov.au

ISBN 978 1 76052 919 2

Set in Minion by Midland Typesetters, Australia
Printed and bound in Australia by Pegasus Media & Logistics

10 9 8 7 6

CONTENTS

FOREWORD

Over the last four years, Australians have learned a lot about our military history as we commemorate the Anzac Centenary and a Centenary of Service by our three great services—the Navy, the Army and the Air Force.

We have read and heard many stories of remarkable Australians who served with distinction in the battles they fought alongside mates and colleagues who paid the supreme sacrifice.

Two of the stories involve Hudson Fysh and Paul McGuinness who, as Lighthorsemen, landed at Gallipoli in 1915 and flew together in combat with No. 1 Squadron Australia Flying Corps. Both were decorated with Distinguished Flying Crosses. After the war, they set up Q.A.N.T.A.S Ltd to provide air services to the community in remote north Queensland. At that time, they could not have anticipated that their airline would play a substantial role in providing much needed airlift capability for Australia through the dangerous and highly challenging flying conditions presented by World War II.

This book records the story of Qantas at war between 1939 and 1945. At the outbreak of war, the RAAF was undermanned with 3500 members and ill-equipped with 246 obsolescent aircraft. The only military airlift capability in Australia was provided by the short-range twin engine Avro Anson with the capacity to lift only a handful of passengers.

Not surprisingly, the Australian government came knocking on Qantas's door for more airlift and surveillance capability. Two of the six four engine Empire flying boats, used for the Sydney to Singapore sector of the service to the UK, were transferred to No. 11 Squadron in the RAAF for surveillance. Pilots and support staff were also transitioned into the Air Force. But much of the heavy airlifting in the early part of the war was done by Qantas civilian crews flying Qantas unarmed aircraft.

In this book, Jim Eames captures the experiences of a small band of brave, professional and pioneering aircrew who confronted the dangers of war, the challenges of unforgiving oceanic and tropical weather and the uncertainty of navigation in unarmed flying boats and conventional aircraft.

I enjoyed reading about the Qantas experience in delivering nineteen Catalinas from the United States to Australia for the RAAF in 1941. With no formal conversion to the Catalina, the prospect of flying long routes over water for hours on end from isolated island to isolated island, and with the uncertainties of navigation and weather, the successful delivery of the aircraft was a major achievement.

I learned a lot about the courageous Qantas crews who flew high risk evacuation flights from Singapore and Java in front of the advancing Japanese forces in 1942. Indeed, Jim records that the costs were very high with two Empire flying boats shot down with extensive loss of life near Kupang and in the Indian Ocean south of Java. The worst period of the war for Qantas culminated with the loss of another two Empire flying boats at anchor in Roebuck Bay, Broome after a bold and unexpected attack by Japanese Zero fighters. Fortunately, on this occasion Qantas suffered no loss of crew or passengers.

As the enemy forces advanced into New Guinea, the next task was to evacuate Mount Hagen, a high-altitude airfield in the Western Highlands. This mission was also very challenging but successfully accomplished with underpowered DH-86 aircraft.

The Empire flying boats continued to conduct military charters to Darwin and then Port Moresby and Milne Bay. On occasion, they were called upon to conduct search and rescue missions. Unfortunately, two more flying boats were lost on these demanding missions. In all, Qantas lost seven of its ten Empire flying boats during the war.

As the New Guinea campaign continued, Qantas obtained three Lockheed Lodestar aircraft which were called the 'Bullybeef Bombers'. They flew continuous missions through the valleys and gaps of the Owen Stanleys, often in appalling weather, to airdrop and airload critical supplies to Australian troops in combat with the Japanese at Buna and Gona.

Towards the end of this most readable book, Jim tells the fascinating story of the Double Sunrise flight, which were established to restore the air line between Australia and the United Kingdom. Using the Catalinas to the limit of their range and capability, Qantas crews flew non-stop in secret from the Swan River at Nedlands in West Australia across the Indian Ocean to Koggala Lake in Ceylon (now Sri Lanka). With difficult winds and weather and the threat of enemy air activity, the flights were successfully conducted without loss.

This is a book about a great generation of Qantas aircrew who served and sacrificed for their nation. While those Qantas aircrew who transferred into the Royal Australian Air Force won recognition for their service and courage, those who stayed with Qantas and faced similar risks and acted with similar professionalism and courage were not recognised by their nation. In my view this was most disappointing and must never happen again in similar circumstances.

I commend this book about Qantas at war to the reader.

Air Chief Marshal Sir Angus Houston AK, AFC (Ret'd)

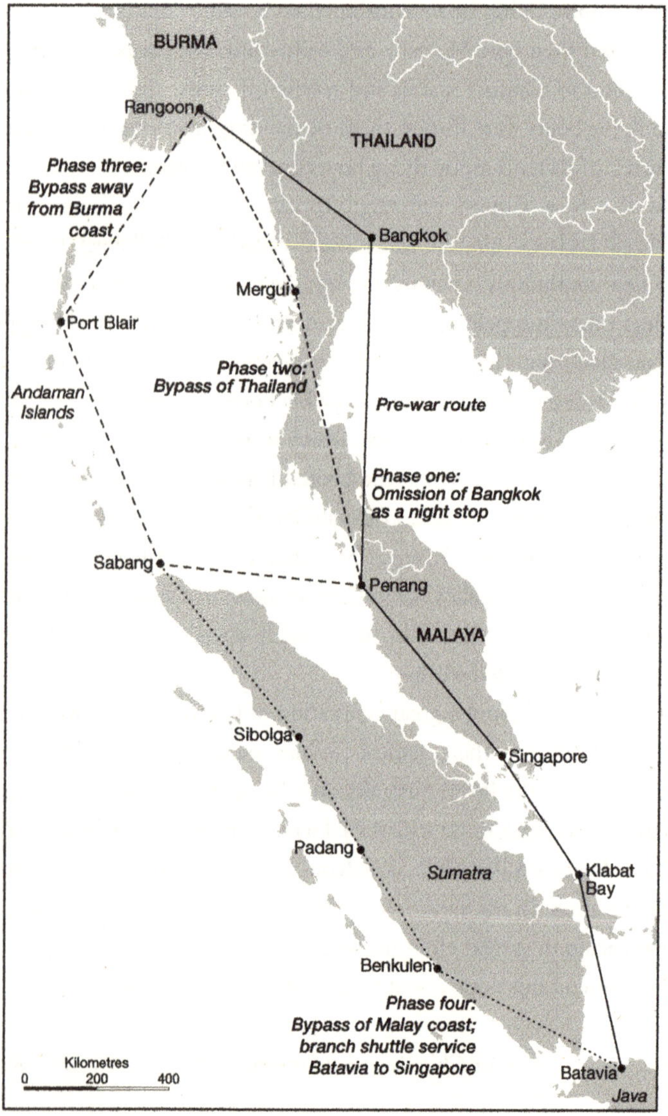

The four-phase plan adopted by Qantas and Imperial when the Japanese entered the war was first to omit Bangkok as a night stop and then move the operation of the flying boats further away from the Japanese as they advanced down through Malaya.

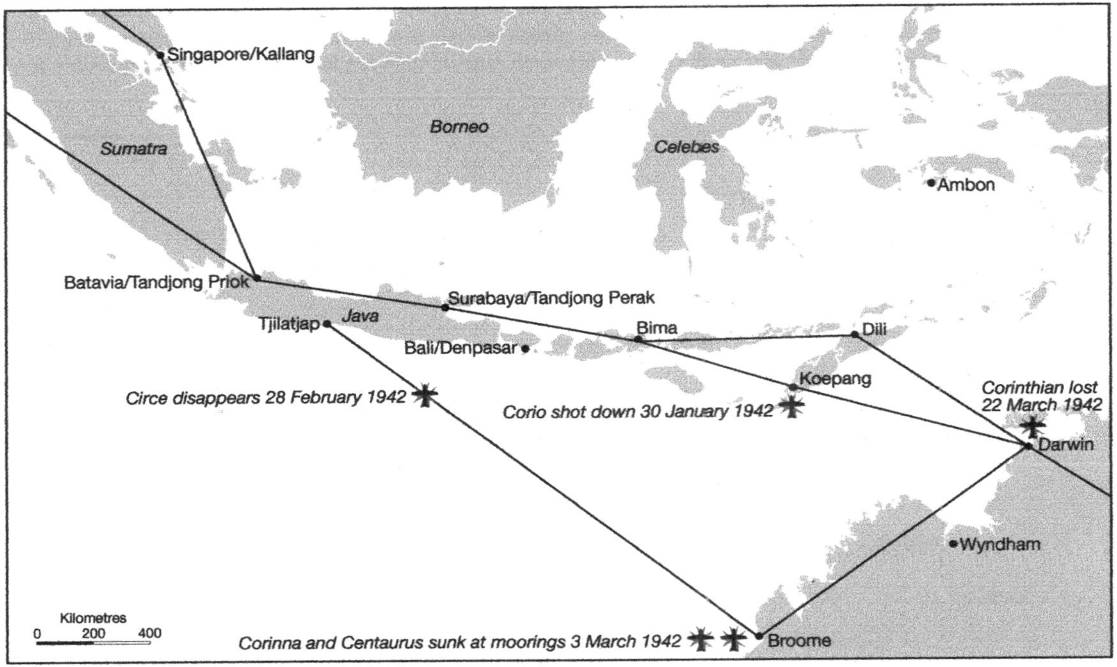

QEA and RAAF Empire flying boats lost in the first four months of the war in the Pacific: *Corio* off Koepang, *Circe* off Java, *Corinna* and *Centaurus* at Broome, and *Corinthian* at Darwin in March 1942.

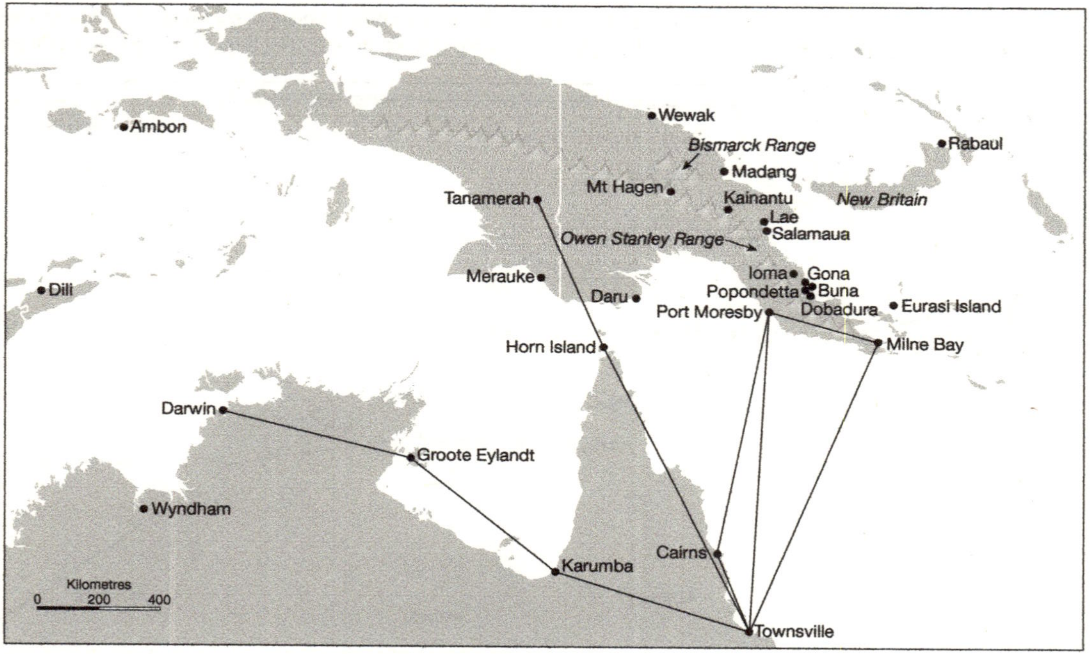

QEA operations in the South-West Pacific from 1942 as the Japanese advanced through Papua New Guinea. While supply operations continued to a devastated Darwin, rescue, support and medical evacuations missions also continued into war zones at Port Moresby, Milne Bay and into Dutch New Guinea.

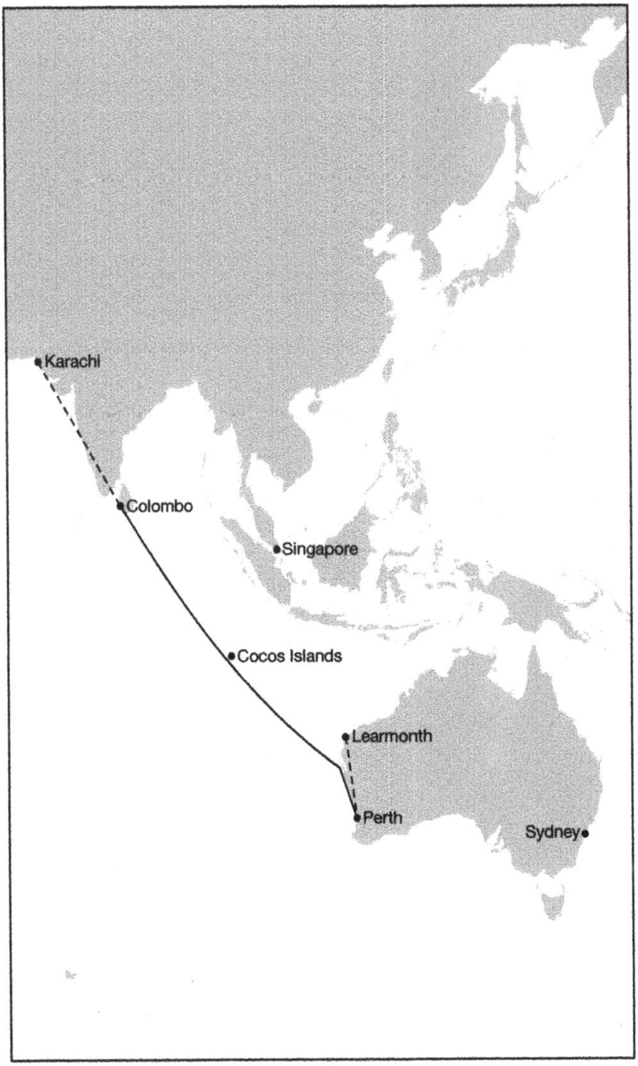

From 1943 the route of Qantas's secret Indian Ocean service, which became known as the Double Sunrise service, re-established the link between Australian and the United Kingdom that had been severed by the loss of Singapore. Qantas Catalinas made 271 ocean crossings in an operation that sometimes required in excess of thirty hours in the air.

INTRODUCTION

As Qantas approaches its one hundredth anniversary in 2020, it remains the oldest airline in the English-speaking world. Its birth in outback Queensland in 1920 might have come just seventeen years after Wilbur and Orville Wright lifted off the ground at Kitty Hawk, but its Australian pioneering heritage can be traced back to Lawrence Hargrave, who in 1894, at windy Stanwell Park south of Sydney, strapped four of his box kite inventions together and flew for sixteen feet.

Hargraves was to be the first of many. Those who followed him—the likes of Charles Kingsford Smith, Charles Ulm, Harry Hawker and a brace of other adventurers—would carve an indelible Australian identity on almost every aspect of world aviation. They would be the first to cross most of the world's major oceans, with the exception of the Atlantic, and be at the forefront of nearly every aspect of aviation development.

Like most of their compatriots, the founders of Qantas, Wilmot Hudson Fysh and Paul McGinness, came out of a war that had forced the world to recognise that this new fighting machine called the aeroplane, which now thrilled a populace with its barnstorming romance, could revolutionise transport for the rest of history.

For Fysh and McGuinness, however, it was something of a false start. They had dreamed of following their First World War involvement by competing for the lucrative 10,000-pound prize offered in 1919 by Prime Minister Bill Hughes to be the first Australians to fly from England to Australia. Indeed, Fysh had sold his car, their wartime mechanic Arthur Baird had sold his garage business, and they were about to board ship for England to choose their aeroplane when their backer died, and with him, their dream.

Fortunately for them there would be a second 'prize'. The eventual winner might earn the 10,000-pound prize by landing at Darwin, but someone had to make the torturous journey halfway across Australia to select the landing fields for the competitors as they crossed the continent to the east coast to complete their journey. The Department of Defence, which then bore the responsibility for aviation, chose Fysh and McGinness for the job, and in August 1919 they set out from Longreach in central Queensland in a Model T Ford to go where no car had ever been: across the featureless plains, through sand and across creek beds to the Roper River and Katherine. There they left their battered Ford and took the train to Darwin, where, in what must have been a joyous but bittersweet moment, Fysh would welcome brothers Ross and Keith Smith as they touched down in their Vickers Vimy on 10 December to claim the prize.

The glamour and success of the air race itself might have convinced Australia of the romance of air travel, but the international aspect of it must have been of less interest to Fysh and McGinness. Coaxing that primitive T Model across desolate plains between far-flung outback stations had convinced them that the aeroplane had a domestic application of immense value to these remote Australians. This, they reasoned, was not simply a barnstormer's instrument to thrill crowds at spectator events. Out here it would bring a whole new meaning of life to isolated communities.

What followed over the next few months was the coming together of a small group of people whose combined vision would lead to the birth of an airline that today spans the world. In contrast to their air race sponsorship disappointment, Fysh and McGinness would have better luck with their next venture after McGinness abandoned a planned picnic to help prominent Queensland landowner Fergus McMaster fix a broken axle on his car. McMaster was so impressed that when the two airmen later presented their proposal to develop an air taxi business, he not only pledged his personal support but lobbied friends and fellow graziers to contribute funds. Finally, on 16 November 1920, Queensland and Northern Territory Aerial Services Ltd was formed, with headquarters at Winton in Queensland and McMaster as chairman.

In 1921 the headquarters was moved to Longreach and the following year Qantas operated its first mail and passenger flight from Charleville to Cloncurry. Soon the fledgling operator was not only flying mail and passengers but, under the watchful eye of mechanic Arthur Baird, was also building its own aircraft at Longreach while stretching its wings to Brisbane and across Queensland. By then, however, Paul McGinness, never one inclined to the discipline of company structure, had left the group to seek fortune elsewhere, a pursuit which would sadly remain unfulfilled.

By 1930 it had become obvious that if the company was to grow it needed to provide coastal and interstate services from a capital city base. Brisbane was the next move and it was from here, in 1931, that Qantas would take its first tentative steps onto the world stage, carrying mail from Brisbane to Darwin as part of an experimental airmail service with Britain's Imperial Airways to the United Kingdom.

But the major leap would occur on 26 February 1935 when, now registered as Qantas Empire Airways, Captain G.U. 'Scotty' Allan lifted off from Darwin on the first overseas departure of a Qantas aircraft, destination Singapore. Allan flew a de Havilland DH 86 aircraft powered by four engines, which Qantas considered essential for overwater operations.

The DH 86 had had a controversial introduction to Australia the previous year and although it was to prove itself on the Empire route, a series of accidents had damaged its reputation leading to its temporary withdrawal shortly before the inauguration of the Darwin–Singapore service. A Holyman Airways single-pilot version had disappeared in Bass Strait in October 1934 with the loss of three passengers and two crew, to be followed a month later by the crash of Qantas' second DH 86 on the last leg of its delivery flight between Longreach and Brisbane. Subsequent investigations and alterations to the aircraft's tail helped alleviate public concern but would lead to a bitter exchange between Fysh and one of the era's famous airmen, P.G. Taylor. Taylor, then in England, had agreed to join Qantas on the Empire route, but gave a press interview stating he no longer had plans to do so, firing off a cable to Fysh that he would not 'in principle' fly the DH 86 under any circumstances.

Fysh, convinced that the aircraft had been well tested both on the ground and in the air, left Taylor in no doubt about his feelings, immediately cabling back: 'Regret your comment without knowledge of accidents. As unwilling to fly aircraft feel mutual wish cancel previous arrangement join us which we now confirm.' The lingering discontent between the pair would reveal itself again in future years when their respective company ambitions merged, particularly in the major task of ferrying Catalina flying boats to and from the United States to Australia on the eve of the Second World War.

Right from its beginning, however, the UK's Empire Air Mail Scheme, initially designed to link the numerous threads of the empire, would be a complicated arrangement born out of competing interests of others anxious to be part of the aviation connections to and from Australia. On one hand was the pressure being applied by the Dutch, determined to extend KLM's Netherlands East Indies air route on to Australia. Looking in the opposite direction to Australia's east, both the British and Australian governments were wary of emerging American efforts to extend their services on from New Zealand. Also in the mix were the efforts of the likes of Charles Kingsford Smith, Charles Ulm and other Australian aviation entrepreneurs who had their own plans for United Kingdom–Australia connections. In the end, Imperial Airways and the newly formed company Qantas Empire Airways (QEA) triumphed, and Qantas, with a government mail subsidy, extended its reach beyond Australian shores as part of what was the longest air service route in the world. Looked at by the standards of the 1930s, its structure appears breathtaking in its concept.

Covering a total of 12,654 miles (more than 20,000 kilometres) over twelve days, the route involved air and surface links operated by three organisations: Imperial Airways from London to Paris, Paris to Brindisi by rail, again by air Brindisi to Karachi via Cairo, then with Indian Trans-Continental Airways from Karachi across India to Rangoon and Singapore and then QEA from Singapore to Darwin and Brisbane. But although operated by an assortment of aircraft types, some carrying other country's registrations, it was a strictly Imperial Airways affair.

The Qantas Empire Airways DH 86 service between Brisbane, Darwin and Singapore would settle into a four-day excursion through Koepang, Lombok, Bima, Surabaya, Batavia and on to Singapore, soon proving that early doubts expressed by some sections of the Australian government about the value of the service would be misplaced. In fact, the demand for faster airmail between the United Kingdom and Australia reached such a level that the DH 86s were often limited to only one passenger, a sore point for Qantas which, under the agreement, received the revenue from passenger fares to Singapore.

Flying low and subject to tropical weather patterns, the DH 86 services must have at times presented mixed experiences for those early travellers, with the initial leg across the 500-mile-long stretch of the Timor Sea providing a bird's-eye view of whales and large sharks, the latter probably reassuring the passengers of the value of the DH 86s four engines! Cabin service was hardly elaborate, limited to a thermos of coffee and sandwiches, but while their in-flight comforts might have been minimal, some compensation would come with the night stopovers involving lavish meals in exotic locations.

Soon, however, the ambitions of both Imperial and Qantas would outgrow the technology of the lumbering DH 86 biplane, and plans were developed to replace it with an aircraft of much greater capacity to absorb the increasing demands of passengers and mail across the empire. These plans would come to fruition in the form of the Short Brothers' S23 flying boat.

The introduction of the Short flying boat was aimed at replacing an assortment of aircraft types with a machine capable of utilising the vast tracts of water available across the route, thus overcoming the necessity for the costly provision of landing grounds. The concept was solely an Imperial Airways enterprise and while it faced little opposition from the colonial governments en route, the Australian government, firmly of the view that the Australia–Singapore sector of the route was Australia's 'patch', rejected it outright. There were also other economic concerns, such as the fact that the British proposal would mean an airmail letter would cost less to send between Australia and London than the current domestic airmail rate between Sydney and Perth. The Australian government could envisage a strident public demand for cheaper internal mail that would cost it dearly.

More seriously from a Qantas viewpoint, however, was the attitude of Australia's aviation authorities. Both the controller of civil aviation, Edgar Johnston, and the chief of the Royal Australian Air Force (RAAF), Air Vice Marshal Richard Williams, were strongly opposed to the flying boat proposal, believing that, at least for the Australia–Singapore sector, landplanes should be used. While recognising Imperial's desire to avoid costly aerodrome construction on the route, they faced the prospect of meeting the cost of establishing flying boat bases along the Australian coastline to Darwin. However, when it came to landplanes versus flying boats, Hudson Fysh was coming from a more practical Qantas viewpoint. With the current DH 86 contract with the Australian government due to expire in 1939, Fysh knew there would be no four-engined landplanes available for overwater operations.

Supporting the government's objections, however, was the report of a 1935 RAAF survey mission, led by experienced flying boat specialist Squadron Leader Arthur Hempel, which maintained no suitable alighting areas for the flying boats existed. While his report may have been negative from a Qantas point of view, one could sympathise with Hempel as, at the time he set out on his survey, he had limited information even on the actual size of the Empire flying boat being developed by Short.

Determined to prove the sceptics wrong about a seaplane versus landplane service, Fysh and Imperial Airways operations director Major H.G. Brackley set off in mid-1936 on their own survey from Singapore in an earlier Short flying boat. Widely known as 'Brackles', Brackley, a former Royal Naval Air Service pilot during the First World War, was a perfect choice for the role, having already been involved in the choice of a proposed flying boat route through India and Burma. Having no illusions about the sensitivity of the issue between the two governments, he elected to say very little publicly about the survey but had no doubts about its future. By contrast, Fysh, never shy of criticising any government when he considered it necessary, made up for his colleague's reticence when it came to supporting the flying boat concept, frequently publicly voicing his support for the flying boat idea.

Their first stop was Bangka Island off Sumatra, then a long 334-mile flight across the Java Sea to Surabaya's Tandjong Perak harbour, at the eastern end of Java, although the lack of suitable water landing areas on this sector would see Batavia (now Jakarta) substituted for Bangka on the eventual route.

From there it was on to Timor to choose a site at Koepang, and then to Darwin, where Squadron Leader Hempel joined the party. Qantas already had an established base in Darwin for its DH 86 services so some company infrastructure was already well established, but the requirement for a flying boat alighting area would now have to take into account the large tidal range that was a feature of much of northern Australia. In fact, Darwin was only one of the unique challenges the choice of alighting sites in Australia would present to the team. An abundance of crocodiles in the water at Roper River in the Gulf of Carpentaria would see one of the crewmen in the party standing by with a pistol as the team went ashore. As Groote Eylandt and Karumba completed the Gulf part of the survey, Brackles appears to be enjoying himself, with photographs showing him smiling while balanced precariously on tiny boats with limited freeboard. For his part, Fysh took every opportunity to go fishing. After the Gulf, the journey down the Queensland coast via Townsville and Bowen to Brisbane, and finally Sydney, must have been something of a milk run.

All the while the argument between the two governments about the use of flying boats continued, although it obviously wasn't bothering Imperial too much. They'd already commissioned Short Brothers to start building an aircraft especially for the task.

The all-metal Short S23 Empire flying boat, which would become known as the 'C' class, was a quantum leap for British aviation. A total of thirty-one would be produced, six of them for Australia. The four Bristol Pegasus XC engines could carry a payload of 3700 kilograms at a cruising speed of 165 miles per hour. Its limited range of 760 miles, far short of the 2500-mile range of those to be operated by Imperial on the North Atlantic, would allow it to carry the largest loads possible between the short refuelling stages of the route, but would have serious implications for Qantas in the future.

With two pilots, a radio operator and three cabin crew, their fifteen passengers would have the comfort of a spacious interior over three decks and quality hot meals made possible by heated containers. Passengers and mail would interchange with an Imperial Airways C Class in Singapore and could be in London in nine days.

Finally, the governments agreed on the seaplane concept and, with the route established, the first of the Qantas aircrew set off in early 1938 for flying boat training in the United Kingdom. The initial Qantas aircraft would carry British registrations but would bear Australian names—*Coogee*, *Corio*, *Coorong*, *Carpentaria*, *Coolangatta* and *Cooee*—and would interchange with their British-named counterparts as they operated along the route. Among the pilots who would fly the Empires were some who would become household names in the history of both their airline and Australian aviation in general.

George Urquhart 'Scotty' Allan, who had captained the first DH 86 flight out of Darwin, had more experience in overseas flying than any of his compatriots. Short in stature and with a broad Scottish brogue that never abandoned him, Scotty had flown in the Royal Air Force (RAF) in the First World War, and later with Charles Kingsford Smith and Charles Ulm. Lester Brain, the airline's flight superintendent, would subsequently rate Allan as the best pilot of the Kingsford Smith era, and believed his legendary Scottish ability to be penny-wise brought immeasurable benefits to the airline. Allan would constantly manipulate the throttles and mixture controls of the DH 86 to get the best possible performance from his engines, no matter the flying conditions. Such parsimony would also extend to the ground when it came to refuelling, easily giving the impression he was paying for the fuel himself as he made sure the fuel dispensers didn't charge him one more gallon than he should have received. The result was his fuel costs to Singapore were less than anyone else.

Brain, the man leading the training mission, had learned to fly at RAAF Point Cook and joined Qantas in 1924. England-born Russell Tapp gained his 'wings' with the RAF in the First World War and had joined Qantas in 1928. Bill Crowther was a former jackeroo who, upon hearing of the arrival of Ross and Keith Smith's Vimy at Darwin to win the 1919 air race, had ridden his horse to a point on the route to watch them go overhead on their flight across Queensland. It made such an impression that he went against his father's wishes for him to study medicine and set off to learn to fly instead. Like Brain and Scotty Allan, he would play a pivotal role in the future of Qantas, particularly during its wartime years when they would be joined by Orm Denny, Lew Ambrose, Eric Donaldson, Bob Gurney, Bert Hussey, Aub Koch and Bill Purton.

Given the historic romance of early aviation, there is a temptation to conjure up a devil-may-care characterisation of these early Qantas men. Certainly they needed courage and an adventurous spirit to be part of those early dangerous years, where death made a rapid appearance if you didn't take flying seriously. But looking back on their careers they appear to have taken few unnecessary risks, and when they did they called on their skill and experience to get themselves and their passengers safely through.

Here too one can see the early development of the Qantas safety culture on which Fysh and his team insisted. Bill Crowther would later recount how, blinded by a dust storm while flying across Queensland, he decided to turn back and land, delaying the service and causing schedule upsets for several days. Later he learned that had he kept pressing on the dust storm would have cleared. When he subsequently arrived in Brisbane and was told Hudson Fysh wanted to see him, Crowther feared the worst. To his delight, Fysh greeted him warmly and, in front of other senior management staff, thanked him for upholding the safety and reputation of the company.

Flying the C Class was a whole new world for the Qantas pilots, however well versed they may have been in taking off, landing and taxiing an aircraft on terra firma. The flying boat introduced a different dimension, even from the basic handling viewpoint: a landplane remained still while you went through the process of warming up the engines, but a waterborne machine started moving at the moment of ignition!

One of their first tasks was to undertake a course in seamanship, sailing yachts around Southampton Water where the vagaries of winds and tides were immediately apparent. The C Class they were to fly was a large aeroplane, and its sheer size meant it could have a mind of its own if wind and tide took over. After the yachts came a course handling a small Short Brothers biplane flying boat before graduating to the real thing. The lessons learned at Southampton and also at training on Sydney Harbour would be critical in the years ahead, helping them tie up to safe moorings in harbours scattered with shipping and in varying weather conditions.

Landing in the rolling open sea was altogether another matter, as Scotty Allan would later describe:

> In the sea, you land along the swell. When you land like that, the swells are going past you. You don't want to land in the hollow between the swells, otherwise the float will hit the swell and be torn off. You've got to land on top of the swell, so you can't just shut the engines off when you come in to land. You've got to 'trickle it on', that is to say you keep the engine going until the swell gets underneath and then you shut the engine off and sit down on top of the swell.

Years later, one of the captains, Lew Ambrose, had occasion to appreciate their training, watching in dismay as the skipper of an American flying boat taking him to the United States, even after landing on smooth water, made numerous attempts to manoeuvre his aircraft to the anchorage before finally giving up in despair, shutting down the engines and inviting a motor launch to tow him to the mooring. 'Lester Brain was the main force behind such training and we were certainly thankful for it,' Ambrose would concede.

Ambrose, born in Melbourne, trained first as a radio officer before graduating as a pilot with the rank of sergeant in 1932. Although he would achieve some remarkable efforts during the war, he appears to have been something of an odd man out in the Qantas scheme of things postwar, never quite fitting in with the management style of his senior colleagues.

However, there could be no doubting his courage and airmanship, both in the days of the Empire flying boats and later on the secret Indian Ocean Catalinas that would re-open the link with the United Kingdom at a critical stage of the war.

In March 1938, with seven captains, two ground engineers and mechanic Arthur Baird having completed their initial courses in England, *Coolangatta*, the first Empire C Class flying boat to be delivered, left Southampton with Scotty Allan in command for Australia.

As Rose Bay in Sydney became established as the major Qantas base, another five aircraft, carrying the C-prefixed names of *Cooee*, *Coorong*, *Carpentaria*, *Coogee* and *Corio*, joined the fleet and by early July were crisscrossing each other on a regular Sydney–UK service, interchanging crews at Singapore. In contrast to the smaller, cramped DH 86s, the flying boats introduced a whole new world to the elite breed of passenger who could afford them.

The main cabin had fifteen seats on the starboard side, with five tables between them, paralleled by a promenade on the port side where passengers could stare out the window at the myriad of islands passing below. More seats were available in a smoking cabin and cocktails took some of the boredom out of time in the air. Roominess and exclusivity might have been the catchwords, perhaps best illustrated by a well-known Qantas publicity photograph of a casually attired passenger practising his in-flight golf swing! Indeed, the remarkable Empire would be first class all the way.

In the earliest days, however, such images could be deceiving. Even after the first service took off from Rose Bay in July 1938 it would take months for some of the base handling issues to be resolved. Fysh's own writings of the years 1937 and 1938, while he and his chairman Fergus McMaster were struggling to establish his airline's role in the Empire Air Mail Scheme, clearly demonstrate the challenges facing the embryonic Empire flying boat scheme, with government delays to the provision of the flying boat bases in Australia matched by a slowness on the part of the

Netherlands East Indies government to do likewise on the route through Java and Sumatra.

Months would pass before many such problems would be satisfactorily resolved, but gradually the Empire C Class would prove its worth. Consequently, it would also be the instrument that would take Qantas to war.

Chapter 1

PRELUDE TO A WAR: THE IMPERIAL–BOAC DILEMMA

Anyone looking back at the two decades that followed the formation of Qantas in 1920 cannot help but reach the conclusion that war itself was, in fact, part of Qantas's DNA.

Both Hudson Fysh and Paul McGinness had won the Distinguished Flying Cross in the First World War. A diary note for 31 August 1918 by Lieutenant Clive Conrick, one of their Australian Flying Corps colleagues, captures the atmosphere of the time and paints a vivid picture of war in the air over Palestine in 1918:

> Hudson Fysh has been awarded the DFC. He came in for a lot of congratulations from all of us as he is a very popular and unassuming bloke.
>
> Today, by shooting down two Hun fighters, Hudson Fysh celebrated his DFC in a very unusual way, which I feel will never be equalled

> again. The facts of the matter are that Dowling and Mumford, with McGinness and Fysh went out on the afternoon patrol along the coast and north towards Haifa. Two Hun L.V.G. two-seaters, also on patrol, were sighted flying a little to the west of Mulebbis and were attacked immediately. McGinness positioned his Bristol Fighter below and a little to the port side of the first L.V.G. thus giving Fysh a good field of fire, whilst Dowling attacked the other L.V.G. from above and head on. Hudson Fysh poured a blast of concentrated fire into the first Hun and he rolled over and spun away and crashed near Kalkilieh. Dowling was unable to engage the second L.V.G. from head on as he found it difficult to maintain his position with the Hun dodging all over the sky, so he decided to attack from below. When he did get into position to attack from below his engine cut out and he was lucky to be able to glide back over the front, where he landed.
>
> McGinness immediately attacked the second Hun in the same way as he had the first and Fysh put such a concentrated burst of machine gun fire into the L.V.G. that one wing fell off and it went into a grotesque spin and crashed about one and a half miles from Diar Alla. Billy Weir and I spent the afternoon with Gordon at the A.A. Battery at Diar Alla and saw the Hun come down. There was great cheering from all the A.A. Battery blokes.

Those first two decades of Qantas's existence would see Fysh surrounded by others who had served in Palestine, on the Western Front, and later, at least in Russell Tapp's case, the punitive expedition against the Mahfuds on the South Asian North-West Frontier in the 1920s. These and other examples go some way to explaining why, in those increasingly fragile years of the late 1930s, Fysh and his Qantas colleagues were perhaps more acutely aware than most in Australia of the reach of the militaristic shadows that were forming over Europe. Indeed Qantas's close partnership with Imperial Airways and the necessity for Fysh to visit the

United Kingdom on a regular basis provided him with the opportunity to judge the mood and see any warlike manoeuvrings by Hitler's Germany at close hand.

Two visits to the United Kingdom—the first in 1937 and the next late the following year—allowed Fysh to identify significant developments in what was taking place. While the 1937 visit was aimed primarily at tidying up the negotiations with Imperial for the establishment of the flying boat services, there were already ominous signs of war. His notes describe the political situation, with Neville Chamberlain as prime minister, as a 'muddle', commenting somewhat tersely, 'While England sleeps, others act.'

In later weeks Fysh would be heartened somewhat by his observations as he visited aircraft factories, finally coming to the conclusion that, at least at the industrial coalface, a great deal of effort was going into the production of fighting machines and armaments.

By the time Fysh arrived for his second visit in late 1938, his Empire flying boat scheme now up and running, Chamberlain had returned from Munich confident of appeasement with Adolf Hitler. Fysh, on the other hand, had no illusions, and neither did his counterparts at Imperial who were struggling with their own problems, the nature of which Fysh realised could have serious implications for its Australian partner.

Qantas and Imperial's aims at this time were relatively straightforward, largely resting on the desire to keep the civil air transport arm flying in the event of war while attempting to avoid its total immersion into the military complex. Passenger travel would still be essential, they argued, as would the carriage of mail, but there was to be a longer-term aim: to look beyond the immediate threat and ensure that when any war came to an end, both airlines would be in a fit state to assume their original roles and at the same time handle the competitive threat that would come, particularly from the Americans.

When it came to his airline's wartime role, however, Fysh wasn't satisfied with flying his Empires in strictly civilian attire. In his discussions with Imperial and right through to the upper echelons of the British government, Fysh not only wanted the Empire flying boats armed but new long-range fuel tanks fitted to replace the short-range versions on the Qantas aircraft. In the end the arming question died on the altar of international law conventions that prevented such steps, and neither could he achieve the long-range tanks, a shortcoming which was to have serious implications for the airline's route structure once the Japanese entered the war.

His one major victory, however, was an agreement to have engine overhaul facilities established in Australia, along with the supply of adequate spares, an achievement not only destined to have a critical effect on Australia's contribution to the Pacific war but also a significant bearing on the airline's very survival postwar. By the end of 1939, Qantas engine overhaul bases would be functioning in Australia with twelve months' spares in hand, a situation which would have been impossible to achieve once Japan had cut the Australia–UK link at the outbreak of the Pacific war.

Fysh's diary notes of his three months in Europe in 1938 reveal his frustrations with the problems his Imperial colleagues were facing. Bitter recriminations at the senior level of government, industrial disputes with staff, particularly pilots, tongue lashings by politicians in the House of Commons and a government-sponsored report detailing a toxic relationship between the airline's management and government departments and calling for an extensive reorganisation of European air services had left Imperial reeling.

Since his earlier visits Fysh now found himself dealing with a whole new regime, including newly appointed full-time chairman Sir John Reith, a former managing director of the BBC, and his senior executive Walter Runciman. Though highly regarded as an administrator, Reith let it be known he hadn't wanted the Imperial job in the first place, considering it a poisoned political chalice that lacked both government and public support. Within two years he too would be gone, shortly before the government approved the immersion of Imperial and its competitor British Airways into the British Overseas Airways Corporation (BOAC), the chosen instrument for international overseas routes. That would not be the end of BOAC's problems, however, and its struggle to maintain its position in British civil aviation would continue for the remainder of the war. Walter Runciman, on the other hand, would develop a close working relationship with Fysh through the difficult years immediately ahead, until he too resigned in 1943.

It was a different story to what was happening on the European continent. Taking the opportunity to visit Germany for talks with Lufthansa, Fysh was able to witness the incredible resurgence of a nation that had been crippled by the peace terms of the First World War. It would further convince him that war was inevitable. Here, in contrast to the squabbles in England, the Nazi regime had grasped the importance of civil aviation. Berlin's new Tempelhof airport boasted an impressive array of modern hangars and administrative buildings, while its civil aviation officials confidently predicted that Germany 'will be the great world centre for air transport'. The fact that said officials 'clicked heels' and 'raised their arms in the Hitler salute' suggested they were confident of achieving their aims. Military uniforms and large portraits of Hitler, Goering and other notorieties were everywhere, leading Fysh to comment later on what a 'topsy-turvey' world it was and one 'terribly dangerous to sleeping democracies'.

Once back in England, the real war work with Imperial Airways began, with Fysh closely involved in the development of British civil aviation's strategies in the event of war. Their efforts would become known as the 'War Book' and would form the template for the role Imperial, as BOAC, would play in the war effort, including priorities such as the provision of transport for the Royal Air Force, selection of locations suitable for flying boat bases and landplanes, the carriage of passengers, freight and mails, and where the airline's headquarters would be located.

The implications contained in the War Book, particularly those giving the RAF first call on the airline's staff and its aircraft, would add to Fysh's own concerns about the role of Qantas as an airline in time of war and its very survival at the end of such a conflict. Did both airlines face the prospect of being taken over by the RAF in the UK and by the RAAF in Australia? Both Fysh and McMaster acknowledged that while Qantas had a vital part to play in support of the war effort, civil aviation needed to be in a position where it could carry on and prosper after the war.

Both men had reason to worry as far as the situation in Australia was concerned, where the RAAF had no heavy aircraft of its own and certainly nothing to match the size and versatility of the Empire Class flying boat. As for the war itself, so many questions remained open. Would Italy come in, thus placing the Imperial/BOAC–Qantas connection through the Mediterranean at risk and necessitating a fallback to what would be known as a Horseshoe Route, providing a service from Sydney to Durban through Cairo? And as for Japan? No one knew.

Despite weeks of discussions, by the time Fysh returned to Australia in February 1939 Imperial still had no precise idea of how its wartime role would play out beyond the fact that the RAF would have first call on its aircraft, with limited consideration for the airline's commercial and postwar interests.

Australian aviation too had undergone significant change while Fysh was away, although not as extensive or controversial as the British government–Imperial upheaval.

In November 1938, civil aviation moved out from under the auspices of the Department of Defence into its own Department of Civil Aviation, to be followed shortly after by the appointment of a director-general. Since its poor pay scale barely matched the challenges of its role, it had not been an easy job to fill, finally falling to Arthur Brownlow Corbett, a former deputy-director of posts and telegraphs in Brisbane. Corbett had no aviation background in a public service career dating back to the

Boer War, hardly an ideal situation for a Qantas desperate to keep its civil aviation identity against the background of the threat of war. Fortunately, the former controller of civil aviation, Captain Edgar Johnston, would be appointed his assistant director-general, bringing with him extensive aviation experience and at times a sympathetic ear to some of Qantas's problems.

Meanwhile, much of the company's efforts were directed towards pushing for government assistance in bringing the facilities along the Sydney to Singapore route up to a reasonable standard.

Fysh was dismayed that the general impression of passengers flying through from England was that the Singapore to Sydney leg was below standard in so many respects that it reflected on Australia's prestige. Even Australia's entry point at Darwin left much to be desired, Fysh describing it to anyone in the government who would listen as a 'lazy and difficult port'. There was no proper accommodation for passengers to undergo customs and quarantine, resulting in them having to risk seasickness and remain on board. Further out, lack of adequate watercraft to support the aircraft at Koepang and other parts of the route needed urgent attention. Too often the launches provided had insufficient power to tow a flying boat to its mooring buoy if required, and even then the moorings themselves were badly positioned or needed replacement. Even Singapore, the important transfer point between Qantas Empire Airways and Imperial, had its shortcomings, lacking adequate operations control and passenger buildings, with Fysh describing it as a 'weak link' in a letter to the Minister for Civil Aviation, James Fairbairn. Perhaps in an attempt to rub salt into the wound, his letter noted the Netherlands East Indies government was in the midst of an impressive upgrade of facilities at its primary ports, which included traffic offices, passenger waiting rooms, a newsstand, refreshment areas and occasionally even a covered walkway down to the water. Landing pontoons would allow flying boats to berth alongside and refuelling to take place from the shore, Fysh pointed out, with a strong inference that, by comparison, the small traffic office and primitive passenger-handling facilities at Australia's main base at Rose Bay made an embarrassing contrast.

But there were bright spots, particularly the establishment of the engine overhaul facility at Mascot. This did away with the requirement for the Bristol Pegasus engines on the flying boats to be returned to the UK for overhaul, an untenable situation anyway should the deteriorating situation in Europe cause the route to be disrupted.

Spurred by this fear, works manager Arthur Baird's team had driven the plans for a two-storey overhaul workshop at Sydney's Kingsford Smith airport with such priority that the building was handed over to Qantas within thirty-nine working days of the turning of the first sod. Not only was it achieved in a commendable time frame but its state-of-the-art facilities provided for quick dismantling, inspection and re-assembly of the engines under a unique arched roof equipped with skylights to make maximum use of natural light for those working inside. The first facility built to specifically handle the airline's engine overhaul, the building opened on 18 August 1939.

It was just as well. The war in Europe was only weeks away.

Chapter 2

A WORLD AT WAR

British Prime Minister Neville Chamberlain's ill-judged confidence in 'peace for our time' collapsed on 1 September 1939 when Hitler's troops stormed into Poland, a fact brought home to many in Britain shortly after by the wailing of air-raid sirens. The sirens might have turned out to be false alarms but they were to be a fearful prelude to what was to come.

Two days later on 3 September, Prime Minister Robert Menzies' sombre tones over the radio announced that it was his 'melancholy duty to inform you officially that, in consequence of a persistence by Germany in her invasion of Poland, Great Britain has declared war upon her and that, as a result, Australia is also at war'.

From now until May 1940, however, at least as far as Britain was concerned, it would be what was to become the Phoney War, where, beyond the tragic sufferings of the Polish people, very little happened. A German U-Boat sank the British passenger liner *Athenia* as it headed for Canada, with the cost of 112 lives, but while in Britain blackouts were enforced, air-raid wardens roamed the streets and shelters were prepared, no bombs fell on London. Indeed the unreal atmosphere was such that after a time the blackouts were eased to allow some street lighting due to chaos on the roads at night. Even some of the children who had been evacuated at the original declaration of war would begin returning to their families.

With the passing of the years some of the memories of that time appear a trifle bizarre. While Hitler consolidated his hold on Poland, the rest of Europe waited and watched, as if not knowing quite what to do next. Part of Britain's 'offensive' moves included the dropping of thousands of propaganda leaflets over Germany to influence the German public's opinion against the war, an effort Britain's wartime leader of Bomber Command Arthur Harris would later describe as an effective way of meeting the continent's 'requirement of toilet paper for the five years of the war'.

When someone suggested British bombers attack the Black Forest to demonstrate to the German populace that any war might impact on their own country, British Secretary of State for Air Kingsley Wood pointed out it was 'private property'. Fortunately for Britain, while he was batting back such demands Kingsley Wood was also directing a massive build-up in British arms.

On the other side of the world, while Australia's early reaction followed a pattern similar to that which existed at the outbreak of the First World War of providing whatever assistance it could to Great Britain, its own situation was more complex. All indications were that an aggressive Japan posed a serious threat to the stability of the region to Australia's north and, ultimately, to Australia itself. While Britain had assured Australia it would come to its aid in the 'unlikely event it would be attacked' and Winston Churchill, as First Lord of the Admiralty, had pledged to divert British arms from its Mediterranean resources if necessary, the Australian government nevertheless still faced the dilemma of deciding how much support it could provide to the mother country and how quickly.

Some of that support had begun in the form of pilots and crews already in England to take delivery of Sunderland flying boats for the RAAF's No. 10 Squadron. Despite their obvious value to patrol duties around the vast Australian coastline, the Sunderlands and their crews were immediately handed over to the RAF to operate as part of Coastal Command, thus leaving the RAAF stripped of any large reconnaissance aircraft, a situation that would have repercussions for Qantas.

These were quick in coming. Within hours of Chamberlain's announcement on 1 September, Fysh and Lester Brain were on their way to Melbourne where they were told of the government's decision to form an RAAF squadron from four of the five Qantas Empire flying boats, and since two of the British-registered boats, *Calypso* and *Centaurus*, happened to be in Sydney that day they were immediately handed over to the air force to be converted to wartime use at the Rose Bay base. They were the first of six that would eventually be handed to the RAAF during the war.

Not that Qantas hadn't seen it coming. At the company's annual meeting exactly twelve months earlier, Fergus McMaster had told the board that, as part of an agreement with the government, all Qantas aircraft and equipment would be at the disposal of the government in a national emergency 'and the engineers and pilots might be required to serve with the Air Force Reserve'.

In fact, in September 1939 the RAAF was in poor shape, its 3500 personnel backed up by a 600-strong Citizen Air Force with no modern aircraft to fly. Lacking any heavy, long-range patrol aircraft, its largest machine was the Avro Anson, little more than a communications aircraft used for training. Its frontline fighter was the Wirraway, a version of the American Harvard trainer aircraft that had no hope of competing with fighters like the Japanese Zero.

Due to the war's extraordinary demand for aircraft, the RAAF was still awaiting delivery of twin-engine Lockheed Hudson medium bombers from the US and was starting to make its own plans to build British Bristol Beauforts under licence to fill the gap.

Added to that, there were very few officers in the RAAF with any practical experience on large, multi-engine aircraft, although in early 1939 press reports indicated they would take control of civil aircraft in an emergency and speculated that provisional arrangements had been made with the airline companies for RAAF men to be seconded to the airlines as second officers. One article in the *West Australian* newspaper pointed out that very few officers had training on modern marine aircraft, 'and none with firsthand knowledge of the "life line" route between Darwin and Singapore.' Likewise, civilian pilots might become part of the RAAF reserve, although the article went on to speculate that this might lead to 'etiquette problems'. Any suggestion such civilians be given a commensurate position in rank to serving RAAF officers was soon dismissed by an army spokesman: 'The Army does not provide commissions in the cavalry for everyone who can ride a horse.' Obviously some in the military command structure still retained a First World War view of what was to come!

Thankfully any such 'etiquette problems' seemed far from the minds of those involved in the transfer of *Calypso* and *Centaurus* now that war had been declared. They would form the basis of No. 11 Squadron while the two Qantas aircraft at the other end of the route, *Coorong* and *Corio*, would be handed over to BOAC and placed on the British register.

Other decisions were also affecting the airline. The day after Chamberlain's announcement and even before Menzies had taken to the radio, pilot Bill Crowther, already on his way to Singapore, was preparing to leave Townsville when the Department of Civil Aviation issued an order that the service between Australia and Singapore be ceased. Bill Crowther headed back to Sydney instead.

Much of this early activity took place amid a prevailing uncertainty as to whether Italy would enter the war on Germany's side, and although Japan had indicated it would remain 'independent', its actual intentions could not be taken for granted. One thing however was crystal clear: if Italy did enter the war, Imperial's route across the Mediterranean would be severed.

Within a few days, however, permission was given for the Singapore service to be resumed, although reduced from three to two flights per week and with the proviso that five of the Empire boats be on the Singapore–Sydney section and immediately available to the RAAF if needed.

Work began at Rose Bay to prepare *Calypso* and *Centaurus* for war. Bomb racks were fitted under the wings, machine guns added in the nose and rear cabin, and extra fuel tanks installed to stretch their range. Hudson Fysh had finally got at least two of his Empires armed—it's just they weren't his anymore!

The flying boats would be escorted to their RAAF base in Port Moresby by fifteen members of Qantas to serve under No. 11 Squadron's commander, Flight Lieutenant James Alexander. Due to its mix of RAAF and civilian personnel, No. 11 would soon become known as 'Alexander's Ragtime Band' after a popular tune of the day.

Temporary Flight Lieutenants Bob Gurney and Eric Sims, Flying Officer Bill Purton and Temporary Flying Officer Godfrey 'Goff' Hemsworth would be the first of Qantas's pilots to be contributed to the war effort. Sims and Purton would later be posted back to Qantas and all four were destined to play significant roles with both the RAAF and Qantas in the years ahead, with only Eric Sims surviving the war.

Bob Gurney was an experienced pilot with more than 3000 hours in the air even before he joined Qantas in 1936, having flown with Guinea Airways during the pioneering years of aviation in Papua New Guinea. Eric Sims, a West Australian, enlisted in the RAAF as a wireless operator in 1926 and graduated as a pilot at Point Cook in 1932. Joining Qantas in January 1935, he flew DH 86s on the Brisbane to Singapore route and took part in the futile search for Sir Charles Kingsford Smith and Tommy Pethybridge, who went missing over the Bay of Bengal in their Lockheed Altair in 1935.

Both Bill Purton and Goff Hemsworth joined Qantas in 1935 as first officers. While Purton would return to Qantas later and resume piloting the company's flying boats, Hemsworth would remain in the RAAF, transferring from No. 11 Squadron to command No. 20 Squadron, piloting Catalina flying boats.

Fighter pilot Gordon Steege, who would ultimately reach the rank of air commodore in the RAAF, was posted as adjutant to No. 11 Squadron at Rose Bay and remembers meeting Hemsworth and Gurney for the first time, 'dressed in their ill-fitting tropical shorts with which they had been hurriedly fitted by the RAAF.' Gurney and Hemsworth, he noted, had spent years flying in New Guinea and were enjoying their international flying, 'so were not exactly pleased to now be sent back to Papua.' Later in Port Moresby he would meet a 'quiet and reserved' Eric Sims and his first officer Bill Purton, 'youngish with a lively sense of humour and an outgoing personality.'

The conversion of the flying boats was achieved in five days and No. 11 Squadron flew to Port Moresby on 28 September 1939. While No. 10 Squadron in England would be able to lay claim to being the first Australian squadron to go into action in the Second World War, No. 11 would be the first to be operational, carrying out a reconnaissance mission on 29 September as the first of a series of flights to monitor foreign shipping in the area. For the next two years, *Centaurus* and *Calypso* would be the RAAF's only long-range reconnaissance flying boats.

As *Calypso* and *Centaurus* donned their fighting colours, the ad hoc nature of the decision-making in Canberra and at the military headquarters in

Melbourne must have given Fysh cause for concern that his fears for the dislocation of his airline were coming true. In a letter to his chairman he told McMaster:

> We are anticipating a commencement of hostilities at any time. Our position over a period, should war commence and last, is still obscure. There seems a chance at the moment that our organisation will become split and scattered. One of the most burning questions is that of ascertaining our new income and adjusting ourselves to it. As the Empire Mail Service will have ceased, we have got to find where our revenue will come from.

In replying, McMaster, though in ill health since a heart attack in 1938, was supportive as usual, and must have been a fillip for Fysh. It also showed McMaster had an astute appreciation of the extreme pressure Fysh was under on all fronts:

> You should endeavour to keep your organisation together whatever work it may be given to do. Keep a careful account of all expenditure and loss.
>
> In so far as QEA is concerned, there must be no defaulting or hanging back if assistance is asked, but be sure that those responsible for asking for that assistance are not over-excited. I wish to compliment you, yourself in getting the extra engines out, and the overhaul base in readiness. This will be a big factor for QEA, and not only for QEA but for Britain also. It is due to you personally that this work has been pushed on.

A few days later Fysh also wrote to Sir John Reith at Imperial, assuring him that he could see no likelihood of any disturbance to the route unless Japan came into the war. 'Our policy here is to keep the QEA organisation together,' Fysh told Reith, 'as long as by doing so the maximum service to the country is being rendered.'

As 1940 arrived the 'QEA organisation' Fysh was referring to, while concerned about where the immediate future was taking it, was in reasonable shape, although it was a mixed bag.

The replacement of the DH 86 landplanes with the Empire C Class on the Singapore route had been successful from the company's viewpoint, carrying almost five thousand passengers in their first year of operations and more mail than the DH 86s had carried in their four years of operations. Coupled with the onboard trappings of ocean liner-style service, exotic ports of call and the romantic flavour of it all, the boats had proved popular with passengers.

Indeed passengers were even provided with a world first: an in-flight news service. In addition to his normal monitoring of the airwaves, the radio operator would listen on short wave for the news and type the main items for distribution to passengers, although the ever-circumspect Lester Brain directed that any news relating to aircraft accidents be edited out!

Meantime, although the airworthiness and grounding problems that had beset the DH 86s were now behind the Qantas and BOAC, its Empire flying boat fleet was rapidly depleting. Even before the transfer to the RAAF of *Calypso* and *Centaurus*, a couple of serious incidents had robbed the airline of two other flying boats: *Coorong* when strong winds drove it ashore at Darwin and *Capella* in a taxiing incident at Batavia.

Of all the flying boat mooring facilities on the Sydney to Singapore route, Darwin Harbour was among the most exposed, and the monsoon season added to the problem. Lester Brain had taxied the *Coorong* to its mooring, and the passengers were taken ashore by launch while the aircraft was fuelled and readied for take-off again next morning. Later that night, however, the aircraft broke away from its buoy and crashed onto a rocky breakwater. Fortunately, Brain and station engineer Norm Roberts were able to marshal a team which succeeded in safely securing the aircraft before water could penetrate its hull, although repairs were beyond Qantas, capability and *Coorong* was dismantled and packed aboard ship for Short Brothers in England, eventually to return to service with QEA.

Capella had no such luck. Bert Hussey, taxiing close inshore at Batavia, hit the wreckage of a submerged vessel not marked on the harbour charts, ripping a gaping hole in the hull of the aircraft. Although successfully beached, it lay there with a hull full of salt water before also being shipped to England, but by then the salt water had taken its toll and *Capella* was scrapped.

Hussey's misfortune at Batavia highlighted the challenges confronting the company in those early days of international aviation, where the vagaries of weather, inadequate charts and limited navigational aids meant disaster could strike at any time. Perhaps no better prewar example exists than the problems which confronted Russell Tapp trying to find storm-ravaged Batavia on Boxing Day 1939.

Navigational facilities were almost non-existent along parts of the route and meteorological forecasts had little hope of contending with rapid changes in tropical weather patterns. This, coupled with the limited fuel range of the flying boats should they be forced to divert due to weather ahead, occasionally made life interesting to say the least, although apart from being bumped around, passengers down the back often remained blissfully unaware of what was really happening.

The primary navigational aid aboard the flying boats was a radio direction finder, a small rotating antenna above the radio officer's station that he would rotate manually to tune into the radio signal from a ground station to fix their position. Even with that achieved, when they reached their destination they often had to look for gaps in the cloud or low-lying fog to identify their landing area on a bay or a river, carefully avoiding any moored ships or moving watercraft.

Surabaya was being buffeted by a severe storm as they took off for Batavia on Boxing Day morning but reports indicated that the weather over the last hundred miles into Batavia was good. Sure enough, around sixty-five miles out *Corio* came through cloud and rain into clear weather, but it was short-lived and they were still in cloud when the direction finder told them they were overhead Batavia. With no breaks visible, Tapp adopted the safe procedure in such circumstances, returning to the clear air behind them over low ground and making another approach at around three hundred feet. Once again they ran into cloud, but not before Tapp caught a fleeting glimpse of a pylon he recognised at the entrance to the port at Tandjong Priok, Batavia's harbour.

With even that limited clear patch closing in rapidly and with his fuel running low, Tapp now was faced with the option of making a blind landing in the open sea, which he knew was littered with fish traps, or onto a narrow river section that ran through the clear patch he had just sighted. Banking sharply, he touched down on a section of the Citarum River, east of Batavia and barely wide enough for the flying boat. More problems were to come when the skies opened up again and the mooring line threatened to break away, risking the prospect of the flying boat drifting downstream towards a heavily timbered bank at a bend in the river. While radio officer Frank Furniss sent urgent messages to Batavia to assure them the flying boat was down safely but needed assistance, Tapp restarted the engines to keep the boat in position.

Finally, one of the crew scrambled ashore and reached a telephone box where he was able to call the Qantas agent in Batavia to the scene to help secure *Corio* to the shore for the night. Next morning the weather had cleared, and with the help of several hundred locals at the end of a rope the flying boat was dragged to the centre of the stream and Tapp took off for the remaining short flight to Batavia.

Despite such mishaps and challenges, as 1939 drew to a close Qantas had a staff of 285, split into administration, engineering and operations. Secretary and traffic manager H.H. (George) Harman had a staff of thirty-five and Lester Brain as flying operations manager had an operational group of forty-three, which included Scotty Allan as chief pilot and ten captains and ten first officers. Arthur Baird controlled the bulk of the employees with 114 engineering staff at Sydney and throughout the network, and a stores and spares section of forty-six was under C.O. (Cedric) Turner. The Brisbane–Daly Waters DH 86 landplane operation, with responsibility for the Flying Doctor Service, had a further forty-six personnel.

Along with such human statistics, QEA had a paid-up capital of £523,000 and had flown a total of 1,707,060 route miles over the year and a total of 5,461,986 passenger miles.

The coming year would see both Qantas and the Australian military forced to quickly adapt to an escalation in hostilities, with Qantas facing the added problem of commercial threats to its international operations. As for the armed forces, the RAAF would continue to scramble to obtain adequate equipment, although the navy was reasonably equipped with ships of the line, including heavy and light cruisers and a batch of destroyers along with several Australian-built sloops. Late in 1939 the Menzies government appointed Major General Thomas Blamey to command its 3000 army regulars and the 80,000 militiamen who had volunteered for part-time training. Blamey would subsequently attain the position of land commander under General Douglas MacArthur after the United States entered the war, but his chequered background as a former Victorian commissioner of police and a series of scandals would make him a controversial choice.

Neither would Blamey win the respect of his subordinates or the bulk of the troops who served under him. However, as with other military VIPs, he would be a frequent passenger on Qantas aircraft. In fact, the airline would be involved on the periphery of one of the incidents which would involve Blamey and one of his subordinates, General Gordon Bennett, after Bennett's controversial escape following the fall of Singapore in 1942.

Chapter 3

THE SHADOWS DARKEN, 1940

The first months of 1940 presented Qantas with a dilemma. More than one hundred Qantas staff were on the RAAF reserve, and either had to stay with Qantas or join the RAAF when ordered. Many at the top also wanted to have a gun in their hand. Lester Brain was already a wing commandeer on the RAAF reserve and Fysh himself a squadron leader, but although their desire to serve would be denied them, the significance of their roles would see them play equally critical roles in the years to come.

Scotty Allan would leave soon, first to take charge of the RAAF's Seaplane Training Flight at Rathmines in New South Wales. Fred Derham, as the company's auditor a senior executive, had already gone to the RAAF, but as fate would have it would later be directly involved with his former Qantas colleagues in the devastating 1942 attack on Broome.

As the position in Europe gradually deteriorated towards the middle of the year, Arthur Baird's team busied itself with consolidating its

Mascot maintenance base while McMaster and Fysh tackled the commercial threats facing the company and coming from opposite ends of the compass. The Dutch, via KLM, now flying modern DC-3 landplanes, were still knocking on the door with ambitions for flying to Australia from the north-west, while the Americans were pushing for Australia to accept Pan American service across the Pacific.

Part of the tactical approach to stopping the Americans would be the extension of the Imperial /QEA service through to Auckland under the flag of Tasman Empire Airways Limited, although Fysh's chairman had his doubts, confessing to Fysh he had never been an advocate of the Tasman service, believing the flying boats could be better used connecting Brisbane with Noumea, while Pan American be permitted to operate between New Zealand and Australia. McMaster's final comment, however, made long before John Curtin's new year message in 1941 that Australia 'looks to America' rather than Britain, once again demonstrated his astute judgement when it came to the coming war and where the future security of Australia lay: 'Perhaps I am pessimistic but I feel that the closer the connection we can make with America, the safer we will be.'

Negotiations continued with the Dutch, all the time having to keep in mind the importance of their co-operation and support of the Qantas service through the Netherlands East Indies. As for the services themselves, the developing crisis in Europe had led to the cancellation of much of the mail uplift which had been such a large part of the airline's early overseas commitment, to be replaced by a rapid increase in service personnel and freight, prompting Fysh to take the opportunity to demonstrate to Minister for Civil Aviation James Fairbairn the increasing military importance of the Qantas role.

Royal Australian Artillery troops, naval officers and RAAF airmen had been flown to postings in Darwin along with twenty Public Works Department carpenters to undertake defence work there. An assortment of stores, including everything from machine guns and ammunition to mosquito nets and bedding, had been delivered to Darwin or dropped off at Karumba and Groote Eylandt along the way. Royal Air Force, British and Indian Army personnel had travelled further north-west to Singapore as part of their movement on to Rangoon, Calcutta and London.

With increased demands on shipping due to the war, Fysh was able to emphasise the speed advantage of the flying boats, explaining that the increasing accommodation available on the flying boats was being eagerly taken by those having urgent reason to travel overseas. He also noted, 'Of the overseas passengers already carried and forward bookings, all, without exception, are urgent and essential travellers—not one is a tourist.'

Taking the opportunity to highlight the Empire's versatility, Fysh detailed a four-hour reconnaissance patrol commanded by Scotty Allan, which patrolled over four thousand square miles of the Pacific to the south and south-east of Sydney.

Meanwhile the ructions continued at BOAC with John Reith, who had made no secret of his belief that the leadership of BOAC was not to his liking, achieved his aim and was appointed minister of information by Chamberlain in January. Imperial Airways operations manager Major H.G. Brackley, that old stalwart of the first surveys of the Empire route, had gone too, taking his organisational talents to RAF Transport Command. Fortunately, however, as the airline struggled to bring its merger of Imperial and British Airways into reasonable shape and at the same time retain the core of its civilian activities, Walter Runciman remained in place as the airline's chief executive, to Fysh's relief, thus maintaining a valuable personal relationship at the top of both Qantas and BOAC.

So the early months of the Phoney War stumbled on through days uncannily quiet, until the German blitzkrieg on Denmark in April 1940 pointed to what was to come.

Then, in early May, German tanks rolled into France and Belgium. Within weeks, British troops were being evacuated from Dunkirk, France had fallen, leaving Britain alone across the English Channel, and Italy had entered the war. Now there would be no going back. Attacks on London by the Luftwaffe saw its civilians spending their nights in shelters or in London's Underground. The Battle of Britain reached its climax in September, fortunately with the contrails of the Spitfires and Hurricanes in the skies over London signifying the crushing of Hitler's ambitions for an invasion of England.

Now, as Imperial–BOAC had feared, with Italy in the war its service to Australia via southern France then Italy and across the Mediterranean to Cairo was cut, bringing into play the alternative track through east Africa to Durban that become known as the Horseshoe Route. With BOAC's increasing commitment to the war it would not be long before even that would be too much for the airline to handle, and Qantas would be asked to step forward and take up the slack.

Chapter 4

CATS ACROSS THE PACIFIC

Australia's government and its armed forces faced conflicting problems as the months passed in 1940, torn between the increasing necessity to assist the British war effort and protection of its own sea lanes from the dangers posed by marauding German raiders. With only the seconded Qantas Empires in its fleet, the RAAF urgently needed to be equipped with long-range reconnaissance aircraft.

It was a vast area to defend. To the west was the Indian Ocean. To the east, the sweeping arc of the South-West Pacific reached from well to the south of New Zealand to butt against Papua New Guinea and the 14,000 islands that made up the Netherlands East Indies across Australia's north-west.

Beyond, one looked nervously at the potential threat posed by Japan.

Japan's aggressive ambitions had been obvious for a decade, beginning with its occupation of Manchuria in 1931 and its subsequent skirmishes along the border with a China already divided between the warring factions of Kuomintang (KMT) and Mao Tse-tung's Communists (CCP).

Finally, the Second Sino-Japanese War became a full-blown conflict in 1937, and although it would see the Communists and the KMT initially unite in a fragile alliance against a common foe, they were unable to stop the Japanese army from capturing key ports and cities in what was to be one of the most brutal campaigns in modern times, one in which atrocities and massacres cost the lives of hundreds of thousands of civilians.

By 1940, however, the struggle had reached a stalemate, with neither side able to make any progress, the Chinese unable to reclaim territory occupied by their enemy, nor the Japanese able to claim victory, themselves now suffering from economic sanctions imposed by a USA staunchly supporting China's defence.

It was against this background that an approach by P.G. Taylor suggesting the RAAF should acquire a Catalina flying boat to survey potential bases for Australia in the Pacific arrived on the desks of Prime Minister Robert Menzies and Minister for Civil Aviation James Fairbairn in early 1940.

That Taylor would approach the prime minister direct was hardly out of character for one of Australia's best-known aviators. Taylor's pioneering accomplishments during an era that proved the value of air transport had provided him with an extensive range of contacts at both political and government level. He had won wide public acclaim for his first crossing of the Indian Ocean by air in a Catalina known as *Guba* in 1939, and before that as a navigator and second pilot on pioneering flights with Charles Kingsford Smith. His courage was unquestionable. On one of Smithy's flights, an aborted attempt to fly across the Tasman, he had climbed out along the wing struts no less than six times to transfer oil from a useless motor to an overheating one, an effort which enabled them to return to Australia and won him the Empire Gallantry Medal.

Taylor's approach led to his appearance before Menzies' War Cabinet in April 1940, where he outlined his proposal for the government to purchase a Catalina for twenty-two thousand pounds and use it to establish air bases in the Fijian, Cook, Marquesas, Ellice and Gilbert islands to form a protective Pacific ring. Such bases would be used to carry out air patrols for the detection of enemy surface raiders. As a corollary, Taylor proposed using the Catalina to conduct a survey for a trans-Pacific air service to Canada or to Europe.

Despite the advantages of his political connections, what appears to have been working against the progress of Taylor's plans that day was the attendance at the meeting of Chief of Naval Staff Sir Ragnar Colvin and Air Chief Marshal Sir Charles Burnett, who were asked to consider his proposal. Both could be expected to have little more than their own services' interests at heart.

Their subsequent report, tabled at the War Cabinet by Menzies in his role as the government's minister for defence co-ordination, brought little good news for Taylor. Any such proposal, their report said, in addition to being 'well outside the Australian sphere of influence', would mean an unacceptable dispersal of effort. 'If any extra effort is obtainable it would be much more suitably employed in supporting our organised service efforts in the more vital areas nearer home,' the chiefs noted. They also pointed out that even if the sovereignty aspects of any bases could be achieved, without adequate protection they could become a 'potential danger and may prove of assistance to the enemy and a menace to ourselves'. Any advantage of an air route across the Pacific was described as 'slight', believing its cost far outweighed its defence value.

Ministerial correspondence between Taylor and Fairbairn in the following months obviously led Taylor to believe that the door was still ajar, with even a suggestion that any diplomatic difficulties with the acquisition of a military aircraft from the US could possibly be overcome, and that Taylor could also be used to train RAAF personnel. This appears to have been a bridge too far for Air Chief Marshal Burnett, who used a departmental minute to his own minister of defence to express his annoyance at Taylor's approaches to another authority: 'I feel that the action taken with regard to Captain Taylor without reference to the Air Board or myself is wrong . . .' Burnett went as far as suggesting that if the cabinet wished to sponsor the flight of Captain Taylor, 'it should be done under the control of the Civil Aviation Department, and the Air Force should take delivery of the aircraft on arrival in Australia'. Fairbairn was quick to clarify his position, assuring Burnett: 'There are still a great many details yet to be worked out in connection with this proposed flight.'

By now, however, other bureaucratic sensitivities had been triggered with the director-general of Civil Aviation Arthur Corbett telling Fairbairn that an extensive survey of the Pacific had already been carried out in 1938 by New Zealand air force and civil aviation authorities.

Corbett also appears to have been still smarting from his department's own support of Taylor's original Indian Ocean adventure, claiming it 'had simply become a channel for passing vouchers to the Treasury . . . Expenditure of large amounts, some of which appeared to be extravagant and unnecessary was incurred before it was possible to control it and no limitations appear to have been placed on Captain Taylor's activities.' He also took the opportunity to be scathing of its legacy:

> As a matter of fact, the Indian Ocean Survey can only be regarded as an elaborate flying picnic at the public expense resulting in a travel talk illustrated with photographs and chart cuttings of little value, demonstrating nothing which was not already known and omitting that which might well have been included.

Such comments must have created some embarrassment for Fairbairn, who had indicated to Taylor early in July that once the government had purchased a Catalina he would be commissioned to deliver it and at the same time survey the route. He suggested to Taylor that he 'crystallise' his views on the issue with a view to further discussions on Fairbairn's return from a twelve-day inspectional flight around Australia.

Their meeting was never to take place, as within weeks Fairbairn would be killed when a Lockheed Hudson carrying him and other VIPs crashed on approach to Canberra airport.

Not only would Taylor lose a valuable ally but it was a crash both the wartime Menzies government and the nation could ill afford, taking, along with Fairbairn, Minister for Army and Repatriation Geoffrey Street, Minister of Scientific and Industrial Research Sir Henry Gullett, Chief of the General Staff Sir Cyril Brudenell White, White's staff officer Lieutenant Colonel Francis Thornthwaite and Fairbairn's private secretary Richard Elford, along with the four-man RAAF crew.

Meanwhile, the procurement of Catalina flying boats had developed a momentum of its own within the RAAF. Initially the aim was for the purchase of seven but as planning progressed the number increased, with the very size of the program taking it beyond the RAAF and into the civil sphere under Corbett's Department of Civil Aviation. Part of the reason for this was the political aspect of the procurement of military aircraft from America, a nation still not yet at war.

The first approach to ferry the Catalinas across the Pacific came to Qantas in September 1940, which must have come as a relief to Fysh who would have been closely watching the ongoing Taylor saga. Although there are no records indicating Fysh's personal thoughts, there is little doubt he would still be harbouring some resentment towards Taylor, finding it hard to forget the problems caused by his compatriot's terse and untimely telegram from London a few years previously when he refused to fly the DH 86 after accidents in the critical formative weeks of the Empire Air Service.

Qantas was quick to respond, immediately assigning the organisational task to the superintendent of flying operations, Lester Brain. His unit, to be known as the Long-Range Operations Division, would eventually involve ten captains, six first officers, eight radio officers and thirteen engineers, all carefully chosen to spread the benefits of the maximum experience the project would bring across the company.

But Taylor had not gone away and Brain's first problem would turn out to be a diplomatic one. Given Taylor's original approach to the prime minister and Fairbairn, a role would have to be found for him on the first delivery. 'It was a little awkward politically,' Brain would later reflect. 'I was approached on the side and told, "Look, we have a little bit of a problem here. He wants to be in on the act, famous navigator etcetera. Would you be happy to have Captain Taylor as your navigator?" I had no problem with it and suggested he could join our staff temporarily and we rigged him out in a Qantas uniform.'

Since nothing of this scale had ever been undertaken before, while Brain developed his operational plan, the government was at work on the delicate task of convincing the United States Department of War to part with the aircraft from the Consolidated Vultee factory production line in San Diego, now fully engaged in producing Catalinas for themselves and the war in Europe.

Since Australia needed to jump the queue, it called for someone with the right contacts in Washington, a job that fell to Brain's former Qantas colleague Scotty Allan, now with the RAAF's No. 23 Squadron in Brisbane. Once the aircraft were delivered Allan had been earmarked to take command of training the RAAF pilots who would fly them at Rathmines in New South Wales.

With at least some of the diplomatic niceties out of the way, one of Qantas's most experienced ground engineers, Dudley Wright, headed for the Consolidated factory to prepare for the delivery while Scotty Allan did the diplomatic rounds in Washington, a chore that would lead to an unexpected meeting.

Using his old aviation contacts, Allan pressed his case for fast approval of the aircraft at meetings with the War Department, insisting that the

South Pacific had every chance of 'being overrun by the Japanese'. The sessions culminated in a roundtable conference involving war service chiefs and the head of the Procurement Board, where Allan was plied with questions about what Australia was doing about the Japanese threat. He was then told to await a decision.

A few days later he found himself being put through yet another series of security checks at yet another imposing building before being ushered into a room to meet 'a gentleman who didn't get up when we were introduced'. It was President Roosevelt.

'I didn't know until then that he was a paraplegic. He asked me what I was here for, and I told him all about it and we had a pleasant conversation. I said it was of the utmost necessity we get aeroplanes,' Allan later recalled. 'It never had occurred to me that the United States would come into the war, but everybody else was getting aid from America, and Australia had a claim to some assistance too. I was there to put in our claim for aeroplanes.'

Within days Allan had approval for nineteen Catalina flying boats for the RAAF out of the seven hundred which had been ordered from Consolidated Vultee, and he was on his way to San Diego to see them being built. By now Brain and a small team were also on their way, but not before Brain had sorted out a problem of his own.

While Brain and his team had accumulated thousands of hours of experience on flying boats, none, with the exception of Taylor, was licensed to fly a Catalina, a factor that Brain feared would create difficulties when the American authorities came to hand over the first aircraft. He put the problem to the controller-general of Civil Aviation, Edgar Johnston, explaining that he'd flown almost every flying boat in existence at that time, from the Qantas Empire to the Cutty Sark, the Calcutta and the Rangoon, so he was pretty sure he could fly the Catalina. Johnston fixed the problem by signing an endorsement for him to fly any multi-engine flying boat, even though Brain had never even sat in a Catalina.

Conservative, quietly spoken and not one inclined to exaggerated descriptions, Brain would later record his surprise on his first exposure to the industrial might of America when it came to aircraft production. For Brain, accustomed to the struggle to get by with limited facilities and manpower that marked the early years of Qantas, the Consolidated Vultee factory at San Diego was something of an eye-opener. Here was a factory with twenty thousand employees, another being built a few miles away which would have a further twenty thousand, both to produce flying boats, with yet another already planned for Fort Worth in Texas for the production of landplanes. 'Aircraft output at the San Diego factory has already outstripped space,' Brain would write. 'In some sections work on semi-complete machines is progressing in buildings which are still in the course of construction.'

Taking advantage of the fine, dry climate, Brain noted that it was common to complete assembly in the open after the hull had been laid down indoors. 'At this moment, there are literally acres of aircraft under construction out of doors. As far as the eye can see there are lines and lines of big, modern aeroplanes. The sight is one I shall never forget,' he would write in his report to Fysh, at the same time marvelling at the hundred motor scooters, known as 'popcans', which enabled executives and engineers to move from one section to another without wasting time.

In fact, eight Catalinas were rolling off the assembly line each week, part of the eighty total aircraft a month, which included B-24 Liberator bombers for Great Britain. Although Brain could not know it at the time, the B-24 would also bear the Flying Kangaroo's colours later in the war.

What Brain was witnessing was the birth of a wartime American military–industrial complex which, on reaching its peak, would overwhelm the war machines of two enemies. It would also be the precursor of America's pre-eminent role in worldwide aviation at the end of the war.

As for the Catalinas and the four-engine B-24 Liberator bombers Brain could see under production, along with Australia and the United

States Navy, large orders had been placed by the British and Netherlands East Indies governments. The French government had also placed orders, although the fall of France now meant that some of those would make up the Australian order.

The Catalina itself was not a new design and had been flying with the US Navy since the mid-1930s, but its engine power had been increased along with the airframe's ability to handle heavier loads, allowing for take-off weights more than double its original design, a factor which would have important ramifications for Qantas in the future.

Its real value, though, was the advantage such increased engine performance and loadings brought to its ability to extend its range well beyond most other aircraft of the time, an ability the Qantas crews would put to the test on the delivery flights in the months ahead.

There were early delays, however. Shortly after his arrival in San Diego in late December, Brain was told that, despite the lobbying by Scotty Allan to slip Australia up the priority delivery list, the first of the RAAF's aeroplanes would not be ready until the first week in February. Brain did not relish the thought of sitting around in San Diego for weeks but was heartened when word came Consolidated did not have the crews available to deliver four British Catalinas that were sitting on the ramp ready to be flown away. Since the British machines were identical in every detail to the RAAF order, down to the camouflage and markings, Brain watched in hopeful anticipation as Australian embassy officials went into action to see if Australia could take them instead.

After lengthy negotiations, the British finally offered Australia delivery of the first two aircraft, one to be taken by the RAAF and the other passed over to the Royal Air Force to fly on to Singapore. That would increase the total to be delivered by Qantas from eighteen to nineteen, but since Brain already had the RAAF's Allan plus several RAAF engineers and a radio officer with him in San Diego to make up extra crew numbers, he accepted immediately and plans were made to fly the first two aircraft out on 20 January 1941.

Hectic weeks of activity followed as Brain's team studied the Catalinas from nose to tail, but by the time delivery day came around Brain himself had managed to fly a Catalina for less than an hour with a company test pilot. Brain found the Cat generally similar to flying the Empires, although with only two instead of four engines, and those two engines closer together, manoeuvring the aircraft on the water called for a different technique. A pilot could no longer use thrust on an outer engine to turn the aircraft on a tight circle, so drogues were used in combination with the engines to slow the aircraft in a turn without gathering too much speed.

By the time departure day came around the British had changed their minds again, revealing that since their own people in Singapore were as yet unprepared for a Catalina delivery, Australia could take both aircraft. So Brain reverted to his original crew plan and, after a weather delay, the first aircraft left for Honolulu with Brain, Taylor, Dudley Wright and radio officer Pat Patterson as the Qantas crew, with Scotty Allan, two RAAF sergeants and three Americans on board. Orm Denny would join as copilot at Honolulu.

Heavily loaded with ten on board, their baggage, emergency rations, and bits and pieces of equipment from the factory, the Catalina took some time to get into the air, Brain describing 'green water over the cockpit for some seconds' in the early part of the take-off run.

Their first sector covered 3000 miles, an extra 500 miles beyond the direct route due to weather patterns, so by the time they set down at Honolulu they had spent twenty-two hours and five minutes in the air. Even then, Brain noted, they still had sufficient fuel for another four hours' flying.

Although they were ready to move on quickly to the next sector to Canton Island, meteorological officers at Honolulu warned them of two cold fronts with turbulent cloud patterns that would make this dangerous at night. So their departure was delayed until dawn the next morning, allowing an arrival at Canton Island two hours after dark, Brain's first landing of a Catalina at night.

The distances for the flight sectors took the Qantas crews into a whole new regime of flying, far in excess of their experiences in the shorter 700-mile range of the Empire flying boats. Pearl Harbor to Canton Island meant over fourteen hours in the air covering 1665 miles, Canton to Noumea fifteen hours to cover another 700 miles, and finally ten hours for the 1069 miles to Rose Bay.

But at least the long hours in the air came with creature comforts the Qantas crews had never experienced before. Reminiscing years later, Brain would contrast the Catalina with the British-built Empire boats they were accustomed to flying:

> The Cat even had ashtrays in the cockpit. I found myself sitting up on a beautiful night above low cloud with the stars all shining brightly like lamp posts and smoking a Cuban cigar and thought to myself: This is the life. Then in addition they had their own little electric stove and while you were enjoying this you could smell the beautiful American coffee percolating. Someone could bring me a coffee and a sandwich.

Along with that were four comfortable bunks, which helped a crew to remain on duty for long periods.

Orm Denny left the aircraft at Noumea to return to Honolulu to command the next aircraft on the delivery schedule, part of a process of exposing as many captains and first officers as possible to the experience of flying the Cats.

The arrival of Brain's delivery flight into Sydney was only the third in aviation history to make a direct flight across the Pacific, the first being Kingsford Smith and Ulm's initial crossing east to west and the second Kingsford Smith and Taylor's from west to east.

In his detailed report to Fysh, Brain paid tribute to the exceptional co-operation of both Pan American and the United States Navy, whose maintenance and meteorological support had contributed to the success of the mission. As for P.G. Taylor's politically driven 'participation' in the flight as navigator, at one stage during the delivery process Brain had commented to Edgar Johnston that maintaining happy relations with the individualist Taylor was 'not easy', although when it came to his report to Fysh he appears to have chosen his words carefully:

> I should like to record that Captain P.G. Taylor, who joined our organisation temporarily and acted as navigator on nine out of the nineteen flights, conceded much from his normal attitude and went out of his way to give to our other navigators the benefit of his previous practical experience.

Many years later, however, in a recorded interview, he would not be quite as diplomatic when asked to put Taylor's participation in context:

> Quite a number of our captains had qualified as first class navigators and some of them were excellent. [Bert] Hussey and [Aub] Koch were really top notch sextant navigators, quicker and more qualified technically than P.G. Taylor. Not to detract from him. He was the pioneer astro navigator but by the time we were bringing those Catalinas out he wasn't near as quick as Hussey or Koch.

Perhaps another anecdote from that first flight in January 1941, although not from Brain, helps describe the delicate atmosphere that existed between some of the exceptionally qualified airmen on board.

George 'Scotty' Allan, regarded by Brain among others as the best pilot of the era, including Charles Kingsford Smith himself, had no peers in his knowledge of engineering, judgement of weather and navigation skills. The story goes that during one of Allan's periods at the controls, Taylor repeatedly passed notes forward giving him course adjustments until

Allan's patience snapped: 'Tell him the wee Scot can see the island ahead with his own bloody eyes!'

Brain would be lavish in his praise of the Catalina's performance:

> No mechanical trouble was experienced. The engines ran perfectly throughout, required no maintenance and had oil consumption less than three pints per engine hour. No cleaning was done but the engine cowlings and wing were spotless on arrival in Sydney, in marked contrast to the British engines of similar type, which have four to six times the oil consumption and throw oil and grease all over the place.

It would later transpire that Brain's report had overlooked one engine change in Honolulu, but given that the aircraft were being delivered straight off the San Diego assembly line, their performance was little short of remarkable. And while he would also pay tribute to the 'exceptional' work of Pan American, the US Navy and meteorological services in their handling of the aircraft and their general support of the mission, he probably remained blissfully unaware of the experience of engineer Jan Aldous on one of Orm Denny's transits of Honolulu.

Aldous had completed his engineer's pre-flight check and was charging the Catalina's batteries when an American serviceman came on board with a spray gun attached to an air hose and proceeded to spray the interior of the aircraft with insecticide. Aldous asked him to avoid spraying near the auxiliary power unit (APU) as it was hot and could be a fire risk, only to be met by a surly smirk in Aldous's direction as the American pointed the spray gun directly into the APU's air intake, causing it to stop.

Since the APU was difficult to start at any time Aldous was not amused, immediately taking the American by the collar and the seat of his pants and throwing him bodily off the aircraft onto the pontoon, and the spray gun after him.

Finally, after a struggle, Aldous got the APU running again and was casting the Catalina's ropes off the pontoon when he saw the spray gunner and two military policemen hurrying towards the dock. Just then he heard Denny shout as they taxied away from the pontoon, 'I don't think that chap liked that. Perhaps you shouldn't have thrown him off.' A few minutes later they were airborne towards Canton Island.

In addition to being the first to arrive in Sydney from an overseas port, the Catalina delivery program would be noteworthy for other reasons, one being that it marked Qantas's first use of flight engineers.

While ground engineers had flown on sectors through to Singapore with the Empire boats, the Catalinas had been designed with a specific flight engineer's station perched four metres behind the pilots in the pylon, to be known as the cabane, which joined the fuselage to the wing. There the flight engineer operated the engine start buttons, fuel mixture controls and fuel flow monitors and other essentials to ensure the aircraft was performing as it should. Communication between pilots and the flight engineer was by intercom or visual signals.

The remote combination, added to the fact that the crews had only limited time to get to know their aircraft before departure from San Diego or Honolulu, could lead to some tense moments.

On one delivery Brain was plugging along at around two thousand feet in cold, drizzling rain and darkness over the Pacific, still hours away from Noumea, when one of the engines started to splutter, followed soon after by the other one. Quickly realising the carburettors might be icing up, he called the engineer on the intercom asking him to turn up the heat on the carburettor. With no reply from the flight engineer and already losing height, Brain called again, to be told by the engineer he was still looking for the control. '"Well, you better find it pretty quick or we're going to be in the sea." Fortunately, he found it, the spluttering ceased and that was that,' Brain would recall.

Far from any criticism, Brain was quick to point out that the succession of engineers assigned to the deliveries could not be expected to know everything about the aircraft after a few short days of looking over it and reading the handbook. Brain knew no such situation would be countenanced in peacetime: 'Just part of the risk that had to be taken as part of the wartime effort.'

Carburettor difficulties aside, as the deliveries progressed and their confidence in the Catalina increased, operating crews took every opportunity to stretch the flight envelope of the aircraft. In the end one particular challenge would become too tempting for several of the captains and would also bring out their competitive instincts.

In the back of the mind of most crews was to overfly Noumea direct to Sydney from Canton Island, a distance of just over three thousand miles, but it would need favourable tailwinds and ultra conservative use of power and fuel.

The opportunity came on 4 October 1941. With the last of the deliveries in sight, three aircraft under the command of Russell Tapp, Bill Crowther and Bert Hussey left Honolulu at the same time, making it to Canton Island that night. The following morning, upon learning that the weather conditions en route might be favourable for a nonstop attempt, Tapp and Crowther arrived at their aircraft to find Hussey had already left. Suspecting that their colleague was trying to steal a march on them and be the first to do the trip nonstop, Crowther and Tapp took off one behind the other and set course for Australia, both determined to operate via their long-range plans, using careful engine operation and closely studying all wind directions to make the most of any tailwind advantage.

Soon after their pre-dawn take-off Crowther and Tapp lost sight of each other but kept in touch via radio, with neither giving away too much information about their position or intentions. Tapp became suspicious when Crowther kept asking him for his position and whether he intended landing at Noumea. 'We were getting a bit cagey by this time, and I'm afraid I gave evasive answers which did not mention our position and said simply that we were not sure whether we would land at Noumea,' he recalled. 'We repeated this answer every time he asked our intentions and position.'

By now, as they were approaching Noumea, Tapp's fuel calculations told him that there was still a bare minimum of fuel left to reach Sydney, but if the situation became critical they had enough to reach Brisbane. It wasn't until Crowther radioed that he was putting in to Noumea that Tapp signalled his own news: they had passed Noumea and were continuing on to Sydney.

Qantas records show that Tapp reached Sydney twenty-six hours after leaving Canton Island, but in later years Tapp would insist it was in fact 'twenty-four hours to the minute'. Whatever the actual time, Tapp had delicately trimmed the fuel consumption down to 190 litres an hour and still had two hours' fuel left when he alighted at Rose Bay. Not only were Tapp and his crew the first to achieve that distance but the lessons learned would be valuable when it came time to operate Qantas's secret Double Sunrise service through enemy territory between Perth and Colombo in 1943.

The delivery flights also led to a request by Lester Brain for all RAAF Catalina aircraft on order to carry duplicate radio transmitters and receivers on board as a backup safety measure, noting that the British aircraft to be delivered already had duplicate equipment while those on order for the RAAF did not. 'For an arrival at night on a minute coral island such as Canton, a crew is absolutely dependent on radio to guide the aircraft in,' he reported.

As for Brain's high praise for the Catalina as an aircraft, it's a well-known fact that airmen are capable of developing a deep affection for a particular type of aircraft they fly, and there is overwhelming evidence that the Catalinas had won the hearts of the Qantas pilots. Although they had no way of knowing at the time, it would be a factor that would carry some of them through different, vastly more dangerous wartime missions not far in the future.

By the time all nineteen aircraft had been delivered in October 1941, Scotty Allan was already back in his RAAF role at Rathmines, near Newcastle in New South Wales, training pilots to fly them. Of the nineteen Cats, however, only five would survive the war.

During the time Brain's team crisscrossed the Pacific between January and October 1941, a great deal was happening on other company fronts, much of it against the background of a rapidly developing nervousness about what lay ahead for Australia.

The long-running war in China between Japan, Chiang Kai-shek's Kuomintang (KMT) and Mao Tse-tung's Communists (CCP) had reached a stalemate, with Japan still unable to claim a victory and the Chinese unable to throw them back into the sea. There appeared little doubt, however, that Japan's ambitions extended well beyond China, and while some believed their heavy commitment in troops, arms and equipment there would make it unlikely they'd turn their attention south in the foreseeable future, some in Australia were not so sure.

The Australian government now found itself on the horns of a dilemma. With Australia's major infantry divisions committed in the Middle East, its naval forces in the Mediterranean and a steady stream of its airmen heading via the Empire Air Training Scheme for service with the Royal Air Force, the European war was taking up the bulk of the country's defence resources.

Hanging like a shadow over it all was the vulnerability of Singapore.

It was with the latter at the top of his agenda that Prime Minister Menzies flew out of Rose Bay on a Qantas flying boat under the command of Captain Ron Adair towards the end of January 1941. Menzies, suitably impressed, noted in his diary:

> The aircraft is so streamlined that looked at from the rear it looks positively herring-gutted, but from inside it is most roomy—comfortable seats in which you may snooze not only post-prandially but all day.

> Chief feature in the air—press the button and the steward arrives with the drinks—the company's compliments in our case. Shedden [Frederick Shedden, secretary of the Department of Defence, War Cabinet and Advisory War Council] and I, each of which dived into his pockets for cash, smile with genuine Scottish pleasure.

Menzies, however, found the stopover in the heat at Karumba not quite such a pleasant experience: 'Silk shirts are hopeless for the tropics. They are wet through in 5 minutes and flap greasily on you for the rest of the day.' Some days later towards the end of the journey aboard a BOAC Empire, his diary reveals a more ominous tone: 'Approaching England we fly low. There is tension in the nerves, a feeling of "running the gauntlet".'

His efforts to get Churchill's government to even acknowledge the Japanese threat were to fall on deaf ears, Britain's leader providing only repeated assurances that the 'impregnable' fortress of Singapore would deter any attempt by the Japanese to threaten Australia.

Nor did the fragility of Australian politics help. Even as Menzies set off for London his hold on leadership of his own United Australia Party was weakening, and by the time he returned it was obvious its days were numbered. Menzies' resignation in August led to a bizarre few weeks where his deputy, Arthur Fadden, became prime minister for a matter of months until, early in October, two independents who had kept the Menzies government in office switched allegiance to Labor and John Curtin became prime minister.

While political loyalties ebbed and flowed, Qantas continued to consolidate its service throughout Australia and the Netherlands East Indies to Singapore. Refuelling and berthing facilities along with suitable accommodation had to be monitored and improved where necessary. Pulling all the threads of an international flying boat service together called for co-ordination and approval from a range of authorities not under the control of the airline. Care had to be taken that launches used for the loading and unloading of passengers and freight, particularly through the Netherlands East Indies stopovers, were of a standard able to avoid the risk of damage to the aircraft. Even at Australian ports, delicate compromises had to be reached if the inevitable flight delays were to be catered for; at one stage the civil aviation controller at Townsville, struggling with limited staff, refused to lay a flare path for unscheduled pre-dawn departures for Sydney designed to make up time on late-running services, although he did agree to lay a flare path when necessary to avoid a night landing at Rose Bay.

Providing enough, and adequate, accommodation for passengers and crews was an ongoing problem, even at larger Australian centres like Darwin where the unscheduled arrival of several aircraft at the same time could strain resources to the limit.

Along with such operational and administrative difficulties, other developments took place during 1941 that would play a significant role in the Qantas story as the situation in Europe deteriorated.

Sixteen Empire flying boats were south of the Mediterranean when Italy declared war in June 1941, and they would now be used to reroute the Australian link, which would follow the original pattern from Australia to Singapore, Calcutta and Karachi to Cairo but then swing south away from the Mediterranean to Durban. From there, passengers, freight and mail would complete their journey to England by ship.

The impact of the loss of the Mediterranean had an immediate effect on Qantas. BOAC, with increasing numbers of its fleet and personnel now assigned to the critical task of ferrying military aircraft from the United States to Britain, was fast running out of aircrew to the point where they could no longer provide enough crews to run their service all the way through to Singapore. Qantas, therefore, would have to take up the slack and extend their service beyond Singapore to Penang, Bangkok, Rangoon and Akyab to Calcutta and Karachi.

Given the extra three thousand miles required to take on the task, and with the extension of the service scheduled to begin within weeks, the original shortcomings in the range of the Qantas flying boats created a problem that needed to be addressed, and work began immediately on fitting each of the Qantas machines with three 250-gallon (1100-litre) tanks to handle the long sector hops demanded by the new route.

As is common with such issues in the airline business, aircraft commitments meant that the new tanks could only be fitted as the boats came into Rose Bay on service, so while extra tanks were made and sent on to Durban for installation there, not all of the flying boats were equipped with the additional tanks when the first Karachi service left Sydney in October 1941, thus adding the unwelcome necessity for additional fuelling stops en route. The one bright spot, however, was that the conclusion of the Catalina delivery schedule allowed those aircrew to be quickly reassigned to take up the extra Karachi flying.

Other essential materials needed for the maintenance of the fleet were now being affected by the impact of the war, confirming the wisdom of Fysh's insistence in the early stage of the Imperial partnership that Qantas should be as self-sufficient as possible at its end of the route. Along with the development of workshops at Sydney and Brisbane, Arthur Baird and his senior engineer, Dudley Wright, had established an instrument-repair department in a makeshift shed at Rose Bay, at times combining primitive equipment with a streak of Australian ingenuity. Even a milking-machine pump was used to provide vacuum when necessary in an organisation that would eventually maintain and repair the delicate instrumentation carried on US Air Force and RAAF aircraft.

But with the extra demands of the Karachi extension, Qantas too was finding itself short of pilots, a problem that was helped with the return to Qantas of Eric Sims and Bill Purton from the RAAF's No. 11 and 20 squadrons. Goff Hemsworth and Bob Gurney would remain with the RAAF, but with tragic results.

Chapter 5

THE AMERICANS ARE COMING: PAN AM

If Hudson Fysh's team was to learn anything in those tense years of 1940 and 1941, it was to never—at least as far as the United States was concerned—let a threat of war stand in the way of a competitive advantage.

There was no secret about the US government's employment of Pan American as an instrument of foreign policy, using it to pioneer its ventures into South America and other parts of the world of interest to American traders. Australia was no exception, and while the British and Australian governments concentrated on the difficulties of maintaining a wartime pattern for the Empire route, the Americans, fully aware of a weakened British aviation sector, were pressing hard to follow Sir Charles Kingsford Smith's flight path across the Pacific to Australia.

By 1941 Pan American's flying boats were already going to New Zealand, but while an extension to Australia might be their next logical step, some within the Australian government regarded it as an exercise in American imperialism. Neither did the British government like the idea, at least without some quid pro quo, such as the right to operate to Honolulu, although attitudes towards Pan Am's aspirations differed even within Qantas.

Fysh, for instance, in concert with Runciman and his colleagues at BOAC, would have none of it, believing the Americans were simply taking advantage of their most difficult circumstances. Certainly the Americans were willing to apply maximum public pressure, at one stage publicly suggesting the somewhat farcical proposal that they would fly to Noumea and from there bring their passengers to Australia by yacht—hardly a practical move, but even the suggestion of it would be guaranteed to create a public relations nightmare for Australia. McMaster, on the other hand, once again foreseeing value in an increasingly close relationship with the Americans, suggested the trans-Tasman be given over to the Americans under a lease arrangement.

Some in the government held similar views, and even as Brain and his crews were taking delivery of the RAAF's Catalinas, Australia's representative in Washington, Richard Casey, was signalling to his superiors that Australia's intransigence was not in keeping with the increasing importance of the American relationship. 'The implication has clearly been that whilst we are seeking very whole-hearted American co-operation in certain future eventualities, at the same time we steadily refuse to grant landing rights in Australia, despite their importance from a defence point of view,' Casey cabled Canberra. 'Compared with the great issues that are at stake, I submit that this matter is relatively trivial.'

When it came to any foreign competitive threat, however, Fysh had his own views on what needed to be done to ensure the future of Commonwealth aviation, telling a board meeting on 15 October 1941:

> There is no doubt the competitive spirit of commercial aviation has not been dulled by the war. In fact, it seems very clear that if British

> Civil Aviation is not to be swamped, the various members of the British Commonwealth will need to stand together with the operation of the trunk routes and so attain the greater strength. Conditions will be difficult and there are many vital questions involved but we have to stand up to the great test of Empire strength and look closely to the future.

He also advised the board that the first service to be flown on to Karachi by Qantas crews would leave the next day, 16 October, proudly adding a historical reminder that in one month's time Qantas would reach its twenty-first anniversary.

For the present though, while both sides had firmly placed their Pacific air services stakes in the ground, the issue would gradually fade away, overtaken by matters of far greater significance.

Chapter 6

ROUTE EXTENSIONS AND SIBOLGA DOGS

The vulnerability of Singapore may not have been Winston Churchill's main priority as 1941 progressed but it certainly was for Qantas and Australia's civil aviation authorities.

By now few doubts remained that whatever Japanese intentions were to the south, contingencies had to be put in place to ensure the continuation of the Karachi service, which operated from Singapore to a night stop at Bangkok and on to Rangoon and Akyab in Burma, before heading across the waters of the Bay of Bengal to Calcutta and on to Karachi.

With this aim Orm Denny set out in August to survey alternative routes from Batavia and Singapore which could be used to bypass Singapore itself if this became necessary, even though there was still belief in some quarters that this bastion of Empire power in the Far East would eventually halt any Japanese thrust.

Using a flying boat provided by the Dutch, Denny flew along the western coast of Sumatra, mapping out a route that would pass from Batavia through Benkulen, Padang, Sibolga and the island of Sabang off Sumatra's northern tip, thus placing the land mass of Sumatra as a buffer between any Japanese threat to Malaya and Singapore.

While Denny's journey succeeded in ensuring the necessities such as handling facilities and fuel for operating the flying boats were in place at each port, it had aspects of pioneering about it, not least with some of the culinary challenges to be found at stops along Sumatra's west coast.

Settling in at the relatively comfortable Sibolga hotel for the evening, Denny was enjoying pre-dinner drinks with the crew when he noticed his Dutch colleagues enjoying a laughing exchange in Malay with the manager of the premises. When he asked what was so amusing they kept him in suspense for a few minutes before finally admitting that the discussion had been around whether a 'very expensive and very scarce local delicacy' might be on the menu.

At first concerned that the joke might be on him, Denny was soon convinced otherwise when the manager took him out the back to reveal the breeding kennels for the dogs used for the table. Though he accepted crocodile and kangaroo might elicit a similar response in Australia, he was determined to draw the line at Sibolga dog, but the manager assured him it wasn't on the menu that night. Denny took no chances and ordered eggs!

Denny's survey formed the template for a four-phase plan to be followed in sequence to keep the flying boat service out of harm's way should the worst happen and the Japanese moved towards Singapore.

The first phase would eliminate Bangkok between Penang and Rangoon as a night stop, the most eastern and therefore most vulnerable part of the route. Phase two would eliminate Thailand altogether and fly direct from Penang via Mergui on Burma's southern edge to Rangoon, while phase three would be to avoid the Burmese coast altogether by flying out across the Bay of Bengal to Port Blair, capital of the remote Andaman Islands, before cutting back north-east to Rangoon. Phase four would omit Malaya and should the worst happen and Singapore became too dangerous as a stopover on the main route, it would remain linked via a shuttle operating between Singapore and Batavia.

Even while the plan was being printed in late November, British troops in Singapore and the Malay states were ordered to move to their battle stations as reports began coming in of Japanese shipping and troop movements in the region.

It was against this background that Fysh left Rose Bay for Singapore on 4 December 1941 to meet with Walter Runciman and John Brancker of BOAC. Two years had now passed since the principals of the airlines had met, and with Runciman nearby in Bangkok on the final leg of an extended tour of BOAC's route the opportunity was too valuable to miss, particularly with the rapidly deteriorating situation now facing them in South-East Asia.

Even while Fysh was airborne, however, Qantas was already dipping its wings into the coming war, with pilot Lew Ambrose engaged in a spying mission over Thailand. Since flying military VIPs was a regular occurrence for Qantas crews, Britain's Commander-in-Chief Far East Sir Robert Brooke-Popham had been a regular passenger on Ambrose's aircraft on flights to Australia for meetings with the Australian government.

Although Ambrose found Brooke-Popham initially shy and retiring, the pair gradually struck up a comfortable relationship after Ambrose invited him to sit with them in the cockpit for several hours during the flights, an experience which 'Brookham', as he was known to his troops, seemed to enjoy immensely.

Early in December Brooke-Popham asked whether Ambrose, on his next trip from Bangkok to Singapore, would check out a report that the Japanese were constructing an airfield close to the Thai–Malay border, a task that Ambrose was only too delighted to accept.

As fate would have it, on his next trip from Karachi to Bangkok one of Ambrose's passengers would be Runciman, on his way to Bangkok and then on to his planned meeting with Fysh in Singapore. As he farewelled Runciman at Bangkok, Ambrose, never backward in expressing his view, couldn't resist offering some friendly advice of his own, suggesting that since the general feeling around the Far East was that Japan was coming closer to declaring war, it might be wise not to delay too long getting back to the United Kingdom.

Ambrose's warning was prophetic considering what was about to happen to Runciman in Bangkok.

Next morning, as he took off on the final two sectors of his scheduled service via Penang to Singapore, Ambrose had his own doubts about the chances of finding any evidence of the Japanese airfield, believing the jungle landscape would mean it was like looking for the proverbial needle in a haystack.

Also working against him was the nervous tension which, in these troubled times, had led to countries like Thailand demanding that all aircraft crossing their territory report their position every fifteen minutes, thus making it much more difficult to stray off course without his manoeuvres being detected. He had, however, secretly revised his flight plan in such a way as to give it his best shot and was going to do something no respectable pilot would ever do in respect to his passengers: rather than climb up through the clouds to smooth air he would fly between fifteen hundred and two thousand feet. This meant a very bumpy ride for his passengers, but by changing course abruptly every ten or fifteen minutes, if there was an airfield out there somewhere he might have a chance of finding it.

It wasn't long before one of his passengers, the bishop of Singapore, expressed his discomfort at the bumpy ride down the back, to which Ambrose weakly explained that he was flying low and changing course to 'dodge the weather'.

Then, with just fifteen miles to cover before they were out of Thai territory, to Ambrose's delight, a brand-new airfield appeared out of nowhere in front of him and, realising he could not alter course for a circuit to get a better view without raising the suspicions of those below, he told his crew to note all the details they could. They could see no aircraft on the strip, nor for that matter many people, before they climbed away into clearer skies towards Penang. When they arrived and he sought out the locally based intelligence officer to report his find, it soon became obvious the man had not been briefed and showed little interest. There was a different reception in Singapore, however, where an RAAF group captain was waiting and rushed off to Brooke-Popham's headquarters with the news. Ambrose would later learn Brooke-Popham had acted immediately to send a battalion of Indian troops to take over the airport, only to have them badly mauled by a strong force of Japanese who had apparently moved into the area later the same day.

Ambrose and his crew went into Singapore for a few days' break before their next flight. The date was 7 December 1941. The world for Australia, and Qantas, was about to change dramatically.

Chapter 7

THE BATTLE FOR SINGAPORE

Soon after midnight on the morning of 8 December 1941, Japanese troops landed at Kota Bahru in north-east Malaya in an assault timed to coincide with a devastating attack on Pearl Harbor and the crippling of most of the US fleet. Landings followed soon after at several points in Thailand.

Around 4 a.m., Hudson Fysh, who had checked into Singapore's Raffles Hotel that night, awoke to the sound of air-raid sirens, a few explosions and anti-aircraft fire. Thinking it was probably a fairly impressive local attempt at a practice alert, he turned over and went back to sleep.

It wasn't until the houseboy arrived with his morning tea a few hours later that he realised it had been the real thing. A stick of bombs had straddled Raffles Square, and although they'd inflicted limited damage, they had made enough of a mess to force the Kelly & Walsh bookshop to offer piles of bomb-hit books at greatly reduced prices. Ever on the lookout for a bargain, Fysh bought three books, one, *The Last Days in*

Paris, having a neat shrapnel hole through it that he thought would make a nice souvenir.

Later he would learn that the airport at Seletar had been the main target, but while the damage there was also relatively slight, it was now becoming obvious the early concerns about Singapore's vulnerability were about to be confirmed. There might be guards with fixed bayonets on the streets, anti-aircraft guns at key points throughout the city, sandbags against buildings, tank traps and barbed wire strewn about, and HMS *Prince of Wales* and *Repulse* on station, but already the abiding question was how long the empire's island outpost could hold out.

The answer would not be long in coming. Within days *Prince of Wales* and *Repulse*, in an ill-judged attempt to intercept the Japanese landing forces on the east coast without any protective air cover, would both be sunk, lost to the bombs of Japanese aircraft, setting in motion a series of events over a few short months that would see not only the loss of Singapore but the Netherlands East Indies as well.

Fysh and his Singapore team now had much to do. Although Qantas itself had few of its own staff in Singapore, mainly those engineers and others directly responsible for the turnaround of the flying boats, the general administrative work for both BOAC and Qantas was handled by an agency arm of Mansfield and Company, a major shipping concern which had been involved with the Empire air route since its earliest days.

Mansfield's man at the centre of all this was Malcolm Millar who, as the threat to Singapore developed, had initially been posted to his reserve battalion but fortunately for Qantas had been recalled to Mansfield to help in the now vital task of keeping the civil air route operating.

As a flurry of telegrams went backwards and forwards to both Australia and the United Kingdom, Fysh and Millar faced several immediate challenges. A decision now had to be made to set in motion the series of phases that had been prepared for just such an eventuality, the first of which was the elimination of Bangkok as a night stop since the enemy landings in Thailand now put that at risk.

For Fysh, however, this was not simply an operational decision but also a very personal one. It would leave his old BOAC colleagues Runciman and Brancker stranded in Bangkok.

With confusing reports coming in from the front lines and the situation changing hourly, Fysh appealed to Brooke-Popham's headquarters to use the Qantas southbound service under the command of Ron Adair to continue to Bangkok and lift them out, only to find out it was too late for that. RAF command had already directed Adair to avoid Bangkok and divert to Mergui in Burma to refuel. To Fysh's dismay, neither could Brooke-Popham's people offer any aircraft of their own to assist.

Meanwhile, in Bangkok itself, Runciman, Brancker and another executive of the company, Robert Linstead, were trying to stay one step ahead of the hundreds of Japanese troops who were now entering the Thai capital. Their aim was to make a dash for the Burmese border, an effort which the monocled Brancker later described with typical British understatement:

> We walked for a while, and then we decided we might as well try the train. No one attempted to stop us. I think the Thais were a little ashamed of their show of arms and wanted to help us out of the country if they could.

The train got them about a hundred miles to Phitsanulok in northern Thailand, where Brancker must have tired of slow surface transport: 'We decided to do things, if possible, in style and went to the airport.' Chartering an American Fairchild aircraft from the Thai commercial airline Aerial Transport Company, they flew to the Thai border where they threw their bags on a bullock wagon and walked across into Burma. From there they travelled by riverboat, car and train to finally reach Rangoon. Their journey to safety must have been particularly hard for Linstead as his pregnant wife was unable to travel and had to remain in Bangkok. Fortunately she would be one of the lucky ones and following the birth of her child would be repatriated in an exchange agreement.

Meanwhile, their original hope of rescue—Ron Adair flying *Castor*—was experiencing his own problems completing his schedule through to Singapore, now of increasing importance due to the fact that one of his passengers was General Gordon Bennett, on his way from the Middle East to Malaya to take command of Australian forces there.

Woken in the middle of the night of 7 December in his hotel in Rangoon, Adair was told that phase one had been introduced and he was to avoid Bangkok and head for Mergui and on to Penang from there. He made it to Mergui without any trouble, but a short time after he became airborne again a radio message warned him that Penang was under attack so he turned and headed back to Mergui. There he watched anxiously as hostile aircraft circled overhead while his flying boat was being refuelled, and rather than expose his aircraft any longer than necessary he decided to return to Rangoon until the situation became clearer.

At Rangoon no one seemed to know what was happening. There were no instructions and he now faced the additional dilemma of route changes that would severely test the limited fuel tanks on his aircraft. In what would become commonplace for Adair and his colleagues, when wartime circumstances changed captains quickly became adept at using their own initiative. Knowing that Aub Koch would be transiting there in *Ceres* heading for Karachi, he decided to swing wide across the Andaman Sea to Port Blair, thus lessening the risk of interception and allowing him to exchange *Castor* for *Ceres* and its longer-range tanks.

Exchanging aircraft, however, would not be quite that simple. While Adair had charts to Port Blair he had no details of moorings there, or, for that matter, maps from there to Singapore. Adding to his woes was the weather, bordering on cyclonic, with heavy rain and low cloud blanketing the region. In the event, with no direction-finding equipment at Port Blair, he was lucky to find the island at all.

As it turned out, he failed to receive a message from Port Blair advising him not to proceed because of the cyclonic weather, so when he did make it no one was expecting him, forcing *Castor* to taxi around for twenty minutes looking for a mooring.

It took three laborious hours to refuel from twenty-gallon drums before they were off again into continuing poor weather, at one stage landing at the wrong island before finally reaching Sabang to once again find no one was expecting them. Remaining overnight, they took off at 6 a.m. next day for Singapore, by now picking up radio messages asking about their welfare. Despite the temptation, Adair chose not to reply because of the risk of giving his position away to the enemy who could be expected to be monitoring all radio traffic.

Finally, almost within sight of Singapore he was told to hold off because an air raid was in progress. Qantas Singapore was pleased to see them. Nothing had been heard of Adair and his flying boat for two days. In his captain's report Adair paid tribute to his crew:

> They were all under considerable strain and each carried out any duty unhesitatingly and it is largely due to the teamwork of the crew that the aircraft reached Singapore safely, without suffering the slightest damage.

Gordon Bennett and the senior air force officers on board must also have been pleased to arrive, although fate would decree that his Singapore assignment would have a catastrophic impact on his future as one of Australia's top military officers.

Meanwhile in Singapore, amid the intermittent air-raid sirens, general chaos and alarming reports coming in from northern Malaya, Fysh and Malcolm Millar tried to plan their next moves while attempting to keep Lester Brain and head office back in Australia up to date on an ever-changing situation. Telegrams backwards and forwards quickly led to the cancellation of the Dili fortnightly call, along with other route adjustments and an increased requirement for military uplifts.

The primary concern now was to ensure the safety of the flying boats already on service by keeping them as far as possible out of harm's way until, hopefully, the situation became clearer. The key to this lay with Brooke-Popham's Royal Air Force headquarters, where decisions about the use of airspace and communications were being made that directly affected the Qantas aircraft.

One thing that was already certain was that the Rangoon–Port Blair–Sabang–Medan–Singapore route, which Denny had surveyed through the Andaman Islands in August, would now provide a reasonable buffer between the main areas of conflict and the unarmed Empire boats. Charts were becoming available and fuel stocks were in place at key points, but with Japanese reconnaissance aircraft already reaching further west, even this route might prove temporary.

The fact that Fysh just happened to be in Singapore at the time now brought with it significant advantages. Having his airline's managing director with him when he pleaded his case for access to the RAF decision-making process quickly led to Millar's appointment as liaison officer for the civil air operations, thus allowing him several visits a day to RAF headquarters to update his information. With things changing by the hour it might have limited advantage, but at least it was something.

Fysh's notes from the time graphically record the reactions of the various nationalities in Singapore at the dismal war news—the shock and amazement of the Americans at the devastation at Pearl Harbor, and then the British when word reached Singapore that the *Prince of Wales* and *Repulse* had been lost.

There was really no good news. On the ground, Japanese troops, many already battle-hardened in China, were quickly gaining ground and, contrary to popular belief, the Japanese pilots were well trained and the Zeros they were flying far superior to the RAF's Brewster Buffalo fighters.

Malcolm Millar's own problems increased, not least his transport situation. Forced to abandon his car when petrol rationing was introduced, he reverted to a motorcycle, only to have it requisitioned. He overcame that by bicycling to work until it too was requisitioned. He then found another car, only to have that bombed.

Despite the air-raid warnings and general mayhem, Fysh's diary notes a few days before he left for Batavia reveal at least a degree of optimism:

> One feels very useless and inefficient and starved for news and longs for action.
>
> The Jap aircraft come from Point Cambodia on the south-west tip of Indo China. Everyone realises the Japs have put up a good show, realise some great Allied weaknesses but have absolute confidence in the final outcome.

After noting some of the air-raid alarms were 'only the result of Jap reconnaissance aircraft', he finds time for a wry comment on their effect on some aspects of the Raffles service: 'An early alarm. The Raffles cook made a mess of his usually beautifully fried eggs for breakfast this morning—a drop in efficiency the Mikado would be glad to hear of.' Later, however, his notes adopt a more serious tone:

> Heard Australia's war effort described today as like unto a half dead fly trying to crawl through a plate of cold porridge. Australians unpopular here owing to our politicians withdrawing our troops from the Middle East . . .

Fysh remained for a week, during which plans were put in place for the Empire stand-by boat in Singapore to be flown out to Batavia with as much of the company spares and equipment as it could carry. Company engineer Bill Bennett and his staff would soon follow, bringing to an end Singapore as a maintenance base.

Chapter 8

RUNNING THE GAUNTLET

In those weeks following the first attack on Singapore, Qantas aircraft operating to and from Karachi faced arguably the most dangerous period in the airline's history as they ran the gauntlet of increasing Japanese control of the skies. In addition to adjusting their flights to avoid bombing raids, everyone on board kept a wary eye out for marauding Japanese fighters and watched anxiously as enemy reconnaissance planes circled overhead at major stopover points. Nor did all the problems lie with the enemy.

Unfortunately, often due to poor communications facilities or mistaken identification by nervous, trigger-happy ships' gunners, Qantas aircraft faced the real danger of being shot down by their own side. Occasionally they just had to hope they'd be recognised as a 'friendly' before the gunners opened fire.

Bob Gurney was challenged twice while approaching Singapore in *Corio*, once by a RAF aircraft and then soon after by a British warship.

On both occasions he flashed his signal lamp and simply hoped for the best, later calling on the armed services to improve their identification procedures, 'otherwise some service enthusiast may make a mistake and lots of them are quite capable of it'.

That same trip he described his approach into Surabaya as 'messy', probably something of an understatement under the circumstances. To avoid such incidents at Surabaya, pilots were instructed to fly around until they received a white flag, but after following the instructions for some minutes without any response, Gurney made his approach towards the harbour only to be shot at by an American Lockheed aircraft as he flattened out to land. 'I took a poor view of this and reported the incident. It seems we are the only people who carry out instructions correctly.'

As the Japanese advanced rapidly down the west coast of the Malay Peninsula, both coasts of Sumatra were becoming increasingly threatened by enemy aircraft, now within easy reach of the alighting areas on the flying boat route.

To add to crews' problems, radio communications, so necessary for captains to be able to make judgements as to the safety or otherwise of their destinations, were anything but reliable, often lacking co-ordination between authorities in Sumatra and RAF headquarters in Singapore.

The radio station at Medan on the north-east coast of Sumatra, strategically placed at the entry to the Malacca Straits, was used as a listening post by crews operating through Sabang and the Straits towards Singapore but often closed down without warning, leaving a 'blind spot' and preventing the RAF from giving any indication of what lay ahead of the flying boats. Crews would quickly conclude that a raid might be taking place on Medan and make appropriate adjustments.

In an effort to find a way of avoiding the risk of flying down the Straits, Russell Tapp flew between Singapore and Sabang in the hope of using a known gap through the Central Sumatran Range, which might open the way for the flying boats to cut directly across Sumatra towards Singapore and thus avoid the northern section of the Straits. Unfortunately, it also turned out to be the same route through the mountain passes regularly used by Japanese aircraft on their way to carry out their attacks on Sibolga and Padang on Sumatra's west coast.

Along with the normal through service, special charter flights for the military could prove equally challenging as desperate moves were made to reinforce Singapore with fighter and bomber aircraft.

While a shipload of Hurricane fighters that had arrived in crates were being assembled to replace the outclassed Brewster Buffalos ruthlessly being shot out of the sky by the Zeros, stocks of fuel were needed at Sabang for Blenheim light bombers flying in from the Middle East, a task assigned to Russell Tapp and *Corsair*. Brimful with drums of 100 octane, Tapp found that even with the extra hundred-gallon (450-litre) emergency tank he had fitted *Corsair* wasn't going to make the distance, forcing him to rob his RAF load and hand pump forty-eight gallons into his tanks to reach his destination.

Once at Sabang the fuel was unloaded, but while preparing to leave the mooring *Corsair*'s hull was holed as they gathered in the anchor. Too risky to have *Corsair* sit on the water while proper repairs were made, they patched the hole enough to allow them to return to Singapore the same day. Ultimately such last-minute air reinforcements for Singapore would prove inadequate. Ranged against a Japanese air arm of more than four hundred aircraft, the Blenheims were able to provide limited offensive action to stem the Japanese tide and the uncrated Hurricanes proved no match for the dominant Zeros.

As the situation on Malaya worsened, the risks to the flying boats increased, and this was perhaps no better illustrated than in a report written some months later by Captain John Connolly.

Sydney-born Connolly had started flying with Qantas on the Empire boats in 1940 after working as a flying instructor and with Airlines of Australia. His account not only vividly describes the very real dangers presented by the enemy, along with the more personal, human problems faced by the crews, but also illustrates the exceptional descriptive talent common among many of his peers.

With just a touch of irony, Connolly described how during most of these flights the weather 'remained beautifully clear', forcing crews to remain in a constant state of uneasy vigilance against the ever-present possibility of running into a predatory Japanese aircraft:

> The trips along the east and west coasts of Sumatra were about the most uncomfortable of the whole route.
>
> After leaving Sabang on one occasion, we skipped along low between Medan and the mountain range. As Medan radio had been silent for an unusually long time that morning, we suspected something was afoot and tried to give the place as wide a berth as we could—about seven miles, I think. Sure enough a Jap machine was shooting the place up, so we kept as low over the treetops as we could and trusted to our camouflage with the hills as the background to escape detection.
>
> When we made our first landing at Sibolga on the west coast of Sumatra we were very annoyed because no one would come out to take us off. Then we heard aircraft in the distance and the reason was clear enough. Discovery at that particular time by the Japs would have been particularly embarrassing, because among our passengers were two crippled men and a very pregnant Chinese woman, together with a party of very sick Indians who had wolfed practically all the food on board, and were then in the process of paying for their gluttony.

Connolly went on to describe a two-hour wait before the agent finally appeared with his native crew to explain the reason for the delay to meet them. A few days previously Sibolga had been heavily machine-gunned by Japanese aircraft, with the result that the sound of any aeroplane approaching sent the locals scrambling for shelters, which they would leave only with 'extreme reluctance'.

With alerts, alarms and raids now constant at points like Sabang, Padang and Sibolga, Connolly explained how it had become necessary to arrange their arrivals and departures in accordance with what he described as the 'Japanese timetable'. This was a reference to the highly predictable timing used by the Japanese aircraft in their missions along the coasts of Sumatra, a factor that was now proving increasingly valuable to the Qantas crews. 'Their appearance over Sibolga each morning to begin their sweep down the coast and shipping lanes was made almost invariably around 8.30 a.m.'

This particular Japanese routine of rigid scheduling would prove common throughout the rest of the war in the South-West Pacific, where often the timing and pattern of Japanese air activity could be anticipated to an incredibly accurate degree, often allowing the Allies to adjust accordingly.

Connolly's report of one flight from Port Blair to Rangoon also reveals how this 'constant state of unease' applied while the Qantas boats were both in the air and on the water as they passed through the region, forcing rapid decisions and route adjustments to minimise risk.

Even with the advantage of its remoteness, Port Blair, in the Andaman Island group, still attracted its fair share of Japanese attention. On one occasion, while Connolly's aircraft was on the water refuelling at Port Blair, a Japanese reconnaissance aircraft appeared but thankfully spent most of its time concentrating on a small bay several miles away. Soon after the Japanese plane flew off Connolly headed for Rangoon (now Yangon), to be told as they approached that the Burmese city was under attack. After flying around in circles waiting for the all clear he decided to divert to Bassein (now Pathein) in the south-east of Burma. Connolly had only been there a short time when he saw another Empire boat approaching to land. It was Orm Denny, who also had been heading to Rangoon from

Karachi when warned of the raid. Denny hadn't quite touched down when the all clear sounded and both Empires headed off again for Rangoon, only to arrive just in time for another raid. Quickly refuelling, both were soon again in the air, Denny towards Port Blair and Connolly towards Akyab. 'We had scarcely left the water when the Japs came over for the third time, but we decided quickly that we were just as safe in the air and on our way out as we would be on the water, and so kept on going.'

Fifteen minutes later, however, an air-raid alarm came from their former diversion port Bassein, which was now directly on his track to Akyab, leaving Connelly no alternative but to return to a Rangoon still under attack.

Luck was with him and the Japanese aircraft were concentrating their attention on the airport at the other side of town, but Connolly still faced the prospect of trigger-happy anti-aircraft gun crews along the banks of the Irrawaddy River as they approached to land, gunners who would be necessarily wary of any aircraft they thought might pose a threat.

Surviving Japanese bombs and twitchy ack-ack gunners wasn't the end of their trials that day. As it would turn out, their stay that night at Rangoon's Strand Hotel was anything but pleasant. 'The bewildered natives had left the city en masse, and the local authorities had been unable to clear away the numerous bodies trapped under the wharf wreckage. The hotel was adjacent to the waterfront and the stench was really bad—and quite inescapable.' You can almost feel Connolly's relief as he concludes his report: 'We were glad to be on our way next morning.'

Looking through the reports over seventy years later, there are numerous other examples of the varying issues crews had to deal with, not all of them related to being shot down by the enemy.

Aub Koch experienced some tense moments while trying to position *Coorong* for take-off from Surabaya due to a series of bamboo structures which had been spread around the harbour to deter any attempt by enemy flying boats to land. The normal procedure for a dawn take-off was for the local harbour control officer's launch to move enough of the structures to allow a narrow lane for him to escort the flying boat to taxi out of the harbour for take-off, but on this particular morning, as they approached the submarine defence boom, eight small vessels sailed into the main entrance leaving it impossible for Koch to proceed without colliding with them. The control boat stopped on one side of the lane to allow them past but that left Koch with the big flying boat now in a lane too narrow to turn around and a row of bamboo structures too close to ride safely at anchor. The only option was to cut the engines and have the control boat tow them, a plan the control boat skipper was taking too long to realise as the flying boat drifted dangerously towards the wharf and among the obstructions.

Fortunately for Koch, Qantas station engineer Bill Bennett was in a second launch and, quickly realising *Coorong*'s predicament, attached a line to the front bollard and held *Coorong* firm until both launches towed her stern-first to a point where Koch could restart the engines and continue to taxi.

As with the case for Connolly, rising tensions and fractious communications meant the Qantas boats created their own air-raid 'alerts', as Russell Tapp experienced. Transiting Port Blair, Tapp tried repeatedly to get a message forward to both Rangoon and Sibolga that his arrival at Sibolga would be delayed, only to find an air raid being sounded as he approached. Given the time of day did not match the normal Japanese aircraft 'attack schedule', Tapp quickly assumed that his *Clifton* was probably the reason for the alert, so went ahead and alighted. 'This surmise was found to be correct,' he commented drily in his report.

Such unreliable and often confused radio communications would remain a constant worry for the crews.

After one trip from Batavia to Sydney, Bill Crowther would report a litany of radio mix-ups which not only made his task more difficult but added markedly to the dangers. Acknowledging that radio silence was desirable as much as possible, Crowther became increasingly annoyed when Dutch radio stations along the route insisted on sending weather forecasts by direct radio transmission to the aircraft, thus forcing captains to break radio silence.

Another of Crowther's colleagues, Captain Frank Thomas, too complained of ground stations calling his aircraft for often trivial reasons as he tried to maintain radio silence, while Bob Gurney was critical of a lack of co-ordination between Indian, Burmese and Singaporean radio stations when deciding which of them was responsible for any warnings delivered to aircraft.

According to Gurney, at one stage the Indians appeared miffed that Burma had 'taken it upon themselves' to shut down civilian aircraft like his heading towards Rangoon, the Indians insisting that even if Rangoon was off the air that was no reason not to proceed, an extremely dangerous assumption, to say the least. Gurney argued that RAF headquarters in Singapore, with their more extensive knowledge of the situation, should be the ones to issue instructions as to whether aircraft should proceed in such situations. He appears to have had no hesitation in making his feelings known to those responsible for what he termed 'departmental squabbles': 'I made myself quite clear.'

Bill Purton was maintaining radio silence out of Darwin only to have his efforts put at risk by prolonged conversations between Darwin, Koepang and Dili concerning his movements, Dili committing the cardinal sin of doing it all in 'plain language'. To add to Purton's disgust, the radio operator at Bima insisted on asking three times for his estimated arrival time there, a bonus for any Japanese pilots listening in.

Crowther also emphasised the importance of adherence to strict corridors on approach to some ports, along with the suggestion that all aircraft be allocated with specific 'letters of the day', pointing out that an American aircraft had been hit by Dutch anti-aircraft fire when it strayed outside the corridor as it approached Bandoeng on Java.

Even friendly aircraft on the water could be a hazard in these hectic days. Bert Hussey watched in alarm as a Dutch civilian aircraft landed alongside while he was refuelling at Tjilatjap in southern Java, despite firing a Very pistol at the intruder as it headed towards him. After the Dutchman still passed within six metres of his wingtip, Hussey sent of a terse signal suggesting, with slightly suppressed Australian humour, 'While we do not mind being "matey", such tactics are undesirable.'

By now the loads carried on all aircraft reflected the rapidly declining state of the war, comprising military personnel, arms and equipment in one direction, and refugees, mostly women and children, in the other, and it was with the latter that the Qantas stewards would come into their own. While the aircrews scanned the skies ahead for danger and darted in and out of clouds, in the cabin behind them stewards tended to the needs of often distressed residents of Malaya and Singapore fleeing to the relative safety first of Batavia then, inevitably as the cards in the Allied deck collapsed, on towards Australia.

Diary notes of the stewards and pursers themselves from those days are a rarity, but the few that do exist show a small group of dedicated men who faced the daily dangers from inside a metal tube, serving their charges often without the benefit of knowing what might be happening outside.

There is one report, however, written by an anonymous passenger, which describes the 'family atmosphere' of one flight out of Singapore under the charge of steward Sid Elphick.

As was common, Elphick's charges were a mixed bag, including an army general from the Middle East, a Sydney businessman, a shipping executive, a commercial pilot, an American technician, the Sultan of Bima and his son and daughter aged around ten and eleven, and four women with nine children between them, the youngest a baby with whooping cough, who, because of the complaint, was required to be separated from the other children.

A lad called Anthony, however, had no intention of being confined to one place and while the other children occupied themselves playing with blocks and toys on the floor, Elphick and the toddler's mother spent much of their time chasing him around the cabin, under and behind seats and in any nook and cranny he could find to escape authority. At one stage the author of the report describes the aircraft's captain coming back to check on his charges and himself making several attempts to get Anthony back into his seat, only to have the lad repeatedly dart off between his legs. Finally, our writer notes, the captain abandoned his efforts and returned to the relative calm of the cockpit!

As the flight progressed, the normally glamorous interior of the Empire flying boat was transformed. It appears nothing was too much trouble for Elphick, who turned the inside of the flying boat into a flying nursery as he strung two washing lines in the forward cabin for the nappies and other small attire and even managed to arrange mini sanitary 'thrones' to cater for the infants' urgent needs, an effort which led to many humorous moments by the watching adults.

Tragically, within a few weeks, Elphick would be one of the first to lose his life in the company's wartime service.

Other diaries of stewards or pursers on the Empire flying boats reveal fascinating insights into the exciting days of early international passenger travel and the gradual, inexorable advance towards a brutal war. One of those who detailed his experiences was Charles Baron.

Baron served throughout the war and his early diary entries show fleeting references to carrying the likes of Australia's wartime minister in London Sir Earle Page and New Zealand Prime Minister Peter Fraser on their way to England, along with a spattering of generals, a Russian diplomat and Duff Cooper, Churchill's resident cabinet minister in Singapore. Landing in Singapore the day Britain declared war, Baron noted somewhat as an aside that they'd 'had trouble' with a German passenger in Surabaya, perhaps a reflection of what was happening in Europe: 'No one wanted him.'

From mid-1941, however, his words adopted a much more serious edge as loads being carried had a more military content and the demands of the job increased markedly, at one stage ruefully mentioning parenthetically after spending four days in Singapore, '(I know more about Sing than I do about Sydney.)'

After a month away flying through the area, Baron's diary entry for 11 December 1941, only days after the bombing of Pearl Harbor and the Japanese landings in Malaya, has him doubting Australians realised the disaster unfolding to the north: 'Glad to be home. Things are much worse up there than people believe. Singapore has no hope, we can see that now.'

There were other signs. In mid-December British military authorities in Singapore issued an order for all civil aircraft operating over Malaya or near its territorial waters to fit blackout screens to their windows, not so much to disguise the aircraft at night but to prevent passengers from seeing too much. As Brain explained in a note to crews:

> It should be noted that this 'blacking out' is not so much a matter of screening lights at night as of preventing passengers by day from possibly observing Naval, Military and Air Force movements and establishments. It must be remembered that the integrity of all passengers cannot be guaranteed and that a careless word spoken about movements of shipping observed from the air might do inestimable damage in the present critical situation.

Chapter 9

IMPREGNABLE NO MORE: THE FALL OF SINGAPORE

Christmas 1941 brought little cheer to those in Singapore, with the intensity of the Japanese raids increasing daily.

Through the air raids, as anxious passengers flooded the company's Kallang airport office, Millar and his remaining staff, along with BOAC's John Brancker, who had now reached Singapore following his misadventures in Bangkok, continued trying to balance schedules against the plethora of changes and confusion created by the rapidity of the Japanese advance.

To Millar and his team the situation had now reached the stage where it had become obvious that, at least as far as Singapore was concerned, its role as an integral part of the 8000-mile Sydney to Karachi service hung by a thread. Even so, when Millar first proposed to the RAF that phase four of the emergency plan serving Singapore to and from Batavia via an offshoot shuttle of the main route be implemented, RAF headquarters was reluctant to do so, finally relenting only when it became obvious that sooner or later one of the Qantas flying boats would be caught on the water and a vital asset lost.

The shuttles began the first week in January and involved the through-service aircraft overnighting at Batavia then operating to Singapore and back the following day, but as this still left the flying boats too exposed in daylight hours, the schedule was soon switched to an arrival into Singapore around dusk and a departure before dawn next morning.

Adding to Millar's woes, Kallang's civil airport, used by Qantas as a transfer point for passengers down to the water's edge, had become a primary target of the Japanese bombers, and although the main terminal remained relatively intact, all window glass had been shattered and the office facing the runway badly damaged. Waiting there for flight arrangements presented passengers with many anxious moments as air-raid sirens sounded and ack-ack guns began firing. Even under such difficult circumstances, the Australian sense of humour appears to have come to the fore, one anonymous passenger describing how 'bombing and dignity did not necessarily go hand in hand':

> One cannot think without some amusement of Captain Koch and his crew all lying on their tummies under a counter at Kallang Airport, solemnly continuing a discussion on operations, punctuated with exclamations, decent and otherwise, when bombs fall on the other side of the airport.
>
> Yet again, lying nose to nose with Mr Brancker of British Airways, in a dry drain, prodding ants with matches, has its amusing side until gross familiarity on the part of the ants forced us to chance the bombs in preference to even fiercer infiltrations.

Despite one heavy bomb dropping within forty metres and others straddling the terminal building, our correspondent paid generous tribute to the calmness of passengers, women and children among them, as the terminal floor shook, windows blew in and plaster was scattered everywhere. There follows a description of vehicles alight outside and ammunition exploding from a burning RAF Buffalo fighter across the tarmac before resorting to humour once again via a description of John Brancker emerging from the dust 'still with monocle firmly in eye' along with a traffic officer in a white suit covered from head to foot in mud, fittingly ending it all with a little homespun philosophy of his own: 'The lessons learned have all been widely publicised, but those mixed up in bombing seem to be divided into the prostrate and quick, and the upright and dead.'

John Connolly also managed to see the humorous side during another attack, describing how one of the passengers, a Royal Australian Navy (RAN) commander, found himself as the sole possessor of a tin hat in a dugout full of females. Ever the gentleman, he handed his hat to the woman sitting next to him only seconds before a bomb dislodged a large chunk of concrete from the dugout roof and onto his head. 'The moral, if any,' suggested Connolly, 'seems to be—when you've got a tin hat, stick to it.'

By the end of December, it was clear that the writing was on the wall and it was only a matter of time before the enemy would be at the gates of Singapore. With the core of Qantas engineering and support staff already in Batavia, the shuttles would constitute Singapore's last remaining link with the outside world.

The introduction of the Batavia–Singapore–Batavia shuttles must genuinely be considered one of the most courageous four weeks in Qantas's long history, with crews not only flying into a hornet's nest but playing a dangerous cat and mouse game with the enemy to get there. Covering the five hundred miles between Batavia and Singapore meant hours of tension in their unarmed flying boats, with the ever-present danger of surprise attacks from behind by Japanese aircraft in complete command of the skies.

Now Thomas's Funkhole, as it became known, would come into play, a secluded river estuary that Frank Thomas had diverted into during one of the earliest shuttles. In the days to follow, it and other remote estuaries among the Dutch islands to the south of Singapore provided secret hiding places for the flying boats; captains, warned over the radio a raid was in progress, would quickly sideslip into the estuaries and land after advising Singapore in code of their intention. Anchored close against the jungle bank, they would wait for the all clear to resume their approach.

Even then there were some narrow escapes. Once, Bill Purton's aircraft was within a hundred miles of Singapore when a pair of Japanese bombers appeared out of nowhere and dead ahead. Quickly turning away, Purton watched with relief as the bombers, obviously without sighting him, altered course to another direction while Purton set down in the mouth of a nearby river. After waiting for a half an hour, he took off again towards Singapore to be greeted by smoke rising from yet another attack. Back he went, this time to Thomas's Funkhole, where he waited until another all clear was given. Even a landing in Singapore was not without its risks as it was not unusual for crews to be challenged by British aircraft or nervous ships' gun crews as they approached the harbour.

While pilots scanned the sky and dodged and weaved along coastlines and between islands at perilously low levels, those down the back in the flying boat cabins did their best to calm their passengers. Steward Lionel Haberland would recall many of his passengers suffered airsickness for most of the journey as the flying boats bounced around the sky at low level. There were contrasts too. While most came aboard with little beyond the clothes they stood up in, Haberland, a former ship's steward, would also remember many of the Chinese evacuees carrying large quantities of gold aboard as part of their personal belongings.

By the last week in January Millar had decided Kallang was no longer tenable and arranged with port authorities to lay a mooring on a section of the harbour known as the Inner Roads, allowing him to transfer to an office in the nearby Ocean Building and thus reducing the risk to passengers. It was a timely move. The day after the company's launches transferred to their new loading point, a particularly heavy attack at Kallang completely wrecked Mansfield's office and another struck alongside the now vacant launch shelters.

When on 26 January 1942 the first of Millar's remaining staff left for Batavia, back in Australia, Fysh and operations manager Brain knew the shuttles would only have days to run.

As disaster loomed for Singapore, an equally disastrous event would strike the airline when its luck ran out and the first of its prized Empire flying boats would fall prey to the Japanese.

Chapter 10

AUB KOCH'S WAR, PART ONE

When *Corio* lifted off the water of Darwin Harbour on the morning of Friday, 30 January 1942 for Surabaya via Koepang, Aub Koch knew there were dangerous skies ahead.

Recent days had seen his refuelling stop at Koepang the target of Japanese air raids and two Dutch civilian aircraft shot down. His first attempt to refuel there the previous day had also resulted in an ominous sign when repeated attempts to raise Koepang radio had received no response, in these tense days a sure indication that Japanese aircraft were about. By the time he had the Timor coast in sight and was still unable to raise Koepang he decided not to risk venturing any further and turned the big flying boat into a wide circle back towards Darwin.

Typical of those flying the Qantas flag, such caution was second nature to Tasmanian-born Aub Koch. Austere and modest to a fault, he'd been a boxer and King's Cup rower in his younger days. He was also a strong swimmer, an attribute that would save not only his own life but those of others in the days ahead.

Originally graduating as a pilot in the RAAF, by the time he joined Qantas in 1938 Koch had already served with the Royal Air Force in England and flown for five years with Guinea Airways in the treacherous skies of Papua New Guinea, gaining some fame when he managed to locate and supply the second Archbold expedition after it became stranded in the rugged Strickland River region of west New Guinea. The expedition, one of three to New Guinea sponsored by wealthy American zoologist and philanthropist Richard Archbold, had lost its own supply aircraft during a storm at Port Moresby. Setting out in a Guinea Airways Ford Trimotor aircraft fitted with long-range tanks, Koch managed to find the camped party and drop supplies of food and petrol by parachute.

Widely experienced in long-range flying, Koch acted as first officer to Brain on the delivery of the first of the nineteen RAAF Catalinas from the United States to Australia in 1940, and had since accumulated many hours on the Empire flying boats on the Sydney to Singapore route.

Koch had tried to leave nothing to chance as far as radio communications were concerned on this second attempt to reach Koepang, advising them in code of his intended arrival time and suggesting Koepang come on air every half hour to advise him all was clear.

Along with Koch, four other crew were on board *Corio* that morning: first officer Vic Lyne from Taree, British-born radio officer Patterson, purser William Cruickshank and steward Sid Elphick, who had earlier won high written praise from one of his passengers for his efforts on the 'family affair' evacuee flight from Singapore. Like Lyne, radio officer Patterson too had been part of Lester Brain's crew on the first Catalina delivery from the US. Purser Cruickshank had only recently returned to the Qantas fold after being retrenched when services were reduced following the transfer of the two flying boats to the RAAF late in 1939.

The thirteen passengers down the back were a mix of RAAF, RAN and civilians on wartime duty, most on their way to Surabaya.

Once in the air, and to Koch's relief, the half hourly reports he requested had been coming in regularly for the first stages of the flight, although the weather was poor, with low cloud forcing him to fly at around five hundred feet and 'feel' his way towards the coast. Koch considered such conditions as something of a mixed blessing, however, making it harder for the Japanese to see him.

Then suddenly the weather cleared and the cloud base lifted to around 5000 feet, and about the same time Patterson told Koch that Koepang had missed its last half hourly radio schedule. Koch, still flying at around five hundred feet, was telling Patterson to keep calling when he heard a strange rattling sound in the fuselage behind him. First officer Vic Lyne for an instant thought it must be something wrong with an engine but that idea quickly disappeared as tracer bullets flashed across the top of the flying boat and ahead of him.

Although Koch could not see them behind him, attacking his flying boat were seven Japanese navy Zero fighters which had left the Netherlands East Indies island of Celebes (now Sulawesi) early that morning for an offensive sweep along the Timor coast. After strafing an RAAF Lockheed Hudson on the ground at Koepang's Penfui military airfield they continued south-east along the coast for the fateful rendezvous with Koch's *Corio*.

With more bullets crashing into the wings and fuselage, Koch slammed the control column forward and dived towards the ocean, already convinced that the only hope his unarmed machine had was to crash-land it close to the coastline, about fifteen miles ahead.

By now the noise of the bullets hitting the metal hull was deafening, while a bullet had grazed Koch's leg and both Lyne and Patterson had also been hit. With no other defence, Koch began to zigzag a few feet above the wave tops, immediately noticing that, with his first zigzag, the tracer bullets splashed into the water well over to one side. Realising that to force the Zero pilots to adjust their aim could be *Corio*'s only hope of survival, Koch flew straight again then swerved hard over towards the direction the bullets were hitting the water, and while he could still hear some hitting the aircraft, he experienced a few seconds of satisfaction as he watched most of them crash harmlessly into the sea.

Koch was now so low that *Corio*'s wingtip floats were at times touching the wave tops, but death had already arrived behind him. As bullets ripped into the cabin, RAN Lieutenant Bruce Westbrook saw the man in front and slightly to the left of him hit and one of the RAAF men die instantly as he reached for his lifebelt. A second RAAF man was also shot as he rose out of his seat, while several others probably saved their own lives by diving to the floor.

Up front, time was also running out for Koch. Two of *Corio*'s engines were burning, and as his speed began falling away he realised he would never make it any closer to the shore. The end came suddenly when he tried to lift the flying boat over a high wave but the mortally wounded *Corio* was no longer capable of any such manoeuvre. Its hull riddled with bullet holes, the aircraft smashed into the wave and practically tipped on its nose. As the nose plunged below the water both pilots were thrown out over the instrument panel and through an opening forced by the impact.

The entire attack had lasted less than three minutes. Koch broke the surface to see seven Zeros circling above them and, fearful they might open fire, slid under the wing now resting flat on the surface. He watched as they circled above for several minutes then, obviously satisfied the flying boat was sinking, flew away.

With the Zeros gone, Koch swam around the wing to discover that although the main fuselage was still afloat up to the cabin windows, its centre section had broken open, leaving the tail section jutting skyward. Just as Koch spotted Lyne, radio officer Pat Patterson, and three others swimming about, another passenger, navy man David McCulloch, pushed out a window and joined them. Although badly wounded in the chest and with a gash to the head, McCulloch had at least managed to get into a lifebelt. But there was no other sign of life in the burning cabin and, with the water around the whole area covered in petrol, some of it already alight, they started moving as far away as possible.

Lyne swam close to McCulloch who asked him to help take off his boots, but soon after that McCulloch disappeared.

Patterson had been badly wounded in the legs so Lyne grabbed hold of a wicker basket from the aircraft pantry as it floated past and propped it under him in the hope that it might help him to shore, but they were soon separated and the radio officer was not seen again.

Other bits and pieces were now drifting by, including a mailbag, a soldier's kitbag and a wooden crate, which Koch, Westbrook and two civilian passengers from Sarawak, Fisher and Moore, thought might help them stay afloat.

Up to now few words had been exchanged, although Koch would later recall Fisher, who had suffered two broken ribs, breaking the silence when he suggested it was 'jolly sporting of them not to shoot us up on the water'. Koch later suggested he would have probably put it more bluntly himself!

While Koch had no doubts about his own swimming ability, he estimated they were about five miles from shore when they hit the water, probably too far for anyone other than a good swimmer, and while he suspected one of his own legs was broken, he felt he could still make it by swimming overarm. Moore agreed to join him with the hope of finding natives near the beach who could return and rescue the rest so both stripped off and set out. Lyne too set off towards the distant shore, but soon the trio became separated.

Koch and Moore had gone about a mile when Koch noticed he was bleeding heavily from a deep gash on his left forearm and began to have doubts he could make it. But then he reasoned that after already swimming one mile he could probably swim a few more.

Moore offered to give him a tow but Koch refused, figuring that would be quite hopeless. Given the distance he decided to simply float until he got his strength back to keep going. He resolved to keep trying until he passed out, but years later he would tell his family he had another incentive that morning. Every now and then he would hear the voice of his youngest son David saying, 'Come on, Daddy, come on.'

Rather than swim ahead Moore regulated his speed to keep pace with the captain.

When at last they reached the breakers Koch's watch told him they had been in the water for three hours, but as he tried to stand his leg gave way under him, the result of the bullet grazing his knee. Moore dragged him just clear of the surf and bound his leg and arm as best he could.

Once Koch was comfortable, Moore set off along the beach to seek help but found his way blocked by a river. After an hour he arrived back exhausted and was sitting beside Koch as they wondered what to do next when they spotted a figure further along the beach.

It was naval man Bruce Westbrook, who had set off for shore using a floating mailbag for support, which had gradually became waterlogged and heavy. He'd also lost his spectacles, something that initially worried him, but he then counted it as a blessing as he was petrified of sharks. If there were any around, he told himself, then he'd prefer not to see them.

Both dragged Koch further up the sand, to be joined a little later in the afternoon by an exhausted Fisher, still in acute pain from his broken ribs. Moore and Westbrook again headed up the beach, this time returning with Lyne. They all helped drag Koch up under the cover of some palms, where they dug a hole to make him more comfortable.

The party's next thoughts were to find fresh water but a search of the surrounding area proved fruitless, so after a short conference it was decided that Moore and Westbrook would head off towards the river mouth Moore had found, leaving Lyne with the two others.

To their horror, they found the river mouth was around 400 metres wide and, although fully aware it was likely to contain crocodiles, they had no option but to swim across. Once on the other side they huddled together for the night in a rocky cave, using some grass for bedding. It rained heavily during the night and they licked water from the leaves.

At dawn they set out again, this time finding some brackish water which showed signs that animals had been drinking there, and as they followed a track they heard a cock crow and to their relief stumbled onto a group of friendly natives who gave them water and some food.

With several of the natives they retraced their tracks to the river mouth where the natives were reluctant to cross for fear of crocodiles, but they helped construct a crude raft onto which Moore and Westbrook loaded the food and water and, waiting until the tide was low, once again dared any crocodiles to swim to the other side.

Later that day, after some rough directions from Koch, the irrepressible Moore set out again, crossing the river to find help then, with the assistance of one of the natives, finally making it to Koepang.

As it turned out, Koch's party had come ashore on a small island called Pulau Manipe, and Dutch authorities in Koepang immediately arranged for a steamer to leave that evening to rescue them. Shortly before the vessel was to depart, a Dutch Dornier flying boat arrived at Koepang and the captain volunteered to take a doctor and bring the castaways back to Koepang.

Night was falling by the time it alighted outside the breakers, so the crew and doctor decided to remain overnight and fly them all out the next morning. When dawn arrived, however, the task of ferrying the badly injured Koch out to the Dornier in the crew's rubber dingy wasn't to prove as easy as they thought.

Each time they tried to launch the surf swamped the dingy, forcing them to return to shore and empty it. Finally one of the Dornier crew struggled out beyond the waves with a rope and held the bow of the dingy steady and above the swell until Koch could be lifted aboard.

Although Koch would later praise the 'extreme kindness' his team received in hospital, the three days they spent there was hardly a relaxing time for them. Each day, at precisely the same time as *Corio* had been shot down, up to thirty enemy fighters and bombers would appear over the town, attacking the aerodrome and shipping in the port. Luckily their aim was poor and little damage was done, although Koch was told that the Dornier flying boat that had rescued them was one of the casualties. Fortunately its crew were ashore at the time.

Watching all this happen convinced Koch that Darwin would be next.

Of the five survivors, Bruce Westbrook was soon aboard a military transport and on his way again to Surabaya, Fisher via Darwin to Perth, and Lyne and Moore on the Qantas inland service to Brisbane and then Sydney. In a letter to his parents in Taree, Lyne would vividly describe the attack and praise Koch's remarkable coolness and flying prowess as he flung the big flying boat from side to side dodging the Japanese fighters. Also confessing that the two and a half days on the island had left him badly sunburnt, he wrote:

> Anyway, don't worry, dad—I am beginning to feel O.K. and itching to be in the air again and help pepper the little yellow chap. I have great admiration for Captain Koch. He is a man of much courage and wonderful experience.
>
> The Qantas Airways are exceptionally good to their officers and I have nothing to complain about.

Ending on a lighter note, he suggested his father pass on a little homespun advice to his surfing friends: '. . . a little early training in life saving such as I had at Black Head is no weight to carry, and, as in my case, may mean the saving of their own and others' lives.'

Koch, too badly injured to go beyond Darwin, was admitted to hospital there, just as the first news of the attack was breaking in the Australian press.

Headlines like 'Japs Down Qantas Air Liner' over a press statement by the minister for air, Arthur Drakeford, would be accompanied by the Sydney *Sun*'s 'Hunted to Disaster by Japs' as other newspapers around the country picked up the story.

The loss of *Corio* and thirteen of its passengers was a massive blow to Fysh and his team. Not only had it come at a time when the airline's role in maintaining the Empire route was becoming more tenuous by the day, but it marked the first incident involving injuries to crews and passengers since QEA had begun, and after more than fifty million passenger miles had been flown. Fysh summed it up to his staff in a tribute immediately afterwards:

> It can be said that our crews these days are right in the war alongside the Mercantile Marine, which, as the world knows, is playing a hero's part most often unheard and unsung.
>
> Qantas Empire Airways deeply regrets the loss of life among passengers entrusted to its care. It is a pleasure that Captain Koch and First Officer Lyne are survivors. The loss of Radio Officer Patterson is a blow as he was the Senior Radio Operator and he had been with the Company since 1934. Mr Cruickshank and Flight Steward Elphick had been with the company for many years.
>
> The last two amply upheld the company's standard and will be missed by all.

Little was it thought when Qantas Empire Airways started its overseas service in December 1934 that its first accident would be caused by enemy action, Fysh said.

Although Fysh didn't reveal it to his staff, it could have been worse. Bert Hussey had been flying *Corinthian* east towards Koepang when he heard *Corio*'s unanswered radio calls to Koepang radio, and when they stopped Hussey assumed Koch had gone elsewhere to refuel. As Hussey was refuelling at Koepang an air-raid alarm sounded and Hussey loaded just enough fuel to get him to Darwin and took off, sliding into the protective clouds as soon as possible.

As for Koch, it would not be long before his prediction about Darwin would come true and he would once again be in the middle of it all.

Chapter 11

LOSS AND RETREAT: THE LINK IS CUT

On 30 January 1942, the very afternoon Koch and his four companions struggled ashore on their tiny island, British, Australian and Indian troops crossed the Johore Strait, the last natural barrier separating them from the advancing Japanese.

In just two weeks the Australians had retreated more than two hundred kilometres, with little respite from ambush, encirclement and bayonet charges. Their commanders, British General Arthur Percival and Australia's General Gordon Bennett, had now pressed upwards of 80,000 troops onto Singapore Island after blowing a hole in the kilometre-long causeway linking it to the Malay mainland. Bennett, who had flown in from the Middle East on Ron Adair's aircraft several weeks previously, had no illusions about what the immediate future held in store for his men, nor much confidence in his British counterparts, a situation that would see him soon make a decision which would haunt him for the remainder of his career.

By the end of January, under captains Denny, Adair, Tapp, Ambrose, Hussey, Gurney, Thomas, Purton, Crowther and even Koch, before his *Corio* was shot down, the QEA Empire flying boats had made fourteen shuttles between Batavia and Singapore, skipping in and out of the besieged city and using their 'funkhole' diversion where necessary. Frank Thomas alone was forced to use it three times in as many days because of air-raid warnings on his way to Singapore, and Bill Purton once after sighting enemy aircraft on 22 January.

Now those civilians who could not make it out of Singapore by the thinning airlift were boarding any vessel they could find and heading away from the doomed city in a desperate scramble to what they hoped was safety. Back in Australia, Brain knew the shuttles would only have days to run before the final collapse of Churchill's 'impregnable fortress'. As it would turn out, Bill Crowther's flight out on 3 February would be the last.

Crowther planned to time his arrival into Singapore late in the afternoon after any Japanese aircraft had returned to their Malayan bases, refuelling and loading during the night and leaving early in the morning. Aware that Palembang in southern Sumatra and directly on their course had been bombed that morning, Crowther kept *Corinna* low across the Sumatran jungle and had covered half the distance when he received a radio warning that the position on the ground in Singapore was so chaotic that there may be no facilities there to handle the flight. Although there was still time to turn back, Crowther's inclination was to continue on, but he considered this was one occasion where democracy should prevail so asked his crew, one of whom happened to be diarist and steward Charles Baron, for their thoughts. Everyone agreed to go. Baron's graphic comments are among the few remaining records of the flight. 'Landed at dusk. All Singapore seems to be burning,' he wrote, noting that all forty-one of their passengers were women.

One of those women was Molly Farthing, wife of well-known Australian jockey Tom Farthing, who, along with a number of other Australian jockeys, had been racing in Malaya and Singapore for some years. Earlier, in July 1940, with war gathering over Europe and the Japanese threat increasing, Molly had taken their two sons, Peter and six-year-old Tony, back to Australia to stay with their grandmother in Randwick. Molly decided to return to Singapore to be with her husband and was now among the hundreds trying to get out.

Tom Farthing had intended to join the army but learned he had to make it to Australia first, so decided in the meantime to volunteer as a driver for the Singapore police. When he received an urgent phone call from a friend alerting him to what might be the last flight out, Farthing couldn't find his wife at home and finally tracked her down in town. With no time to gather any belongings, Molly made it to Crowther's *Corinna* with only the clothes she was wearing. Her husband, along with several of his racing colleagues, would spend more than three years in Changi as prisoners of war. (Ironically, their rescue airline would continue to play a major part in the future of the Farthing family. Young Tony would join as a steward in the 1950s and retire as a flight service director in the 1990s. His daughter Tracy is still flying with the airline.)

The take-off from the Inner Roads early the next morning was a daunting prospect for Crowther, so much so that the local civil aviation chief himself went out in the launch to help him to choose a take-off path between the minefields, fish traps, anchored ships and the plethora of other smaller vessels scurrying back and forth across the mooring.

At 2.30 a.m., and with just enough moonlight filtering through the clouds to guide him, Crowther opened the throttles and *Corinna* left the fires of Singapore behind as he set course for Batavia. For the first hour or so those on board watched flickering lights below, not knowing whether they came from gunfire or the emergency flashes of some of those hurrying to safety. Once during the flight they heard Tokyo radio announce their departure. Baron's diary had the final word: 'We can help no more.'

Crowther's flight marked the last of fourteen Qantas shuffles between Batavia and Singapore, carrying a total of more than five hundred passengers and twelve tons of freight into and out of the besieged city.

Several days later those few staff still remaining, including Millar's Mansfield colleague Frank Lane, received a message from Batavia that military headquarters on Java had decided the shuttles should be terminated. Now unable to escape by air, Lane and his team waited apprehensively as the Japanese closed in on Singapore itself, bringing most parts of the city within range of their shells.

Lane's problems were many. Food became harder to get as Chinese shopkeepers refused to stay open during the daytime bombings, his car had been put out of action by bomb damage and the local bus service was now unreliable as drivers refused to turn up for work, making it difficult for staff to reach the office. Garbage littered the streets, largely caked in black oil dust as a result of the smoke from the island's oil storage depots which had now been burning for days. On 9 February word came that the Japanese had landed on the island itself and Lane decided to move out of his house in the suburbs and into the city. Word reached him that the Japanese occupied his house the following day.

But while he struggled to clean up the office loose ends he ensured the company passenger launch was moved to a safe mooring well away from the waterfront. That launch, he knew, would now be their only hope of getting out. For added insurance he kept its starting handle in the office.

Unknown to anyone but those closest to him, General Bennett was also planning to leave an overall defeatist military situation poisoned by poor command and often mutual distrust. Many of the Australians were critical of Percival and his command, while one British officer countered by describing the Australians as 'the most egotistical conceited people imaginable . . . so highly critical of everyone else'.

Bennett, never one to hide his feelings, had little confidence in his British counterparts, considering many of them incompetent and frequently critical of their lack of aggression and their tendency to fight battles from fixed positions, which allowed the Japanese to consistently infiltrate or encircle them. His decision to leave, however, while the rest of his men went into captivity, would, in small part, implicate Qantas in one of the most controversial episodes to engulf Australia's military leadership in the Second World War.

With Singapore cut off, Qantas's attention now focused on the fragility of the through route to Karachi, as not only were the flights down the west coast of Sumatra becoming increasingly dangerous but both Batavia and Surabaya were under air attack and reports were coming in of a large Japanese convoy heading towards Java from the South China Sea. These developments, coupled with the loss of *Corio* off Timor and the vulnerability of Darwin, turned Lester Brain's attention to the use of Tjilatjap on the south-central Javanese coast as the final Netherlands East Indies link point.

To have Tjilatjap as a fallback once again demonstrated Brain's foresight. Some weeks before Zero fighters had downed *Corio*, Brain had sent Lew Ambrose to Batavia to talk to the Dutch authorities about the possibilities presented by Tjilatjap should Singapore fall and Sumatra become untenable.

Ambrose and a senior executive of the Netherlands civil aviation department then set out by road over the range via Bandoeng to determine what would be required to bring Tjilatjap up to the task. Ambrose arrived to find a relatively small port, and the only one of any significance on the southern coast of Java, a population of around seven hundred people and not much else. With the aid of the port's harbourmaster, Ambrose defined the positioning of market buoys, studied wind and tidal movements and determined take-off and alighting paths, taking into account the rising ground on one edge of the harbour.

As was common in some areas of the Indies, the local radio station, which would be expected to play an important role in any evacuee movements, was used mainly for shipping and was under the control of the local postmaster. With additional staff it could provide an air watch on short wave on a 24-hour basis, but there were no direction-finding facilities to help guide aircraft in.

Weather reporting too was a concern, and as there was no meteorological officer the harbourmaster would have to supply weather forecasts, and without direction-finding assistance any significant weather build-up in the late afternoon could make it impossible for flying boats to alight. Ambrose was also alarmed to learn should that happen there were no other suitable emergency alighting areas for flying boats on the south coast of Java, leaving the only option in an emergency to put down in the sea, a hazardous operation in its own right.

Ambrose was convinced nothing was ideal about Tjilatjap, but as the last evacuee point between Java and Darwin or Broome, it would have to do.

Before that took place, however, the death throes of the UK–Australia Empire route would begin to be acted out on 8 February in a dramatic last flight out of Karachi for Batavia. As well as marking the end of the Empire route, Russell Tapp's flight would present him with a whole range of difficulties beyond his control, from engines failures and last-minute diversions due to air-raid alerts to narrowly avoiding Japanese reconnaissance aircraft and, in the very final stages, coming under 'friendly fire'.

For the first sectors of Tapp's journey, via Calcutta and Akyab, everything went according to plan until Port Blair, where one engine gave trouble and the take-off had to be abandoned. With a heavy load and prevailing high temperature, there was no chance the aircraft could operate on three engines so they had to return to the mooring. Fixing the problem would now leave them exposed to the regular daily visits by the enemy.

Sure enough, just after midday a Japanese aircraft flew directly overhead but showed no interest in the flying boat, and by late afternoon an engine test run convinced Tapp the problem had been fixed. Rather than leave immediately Tapp decided to wait until midnight, which would mean arriving at Sibolga early in the morning, refuelling before the usual Japanese sweeps along the coast, and continuing to Batavia.

But the engine gremlins had other ideas and once again the problem occurred on take-off, so back to the moorings they went. Tapp, however, had something in his favour: one of his passengers happened to be BOAC's engineering superintendent, who even though he'd spent all the previous day out on the wing trying to remedy the fault, stripped off his jacket once more and worked until 4 a.m. to get the engine running again.

Although tempted to take off immediately, Tapp realised that to do so would place him at Sibolga at around the time of the daily Japanese bombing schedule, so he delayed until 9 a.m. and set a course as far to the west as he could to avoid enemy patrols. Even then, as he turned in towards Sibolga he received two air-raid alerts requiring him to stand off until the all clear was given.

By the time they approached Sibolga for the third attempt, Tapp was so short of fuel that if they didn't get down this time he was in serious trouble but, given the nervousness of locals and the unreliability of radio messages, he now suspected his own aircraft might be the reason for the alerts, so he decided to risk continuing. His hunch proved right and the flying boat landed without incident.

Next morning they set course again well to the west and away from land with the idea of turning in towards a known corridor of entry north of Java to minimise the chances of detection, but when reports came in that Japanese aircraft were active ahead of them Tapp made for South Pagi, a small island off the west coast of Sumatra. Alighting in a backwater surrounded by trees and other vegetation, they threw out an anchor in a near perfect hiding place. South Pagi would now be the last 'funkhole' to be added to the list.

There they waited for over an hour before setting off again towards the Sunda Strait, at one stage passing over a small convoy which seemed to be headed in the direction of Java. Passing low overhead, Tapp recognised one as a small Dutch vessel that he had often seen at Batavia, only this time it greeted him with several bursts of machine-gun fire. 'We moved over a little and were beyond her in no time.' An inspection of the hull revealed no hits and they continued on to Batavia. Within days of Tapp's flight, RAF fighter operations at Bandoeng ordered that all flying boats were to stop at Calcutta and Batavia as enemy paratroops had landed at Palembang on Sumatra.

On 15 February 1942 British forces in Singapore surrendered to the Japanese, making it one of the most devastating defeats in British history and turning 130,000 British, Australian and Indian troops into prisoners of war. With the Empire route broken, the makeshift port of Tjilatjap would become the last hope of escape from the Netherlands East Indies.

If there was any good fortune in this debacle for Qantas it was that none of its crews had been trapped west of Batavia when the end came.

Chapter 12

MEANS OF ESCAPE

The months of January, February and March 1942 demonstrated just how poorly prepared the Allies were for war in the Pacific, as defeat followed defeat across an arc reaching from the westernmost islands of the Netherlands East Indies, through the Malay Peninsula and beyond to the Philippines.

The whole area under the Allied joint American, British, Dutch and Australian control, known as ABDA, with headquarters under General Sir Archibald Wavell in Java, never had time to concentrate its meagre forces as the relentless Japanese drive continued southwards. Formed in late January and charged with defending what was titled the Malay Barrier, ABDA would last little more than four weeks, its end marked by the sinking of the cruisers USS *Houston* and HMAS *Perth* in the Sunda Strait in the last week of February.

Even before Singapore fell, key points in Java like Batavia and Surabaya followed the pattern the Japanese had employed for the length of Sumatra, concentrating attacks on shipping in harbours and aircraft on aerodromes, disrupting communications and cutting across the Allied lines of retreat.

The strategically planned Japanese assault left little chance for any concentrated defence as they overwhelmed one isolated outpost after another.

They were everywhere, and all at once. In a whole series of attacks, the Japanese swept across the island chain to Australia's north-west to due north, captured most of Australia's Gull Force Battalion on Ambon and rained bombs on Port Moresby the same day. Timor and Darwin were to come.

Through it all came the mad scramble of Americans forced out of the Philippines, along with Dutch, British and Australian troops and civilians using any available form of transport to reach an evacuation towards Australia.

Eventually, with Sumatra gone and Japanese forces landing on the north coast of Java, the focus of the evacuation swung to the tenuous last thread of Tjilatjap, and while the Qantas boats kept flying, some of the Qantas staff supporting them would have harrowing escapes from death or capture.

In January 1942 Qantas staff on the front line comprised Mansfield and Company's people in Singapore, Malcolm Millar, Frank Lane and their support staff, who had stayed at their posts to load evacuees onto the flying boats heading away from the war zone. As the emphasis shifted to the Batavia–Singapore operation shuttles, Millar had moved to Batavia while Frank Lane remained.

Already in Batavia were engineers Bill Bennett and Charlie Short, who had moved there in mid-December to set up an emergency maintenance base when Japanese air raids made the Singapore base untenable.

To the east in Surabaya were senior station engineer Eric Kydd and two other engineers, David Thomson and Jim Lamb. Tall, taciturn Eric Kydd, the airline's first indentured apprentice, had joined Qantas at fourteen in 1929 and was posted to Surabaya in 1936 to act as flight engineer on the Empire air route DH 86s operating between Surabaya and Koepang, one complete trip a week. After engineering instruction on the C Class flying boats in England he returned to Surabaya in 1939 to open the base as an overnight stop.

While a work schedule of six days a week at Surabaya was quite normal, the oddity about their Surabaya posting was that all three had their wives with them. Allowing wives on postings was not common in the Qantas scheme of things in the days before the war, but Eric Kydd's wife, Ruth, had broken the mould. As Ruth Trickett she had been a Qantas secretary at Archerfield when she left to marry Kydd in Surabaya in 1939. And since there was no free travel for wives in those days, Ruth had to pay her own way. Not only that, but the mores of the time meant that she had to be chaperoned by the local Burns Philp manager and his wife prior to their marriage!

When Thomson and Lamb arrived on posting in 1941, their wives Rona and Stavranay had followed Ruth's precedent and were able to enjoy the idyllic existence which was Surabaya in the years before Pearl Harbor. Ruth Kydd was already fluent in Javanese and when not enjoying an active social life the three women worked as volunteers for Dutch charities and the local Red Cross. All that was to change with the mid-December arrival in Batavia of Hudson Fysh, on his way back from experiencing the early bombing of Singapore: 'Get the women out as soon as you can,' was his order to Kydd.

In the weeks that followed the three wives experienced a range of emotions as the war news worsened and they watched aircraft pass through Surabaya loaded with refugees on their way south. They did notice that there was something unreal about it though. Even as Malaya fell apart they were taken aback when their Dutch and English friends occasionally expressed surprise as to why they would be thinking of leaving, presumably unable to contemplate that the British paper tiger that was Singapore would fall. Soon, they too would be scrambling to safety in India or Australia.

As the days passed, however, Rona Thomson began to notice the local Javanese had no such illusions as shops and small stores began closing down, their owners and staff simply fading away. Finally, in the second week in January their own chance came when the service out of Batavia would hopefully have enough seats for them to be able to join it at Surabaya.

Qantas Batavia engineer Bill Bennett was already aboard on his way home to be married, but when the Surabaya seats were allocated they found that Sir Charles Vyner Brooke, the 'White Rajah of Sarawak', who was also an evacuee, had been allocated a priority seat and one of the Qantas wives would have to stay. It was decided on the toss of a coin and Stav Lamb was the unlucky one, left to hope for a seat on a following flight.

On top of her concern for Stav Lamb, the departure was an emotional moment for Ruth Kydd. 'Imagine our feelings as we flew out, leaving our husbands behind, wondering when, if ever, we were to see them again.' Fortunately Stav Lamb managed to make it out next day.

The passengers on board Ruth Kydd's flight were mostly evacuees from Singapore, many of them pregnant women and mothers, so Ruth and Rona spent the flight assisting steward Dennis Egan with the infants and small children on board. Rona Thomas would later describe the trip as 'horrendous': 'We arrived at Darwin with nearly all the women hysterical.'

Once out the windows they saw a large convoy of ships beneath them, thought to be American, and were immediately sworn to secrecy, an order repeated at Townsville where a large contingent of press had gathered to meet the aircraft and began bombarding the passengers and crew with questions. Gratefully the two wives looked on from the background as Sir Charles stepped forward to meet the onslaught.

By 20 February, with Batavia now the subject of increasing bombing raids, Brain decided to bypass Surabaya and move the maintenance and evacuation operations direct to Tjilatjap, while he left immediately for Broome to prepare what would now be the main Australian reception point for the withdrawal from Java.

With air raids daily, it was now up to Kydd, Thomson and Lamb to find their own way out, and the sooner the better. During one concentrated attack on Surabaya's port and its Qantas base, the three engineers, with no air-raid shelters nearby, lay prostrate in a gutter as they watched the Japanese aircraft tear everything above them apart. After that they needed no further prompting and, loading all the spare parts, their few personal effects and Kydd's dog Looky into the company's 1941 Ford station-sedan, they set off on the several hundred kilometre journey across primitive Java roads towards Tjilatjap. Despite their haste, it appears they were still determined not to let the Japanese deny them the opportunity to do a bit of sightseeing on the way as a family album shows the three posing in front of the magnificent ninth-century Borobudur temple near Yogyakarta! Once at Tjilatjap they joined Charlie Short to oversee the engineering needs for the last desperate airlift out of Java.

But of all the difficult situations those serving Qantas found themselves in immediately before and after the fall of Singapore, Frank Lane's must rank as the most desperate.

By 10 February, with food now difficult to find due to the daily air raids keeping everyone under cover, transport all but non-existent and artillery shells falling on the town, Lane began collecting extra fuel and oil for the Qantas launch he had hidden away from the waterfront. He soon learned that his decision to keep the launch's starting handle at home had proved prescient. When he went to check the vessel he found blankets and suitcases on it, obviously left by an evacuee family who had been unable to start it. Daily the Qantas office was flooded with anxious people who hoped to get out by air, but it was now too late for Qantas to help.

Flights by the Dutch had stopped much earlier and Bill Crowther's flight seven days previously had been the last.

News now reached Lane that the Japanese were machine-gunning and dive-bombing the main roads on the edge of the town, had taken Tengah airport and the wireless station and were now within twelve kilometres of the Qantas office. The night of 11 February was the most uncomfortable Lane and his team experienced. Shells were straddling the office and they could hear intermittent rifle fire in the distance, although he surmised this was more to deter looters than actual street fighting. Whatever the firing might be, it was time to go.

After making his way from the office to the launch, Lane was preparing the launch to leave its hiding place when a bombing raid on the Inner Roads narrowly missed both him and the launch, but he was soon underway to a prearranged spot near the yacht club to collect others who were leaving with him.

At noon on 14 February, with thirteen on board the launch—eleven civilians and two army officers who had been ordered to leave—they sputtered out of the Inner Roads towards Pulau Samboe, the Dutch oil refinery island to the south that was now burning fiercely, its thick black smoke adding to the fires raging over Singapore itself. Taking stock of what was on board for the journey ahead revealed they had very little beyond a quantity of fuel and enough charts to get them across and then down the east Sumatran coast. They had no food and only the clothes they had on when they left.

Two and a half hours later they paid the price of not keeping an adequate lookout and ran aground on a coral reef on the receding tide off Pulau Samboe. It took four hours before the tide rose enough to lift them off again, plenty of time to take in the dismal view behind them.

Singapore was now a sorry sight. The whole island except the eastern end was covered in a pall of smoke as the oil tanks at the naval base, Kranji, Pasir Panjang, Normanton, Pulau Bukum and Pulau Sebarok burnt

Fire and smoke streamed skyward from a military depot at Alexandria and parts of Blakang Mati with smaller fires scattered about in the town itself, most of the latter the result of a succession of air raids during the afternoon. The scene was made even more depressing by the fact that although it was a fine, clear day, any sunlight was totally obliterated by the smoke above them from Pulau Samboe.

It was dusk before they were moving again, keeping a close watch this time for reefs, until they decided to anchor for the night. But even while two kept an anchor watch the remaining eleven found it impossible to sleep due to the limited confines of the launch, the tragic backdrop of the flickering flames of a burning Singapore and the occasional muted explosion.

The food situation improved next day when they managed to collect rice, mangoes, pineapples, coconuts, bananas and even eggs from natives on islands they passed as they made their way across the Durian Strait, all the time fearful of earlier stories of vessels being machine-gunned there in open waters. They were also aware that the strait had been mined but fortunately the shallow draft of their launch worked to their advantage and they made it to Tandjong Batu, a small village on an island off the Sumatra coast. Their escape plan could have ended right there when they were confronted by a British Army officer with a Tommy gun who was determined to take over their boat. Tense moments followed until a more senior officer arrived to overrule his subordinate and they set course again that afternoon for the mainland of Sumatra. In the days that followed they would travel for most of the day along the coast then anchor at night, determined not to press their luck by running into another reef in the dark. They had covered 130 kilometres to reach Kateman on the east coast when the launch engine stopped due to choked jets. This time, however, the military came to their aid, and soldiers helped them clean the jets and get the engine running again. Here they were told that Japanese had landed at Palembang, 320 kilometres further south in the direction they were travelling, but were reassured the enemy had been 'satisfactorily dealt with', a report which would prove to be false.

With food and water still in plentiful supply they reached their destination, Tembilahan at the mouth of the Indragiri River, on 18 February where they planned to cross by road to Telok Betong on the south side of Sumatra and catch a ferry to Java, then on to their eventual destination, Batavia.

At Tembilahan they were met with the news that not only was there no road to Telok Betong but Palembang, with its valuable oil fields, had fallen to the Japanese in the first large-scale use of parachutists by the Japanese in the war. The earlier information they received at Kateman had been incorrect and their path down the east coast of Sumatra had been cut. Their only hope now was to take the launch 130 kilometres up the Indragiri to Rengat and from there make their way down the west coast.

Lane would admit later that it was with some trepidation they set out up the river. They were low on diesel and to run out of it midway up a river unknown to them would leave them stranded. Fortunately, not long after they set out a passing Chinese riverboat offered to give them a tow, finally arriving at Rengat early the next morning.

It had now been five days since they had left Singapore and their launch had carried them around four hundred kilometres, but since they had no more fuel they handed the launch to the Royal Navy, who added it to the assortment of evacuee vessels they were using on the Indragiri. Lane and his party would join other evacuees on army transport for the rest of the journey. After living days and nights within the launch's cramped confines, Lane would later confess he was not sorry to see it go, but given their earlier experiences, being placed in the hands of the British Army didn't fill them with too much joy either. They had no choice, however, as the army had requisitioned all the land transport and were soon themselves bouncing through the picturesque Padang Highlands on a bus and then in the luggage van of a train to Padang.

Now short of money, Lane attempted to get some funds from the local BOAC agents, although he would later be forgiving of the agent's refusal, saying 'our appearance was no doubt against us as we hadn't shaved since leaving Singapore ten days before—and the luggage van of a train does not make one look particularly clean'.

At Padang, however, they did manage to get word of their whereabouts through to the flying boat base at Batavia, only to learn when they reached the capital that the last flight had left some days before. But once more the army came to their rescue and arranged space for them on the deck of a small coastal steamer bound for Tjilatjap. Again they were too late: the last plane from Tjilatjap had already left and they continued on by ship to Fremantle and safety.

It had been three weeks since they sailed the Qantas launch out through the Inner Roads. By now not only was most of the Netherlands East Indies in Japanese hands but the war had come to Australia's shores.

Chapter 13

NEAR MISS AT DARWIN

Shortly after eight o'clock on the morning of 19 February 1942, in the Arafura Sea 350 kilometres north-west of Darwin, a Japanese task force under the command of the architect of the attack on Pearl Harbor, Admiral Chuichi Nagumo, turned his four aircraft carriers into the wind ready for launch.

Nagumo's attack force, comprising 188 fighters and bombers, was not only the largest carrier assault force since Pearl Harbor but was one of high morale. In little more than two months his country's military had conquered all before it through south-east Asia and was within days of reaching the zenith of its new empire.

Although there would be initial fears that Nagumo's Darwin assault would be the precursor of an invasion of the Australian mainland that was never the case. Rather it was designed to neutralise Darwin itself and thus prevent it from offering any threat to the invasion of Timor, which was to take place at the same time.

Not that Darwin was much of a threat. Australia's northern frontier was thinly defended and poorly prepared for war, the result of years of complacency that had now been overwhelmed by the speed of the Japanese war machine. Certainly the danger was recognised. Between mid-December and early February most of the women and children had been evacuated, but not much else had happened despite the warning signs, one of which had been sent from Dili by the Australian consul and honorary Qantas representative David Ross.

Several days before, Ross, alerted by Portuguese officials that groups of up to forty Japanese aircraft had flown over Baucau, immediately sent a coded message to Darwin. Those responsible for Darwin's defence were still assessing his signal when the first bombs fell on 19 February.

Even the Americans, desperate to regain some slim foothold after the Pearl Harbor debacle, thought it so vulnerable and inefficient as a port that they'd moved some of their naval support vessels forward to Java a few days previously. The Allies in fact were caught in a Japanese pincer movement that would see Bali assaulted at the same time as Japanese convoys approached Dili and Koepang in Timor.

Neither did Qantas have any illusions about Australia's gateway to the world. On the very morning Nagumo's aircraft set course for Darwin, Lester Brain was signing an urgent despatch to the director-general of the Department of Civil Aviation, Arthur Corbett, outlining the company's knowledge of how the Japanese operated and its suggestions for the continued use of Darwin, calling on lessons his company had learned the hard way. Brain explained:

> Our experience in operating through Sumatra and Malaya recently leads us to believe that in present circumstances air raids on Darwin are likely to occur only between certain hours of the day, and that outside these hours civil aircraft should be comparatively safe in calling at Darwin, proceeding and continuing on their way.

Brain suggested that given the likely bases to be used by the Japanese and the prevailing monsoonal conditions, any attacking aircraft would probably not depart from their base until daylight and would plan to be back at base before nightfall. 'It would seem that the most likely period for bomb raids on Darwin would be between the hours of 10.a.m. and 2 p.m.,' an assessment that was to prove deadly accurate. Brain also stressed the urgency of the establishment of moorings at Wyndham as an alternative on the route between Darwin and Broome.

His memorandum reflected the changing role of Darwin for Qantas. While it may have been a critical part of the Australian airline's Empire route since the mid-1930s, it was certainly no paradise as a stopover but functioned more as a convenient split entity, handling the regular landplane DH 86 services from Brisbane and Sydney at Darwin's aerodrome along with the flying boat base on Darwin Harbour.

By now, however, with the Empire route cut, the retreat through the Netherlands East Indies and the shooting down of Koch's *Corio* off Timor several weeks before, the focus of the evacuation of Java had switched from Darwin to Broome, with Darwin remaining a key link between Broome and the east coast of Australia.

Brain's engineering counterparts were also active. Works manager Arthur Baird had warned Darwin's station engineer Norm Roberts of the urgency of moving most of the company's maintenance equipment to Broome and to liaise directly with his Broome counterpart Bill Bennett to retain only what was necessary to handle aircraft transiting Darwin. 'There is a feature here,' Baird told Roberts, 'which, of course I feel certain you have not overlooked—the fact that you might have to hurriedly remove from Darwin all or as many of our spares as possible, at some subsequent period.'

Baird also expressed his concern that Roberts' wife, 'Honey' Roberts, was still in Darwin and had not been evacuated with the rest of the womenfolk. Norm Roberts, who had joined Qantas in 1934, was one of twenty-four Qantas staff manning Darwin on 19 February, and up to that time his exposure to the war had comprised the untidy scramble to evacuate most of the women and children, the odd air-raid siren wailing with no result, and taking the precaution of fitting his car with narrow slits across the headlight glass.

Along with the local staff this morning were two crews standing by awaiting movement instructions for their flying boat *Camilla*, moored in the harbour just off from the Qantas flying boat base.

Bill Crowther and Bob Gurney had arrived with *Camilla* from Broome the night before after operating a series of shuttle trips between Tjilatjap and Broome over the previous two days. They had used their flight into Darwin to look for an alternative flying boat base between Darwin and Broome and were now waiting for severe weather at Townsville to improve before continuing on. Bert Hussey, recuperating from dengue fever, was on his way back to Sydney after seven weeks away, along with first officer Don McMaster.

There was little warning of an attack. At 10 a.m. Hussey was waiting his turn for a haircut in a barber shop in the Roslyn Court building when the noise of the first air-raid sirens merged with the throb of aircraft engines overhead and bombs exploding. 'There were two soldiers being shaved at the time; they had to complete their own shaves as the barbers' hands were shaking too much,' Hussey would recall.

Hussey ran out of the building and into the yard of the Victoria Hotel, desperately seeking some open space away from the buildings. As he reached the block at the rear of the hotel, vacant aside from a large raised tank which housed the town's water supply, he caught his first sight of the Japanese bombers approaching from the south-west across the roof of the Hotel Darwin. Determined to get as far away as he could from the large water tower he ran towards a concrete gutter in front of the hotel as bombs whistled down and exploded in the direction of the harbour. He arrived at the gutter at the same time as Bob Gurney and Qantas Darwin secretary Val Hansen, and all three took refuge in the stormwater drain as a second wave of bombers passed over, debris flying everywhere as their bombs hit the post office a few hundred metres away. Mrs Hansen had heard the sirens and went out into the street to see what was happening. Looking up she saw aeroplanes and remembered saying to herself, 'I wonder if they're Japs.' Now, huddled in what she would later describe as 'a very unpleasant culvert', she had her answer.

Further down the street Qantas traffic officer John Morris had also run out into the open, just in time for a bomb to land seventy metres away, covering him with debris and wounding him in the shoulder. Purser Charles Baron had the luckiest escape of all of them: he'd walked out of the Darwin post office only minutes before a bomb hit, killing all nine inside.

In the middle of it all, the trio in the culvert saw Bill Crowther appear around a nearby corner, his shirtfront open and soap around his ears, running half sideways as he looked behind him for falling missiles. Crowther had been shaving when the attack started.

Still determined to get into the clear, the group moved towards an open allotment as the next wave of bombers arrived overhead, their projectiles landing towards the hospital. Hussey immediately became concerned for Aub Koch, who was still recovering there from his Koepang wounds.

By now it was obvious the Japanese were concentrating their main forces on the harbour and the civil and RAAF aerodromes while dive-bombers and fighters were strafing ground targets.

As the minutes passed and the bombing began to ease, the little Qantas group made its way back to the Hotel Darwin where they found the Qantas car still intact. With Mrs Hansen at the wheel they headed for the flying boat base.

The sight that met them was one of devastation. The two ships tied at the wharf adjacent to the base, *Neptuna* and *Barossa*, were both burning fiercely, but to Hussey's amazement *Camilla* was still rocking gently at its mooring a few hundred metres away. It was obvious the black smoke billowing across the flying boat from the burning vessels had hidden it from sight.

The jetty leading to the wharf had been broken in two, its small locomotive and trucks used to haul cargo along it blown into the sea. Fractured oil lines were pouring black liquid into the sea, setting the water on fire and beyond it launches could be seen picking people out of the water and bringing them ashore. Hussey now learned that the burning *Neptuna* was loaded with mines, so two quick decisions were made: Mrs Hansen would head for the hospital with the car to check on Koch and Crowther and Hussey would use the lull in the bombing to get *Camilla* as far away as possible from the blazing *Neptuna*.

Since the Qantas work launch *Naiad* was nowhere to be seen, they hurried down towards the boat ramp where the Department of Civil Aviation launch with coxswain John Waldie at the helm was bringing survivors in, some suffering burns. Waldie took them out to *Camilla* where they first unhooked the storm pennant and then unloaded the two pilots at the port side door of the flying boat. To his amazement Hussey's quick pre-flight inspection revealed the only damage to *Camilla* appeared to be two small shrapnel holes in the elevators. He checked the fuel and the starting batteries while Crowther hurried up to the flight deck and soon had one engine running.

The instant Hussey cast off from the mooring Crowther had the big flying boat moving, now with a second engine started, anxious to get as much distance between them and *Neptuna* as soon as possible. With only the two engines running and with Hussey beside him in the first officer's seat, Crowther headed towards the mangroves at the far end of Darwin Harbour's East Arm, all the while trying to keep *Camilla* under the protective smokescreen still spewing from *Neptuna* and *Barossa*.

Once there, Crowther cut the engines and they discussed what to do next. Crowther's first thought was to hide in the mangroves for the rest of the morning but they both soon agreed to discard that idea, mainly because the water was shallow and there was the risk that *Camilla* would be left high and dry when the notoriously high Darwin tide ran out, making her a choice target should the Japanese return.

A brief inspection convinced them that despite the concussion from the bombing *Camilla*'s hull was undamaged, and there appeared to be no real reason why she wouldn't fly. With the decision made, Crowther restarted the engines and, this time with all four of its engines at full throttle and Hussey keeping a watch for enemy aircraft out the roof hatch above the cockpit, *Camilla* leapt into the air. As she climbed away to the south, a shattering explosion blew *Neptuna* apart.

While Crowther and Hussey were scrambling to the wharf to get *Camilla* out of harm's way, station engineer Norm Roberts had been dicing with death aboard the launch *Naiad* in the middle of Darwin Harbour. In fact the reason *Naiad* wasn't at the jetty when Crowther and Hussey arrived was because Roberts and several other Qantas staff members had taken it out to *Camilla* to gather some gear. They were heading back to the wharf when a bomb landed in the water ahead of them.

Looking up, Roberts was greeted by the sight of flights of bombers in formations of seven, all approaching Darwin in line astern, with further sticks of bombs already on the way down. He instantly decided their only chance was to move in the opposite direction, so he opened the throttle and headed for the open areas of the bay. They'd gone only about a kilometre when *Naiad*'s engine cut. The trouble proved to be water in the petrol, but the engine was hot, making it difficult to remove the carburettor while trying to keep an eye out for the low-flying Zeros that had joined the bombers. By the time they had the carburettor working Darwin's fast runout tide had carried them into the midst of the shipping in the harbour, and they watched as the stricken oil tanker *British Motorist* began to heel over while other ships were burning.

Then Roberts noticed a Zero turn sharply towards them and approach from astern. As the Zero opened fire, Roberts calculated their best hope was to drop speed to foil his aim. It worked: the Zero was too low and the bullets went over their heads.

The other choice they had was to minimise *Naiad*'s attractiveness as a target, so Roberts slowed the launch just enough to hold it against the tide and lifted the floor panels so those aboard could crouch in the bilges. Roberts then covered their backs with the boards to give the impression *Naiad* was empty.

The ruse was successful and they gradually made it to the mangroves to the east of the bay where the crew were able to come out of hiding. Their relief was premature as another Zero turned towards them and opened fire, but again its aim was high, the bullets shearing off branches from the mangroves as it roared overhead. The pilot, however, had done them a favour. Quickly gathering the branches, they used them to conceal the boat and then dispersed among the mangroves themselves, from where they could see for the first time the disastrous effect of the raid.

The *British Motorist* was already on its side, the water around it ablaze from its ruptured tanks, and *Neptuna* and *Barossa* were well alight, but although *Camilla* was difficult to make out through the smoke, miraculously it was still afloat and appeared to be unharmed.

Their attention now turned elsewhere and they watched in awe as the American destroyer USS *Peary* attempted to fight off a ferocious attack by dive-bombers and Zeros until a massive explosion engulfed it in flame and smoke. Their final glimpse was of its stern going down and when the smoke began to clear nothing remained of the ship.

Once the fury of the attack subsided they boarded *Naiad* and headed back towards the flying boat base, but with *Naiad* now low on fuel Roberts decided to beach her and they headed off on foot for more petrol, figuring they could use *Naiad* to tow *Camilla* to a safer anchorage.

With *Naiad* refuelled they arrived just as the *Neptuna*'s cargo of two hundred mines exploded in a sheet of flame, throwing a mass of heavy objects all around them. Until now the Qantas building had escaped virtually unscathed but the force of the explosion blew it apart. It was then Roberts noticed for the first time that *Camilla* was no longer moored and with a brief feeling of satisfaction he caught a glimpse of her taking off across the harbour and heading south.

Concerned now for his wife, Honey, Roberts set off in the damaged company Ford for their home in the suburb of Vesteys, relieved to find that part of the town had suffered no damage and his wife in the kitchen preparing a cup of tea for several soldiers who had taken her into cover under a tree. At the first sound of bombs, Mrs Roberts had ran upstairs for her tin hat and then out towards a makeshift air-raid shelter made of sandbags in the backyard, but when the two soldiers arrived they considered the shelter too obvious and thought under the tree would be safer.

Fortified by his own cup of tea, Roberts drove back to the flying boat base to be met with the news that the drum he'd used to refuel *Naiad* had not contained petrol but white spirits, which had caused the engine to almost seize. Since the only other Qantas launch, *Halcyon*, used to take passengers to and from the flying boats, had been wrecked, they now had to dismantle *Naiad*'s engine and replace a cylinder head.

Leaving Qantas mechanics George Lake and Roy Carr at work on the engine, Roberts, anxious now to trace the movements of *Camilla*, set off for the DCA Aeradio station at Fannie Bay airport to see if Crowther and Hussey had reported in. He was halfway there and passing the town's anti-aircraft batteries when they opened up. The second Japanese raid had arrived overhead and from a trench on the roadside Roberts could clearly see the bombers at around 18,000 feet, now concentrating all their efforts on the RAAF aerodrome.

It was around midday by the time he arrived at Fannie Bay to more disappointment. The Qantas hangar had been shattered, its steel structure riddled with shell holes and nearly all the sheeting torn from the roof and wall. All adjacent buildings were on fire, setting off bursts of exploding ammunition, and although the Department of Civil Aviation building remained largely intact, the shock of the bomb blasts had put the Aeradio equipment out of action. Some hours later he would learn that *Camilla* had landed on the island of Groote Eylandt about six hundred kilometres away.

Groote Eylandt, in fact, hadn't been Crowther's first choice. He'd originally intended to head for the closer Alligator River but then realised there would be no fuel there, and if the Shell barges at Darwin were now out of action there might be no fuel there either, essential if he was to return to Darwin to lift out staff and any evacuees. At Groote they could get enough fuel to easily fly back to Darwin and out again. When they eventually touched down on Groote waters Hussey noticed Crowther still had the remnants of shaving cream on his face!

After taking 6000 litres of fuel aboard they went to the local base to learn that until communications were restored no civil aircraft were permitted to return to Darwin. They sent their own message saying they proposed coming back at sunset anyway and requested Darwin signal each half hour to assure them all was clear. Then they waited.

Back at Darwin on her way to the hospital to check on Koch, Val Hansen was battling with her own problems. Confronted by wires across the road near a large bomb crater, she got out of the car to investigate when she heard someone call out and saw a man with his arm almost torn from his shoulder. She knew only enough about first aid to realise that she must stop the bleeding, so she used part of her underclothes as a makeshift tourniquet. By now the injured man was almost unconscious and so heavy she was struggling to drag him towards the car, but another man came along on a bicycle and helped her get him into the vehicle.

At the hospital she found Aub Koch on the nearby beach trying to cheer up other patients. Like everyone in Darwin, Koch heard the sirens and aircraft engines simultaneously: 'I knew what that meant. I had been bombed before.' Nursing his broken leg and an arm wound, he climbed under the bed, thinking the mattress might protect him from splinters as three bombs landed close, one striking the wing of the hospital. He saw the nurses following his example by diving under the beds where they stayed until the initial attack had passed and then began gathering the patients to get them out.

One of the nurses helped Koch, who could hardly walk, about two hundred metres to a clump of bushes near the beach. From there he saw what looked like an RAAF Wirraway being chased by a Zero, while other machines swept in low over the harbour to drop their bombs and then turn to machine gun the streets.

When the first raid ended a nurse brought a mattress to cover him and something to eat. Several of the patients wanted to return to the hospital but Koch warned them against it as his experience had convinced him the Japanese would return. He was right, although he confessed he didn't see much of the second raid, crouching low in the bushes in case they machine-gunned the beach.

Camilla arrived back in Darwin at dusk and Roberts and his team—operating under blackout conditions, without power and with only pencil torches to aid them—toiled through the night preparing it for take-off early next morning, all the while with rescue and salvage work taking place around them on the harbour.

At one stage Roberts watched a steady stream of trucks from the army's Larrakeyah Barracks pass nearby on their way out of town, leaving Roberts unimpressed as those aboard shouted alarms that a landing was imminent.

Later he was to learn that widespread looting had broken out throughout the town and during the afternoon a group of military police ransacked the freight parcels stored in the Qantas office at the Hotel Darwin, one of their number holding Qantas staff at bay with a broken bottle, the irony not lost on Roberts that many of the parcels contained gifts the troops in Darwin were sending to friends and relatives down south.

Through the early hours of the morning Crowther, Hussey, purser Tom Low, injured traffic officer John Morris and their other passengers spent a miserable night in the reception area of the abandoned Hotel Darwin, hordes of mosquitos making sleep impossible. When they arrived at the base an hour before dawn there were no boats to get them out to *Camilla*'s launch until Crowther noticed an overturned dinghy. In it they rowed to the Department of Civil Aviation launch which they intended to use to load *Camilla*, only to find the launch's engine wouldn't start. Against a background of searchlights crisscrossing the sky for enemy aircraft, they wiped the launch's ignition dry with their handkerchiefs until the engine fired. With more daylight appearing and the tide rapidly receding, crew, passengers and a stretchered Aub Koch were hurriedly loaded aboard *Camilla* and they were soon in the air.

They left a Darwin mortally wounded, with those first two raids killing 235 people and injuring more than 300. Eleven ships had been sunk and thirty aircraft destroyed, nine of them United States Army Air Corps and RAAF fighters defending the town. Numerous awards for exceptional bravery would follow, one of which would go to the DCA coxswain John Waldie, who pulled scores of injured from the burning waters of Darwin Harbour. Sadly though there would be another side, exemplified by the tactics of the provosts who raided the Qantas office and many other members of the Australian armed services who, fearful of a Japanese invasion, abandoned their posts. Such failings, however, were more than compensated by the valiant efforts of others like those manning the anti-aircraft guns, who continued to blaze away while under repeated attack.

The raids of 19 February 1942 would be the first of many. Darwin would suffer over sixty more in the next two years.

The press were waiting for *Camilla* when she arrived in Sydney. Some of the passengers, including Koch, still in his pyjamas, talked briefly of their own experiences, but it was obvious from the questions being asked that few in the south realised the full extent of the Darwin raid. It was equally obvious the authorities were intent on understating the loss of life and the damage.

Crowther would later recall his concern that no one had the slightest idea what was really happening at Darwin, and when he tried to pass the message on of the extent of the attack he was taken aside by a government official who counselled him against saying too much. Crowther left him in no doubt of his annoyance, suggesting the country needed to know so that it could prepare to defend itself.

Crowther himself was soon to head back north to assist in the aircraft operations which would support the New Guinea campaign, but before he left he packed the family Oldsmobile with food and other essentials, telling his wife that if the worst happened to get into it and head west!

Thanks largely to the courage, quick thinking and dedication of aircrew and ground staff, Qantas had managed to escape the carnage at Darwin with *Camilla* still intact and only minor injuries to several of its staff, but the airline had little time to ponder its good fortune. Its luck was about to run out.

The following morning, within minutes of taking off from Brisbane's Archerfield airfield on its scheduled service to Roma, Charleville and Cloncurry, Qantas DH 86 RMA *Sydney* spun out of the clouds and crashed near Belmont, twelve miles out of the city, killing the two crew and seven passengers aboard. It was the first fatal DH 86 accident in the seven years since the type had been introduced on the inaugural Empire route service and the first crash involving loss of passengers since the airline was founded twenty-one years before. The DH 86's captain, Charles Swaffield, was an experienced pilot, joining Qantas in 1937 after some years as an instructor at the Royal Queensland Aero Club, while the first officer, Lindsay Marshall, also from Brisbane, had joined Qantas several months previously and since had been a regular first officer on the airline's inland route.

Eyewitnesses told investigators they heard the aircraft's engines sound strange then saw it come out of a cloudbank and crash vertically into hilly terrain, once again raising the vexed question of the airworthiness of the

DH 86 following several serious accidents on its introduction to Australia in the mid-1930s.

A civil aviation inquiry continued for several months but its findings were inconclusive, leaving the question open as to whether Swaffield had become disoriented in cloud or the aircraft had suffered an instrument malfunction. The primary initial concern, however, was that an original problem involving the structure of the tail fin had resurfaced, but no evidence was found of this even though some reports indicated that the fin itself had been found some distance from the site of the crash.

Chapter 14

THE RELUCTANT SPY: DAVE ROSS'S DILI DILEMMA

Within hours of the first attacks on Darwin by Nagumo's fighters and bombers, Japanese transports were landing troops in a two-pronged assault on Timor, aimed at capturing both Koepang in Dutch Timor and Dili in Portuguese territory.

Only 450 kilometres north-west of Darwin, the closest foreign point to Australia and therefore a vital first stopover point on the Empire route, control of Timor had long been an important part of Japanese war planning.

The first alarms were raised in 1940 when the Japanese moved to activate a trade deal with the Portuguese outpost via a series of six survey flights by flying boats of Dai Nippon Airways between their base on Palau in the Caroline Islands and Dili. Clearly part of Japan's extensive drive for influence to the south, the first of these flights arrived in Dili's harbour in October 1940, accompanied by promises of boosts to the economy of the struggling colony from Japanese investment and the export of the colony's coffee, at the same time increasing the colony's commercial interests in trading and agriculture, which were gradually passing into Japanese hands.

The Portuguese themselves appear to have been ambivalent to the Japanese approach but were only too aware of Dili's strategic significance in aviation terms as the only territory between Australia and Singapore not controlled by the Dutch. It was a fact not lost on Australia or particularly Britain, which was anxious to thwart any attempts by the Japanese to gain a foothold across links with its colonial empire.

Timor's strategic importance as far as the Japanese were concerned was, however, nothing new to Qantas head office as the Empire route became established during the second half of the 1930s. In fact Fysh himself had noted Dili's significance on several occasions, once writing to Fergus McMaster while on his way to London back in 1937, pointing out to his chairman the importance of an air connection 'in regard to possible Japanese aggression'.

Shortly before the war he had taken the time to write to Menzies on the topic, suggesting Australia should consider purchasing the colony from the Portuguese in the same way as the United States had purchased Alaska. Other aviation figures were similarly impressed. On a visit to Dili around that time, the *Sydney Morning Herald*'s aviation journalist Jack Percival wrote: 'I felt sorry I did not have enough money to buy it and present it to a national museum as a relic of the 16th century.'

Even though Fysh's prescience as far as Japanese military aims might turn out to be accurate, Dili, unlike the Qantas Empire route station at Koepang to its west, had few attractions as a stopover point in its own right, having no airport capable of handling the DH 86.

By 1939, however, amid rising concerns about Japanese ambitions, the situation began to change rapidly. With Qantas now operating flying boats on the Empire route, the lack of a land airfield no longer mattered and a visit to Dili by Australian government officials paved the way for an agreement with the Portuguese, allowing a regular call at Dili fortnightly in each direction.

Fysh himself was there for the arrival of the first service as Bert Hussey touched down in *Coriolanus* on 19 January 1941 and his subsequent account provides an amusing insight into the challenges of operating an air service to such a remote outpost in those days.

Fysh had flown down from Koepang several days before with Andre de la Porte, a Dutch aviation official who would assist him in finalising arrangements, one of the most important being the procurement of a suitable launch to attend the aircraft. As Hussey landed, Fysh, intent on making the most of the opportunity to wave the Qantas flag, was at the Portuguese governor's residency about to escort the official party on board the aeroplane when an attendant arrived and handed Fysh a sodden piece of paper which read: 'Refuelling launch broken down—send help. Andre.' The messenger, a local, was standing outside the door still dripping wet after swimming ashore with the note held between his teeth. Help in the guise of a replacement vessel soon arrived, but earlier visits had shown that Fysh's experience was nothing out of the ordinary as far as Dili was concerned.

Some months before, when Department of Civil Aviation engineer Bill Bradfield arrived to inspect the airport facilities, he was standing in the doorway of the flying boat when a man dressed in singlet and shorts fishing nearby in a small open boat came over to inquire who they were. When told, he rapidly rowed away to alert the harbourmaster, who arrived by launch a half hour later to take them ashore. There they were given an official welcome by a guard of honour, led by the former singlet-clad fisherman now in uniform and resplendent in epaulettes and gold braid!

Bradfield's visit was, in fact, all part of the elaborate ruse engineered by the British. Rather than send Bradfield on his own, it was given the appearance of an official Australian 'delegation' also comprising Civil

Aviation's Edgar Johnston and the department's superintendent of flying operations David Ross. Little did David Ross know at the time what he was letting himself in for!

Early oddities overcome, Qantas traffic officer Bill Nielsen and engineer Doug Laurie soon had the flying boat transits operating a regular fortnightly call in each direction, although one of the first concerns was to provide adequate radio facilities to handle the new service, solved by the Department of Civil Aviation sending radio inspector Ivan Hodder with new equipment to bring the primitive Dili radio up to date. Assisted by local radio operator Pat Luz, they established a radio room in the Dili post office and soon had it providing reliable communications with Darwin and even as far away as Karumba, two thousand kilometres to the south-east. Of course, Hodder's radio had another role beyond helping Qantas with communications. It too would be useful as part of the British and Australian plan to report on the Japanese, and was destined to play a significant role in Australia's Timor involvement when the Japanese army arrived in force the following year. So, as it turned out, would Dave Ross.

By early 1941, as Japanese interest in Dili increased, suggestions about how to handle the situation led to a flurry of cables between Australia and the United Kingdom. Menzies at first suggested that to strengthen a presence in Dili the British should appoint a British consul from their own diplomatic service, whose primary role would be to spy on the Japanese. The British, however, felt that this would merely place the Portuguese, a neutral country in the war, in the awkward position of having to agree to any Japanese request to appoint their own consul. Their suggestion was for the Australians to appoint someone under the guise of the Darwin–Dili air service who would use his role as cover to report on Japanese activities.

The matter went before the Australian cabinet in February 1941 with the recommendation that the ideal man for the job was Dave Ross, since he had already been involved in the Timor negotiations and had the appropriate aviation background to conceal his true role. Over the following weeks the issue bounced backwards and forwards between London, Canberra and Lisbon until finally Ross was appointed not only the British consul but the Qantas representative as well. To suggest Dave Ross was unhappy with the whole idea would be an understatement. Never afraid to speak his mind, years after the war he would put it this way: 'Some silly old fool in the External Affairs Department wanted someone to go to East Timor to see what the Japs were up to, if anything.'

By the time Ross arrived in Dili early in April 1941, Qantas's Bill Neilsen had already returned to Sydney with the result that Ross soon found himself overwhelmed by the administrative demands of his combined roles of Qantas representative, aviation expert and spy. Assistance soon arrived in the form of 'civil aviation officer' F.J.A. Whittaker, who was in fact a naval intelligence operative but was at least able to take some of the load off Ross.

As it turned out, however, Qantas was a perfect cover. Working in the post office, Pat Luz would hand the content of Japanese radio messages to Ross and Whittaker, who would pass them through in handwritten form via the Qantas flying boats. In between they used coded radio messages between Dili and Darwin, ensuring the messages were kept as brief as possible to avoid suspicion.

By October 1941, their six proving flights behind them, the Japanese announced plans to introduce a regular air service between Tokyo and Dili, the first to operate the following month. Now, against a background of the war clouds that were gathering, Fysh himself stepped in to lead the charge against the Japanese proposal, describing Dili publicly as 'the Japanese listening post in the South Pacific'. 'Beyond giving her a bird's-eye view of what's going on in the South Seas, this post has no great commercial value . . . therefore trade cannot be the reason for the new service,' he said in a press release.

Prompted by such concerns, the British and Australian governments were already discussing the possibility of occupying Portuguese Timor by force. On the other hand, considering his main role was diminishing and fed up with the whole idea, Dave Ross was agitating to return home, but it was too late. Still there when Pearl Harbor was attacked on 7 December 1941, he reluctantly occupied a grandstand seat as he watched the dominoes collapse through Malaya, Singapore and the Netherlands East Indies.

Now, on top of being desperate to get out he found himself as a Qantas representative without an airline. In the following weeks he would also achieve something else unique in the annals of Qantas's overseas representatives: playing a key role in negotiating the takeover of a foreign country, with the result that Ross found himself in Dili when Australian and Dutch troops arrived there to defend East Timor on 17 December.

The very fact that he was still there when the Japanese landed in February 1942 reflects poorly on an Australian government that was still reluctant to remove him because of the value of his Dutch and Portuguese contacts. Despite his parlous situation, when the Dutch also began to leave Ross could at least see some humour in their farewell dinner. 'Being the Dutch, the first thing they wanted to evacuate was the gin—and the ammunition second—before they shoved off.'

Soon after, asleep at his residence close to the beach, he awoke to a flash of light from offshore and shell bursts, along with a substantial hangover. 'I thought this was not a good place to be but I was caught,' Ross would later reflect, 'for the simple reason I had nowhere to go and all my friends had left me.' Shutting the house down, he walked three or four blocks to get as far away as he could from the gunfire, seeking refuge in a native dwelling surrounded by coconut trees. There he waited to find out what the Japanese would do next.

In any event the defence of Timor was short-lived, the majority of the outnumbered Australian battalion surrendering to the Japanese while the other part of the force, the 2nd Independent Company, known as Sparrow Force, took to the mountains, from where they were to harass the Japanese for the next eighteen months.

When things quietened down after several days, Ross returned to his residence to find it had been ransacked while occupied by the Japanese. Cheekily, and showing considerable courage, he sought out the Japanese consul and demanded his house back. The consul explained he would be only too happy to oblige but he had no control over the army sentries around it, at the same time accusing him of being an intelligence officer. 'I'm Qantas. Are you going to dump me with intelligence though I'm a civil aviation officer?' Ross countered. 'Anyhow, he wasn't a bad bloke, Roman Catholic, educated in Spain,' recalled Ross.

The result was Ross found himself back in the house and able to get a note past the guards to the Japanese officer of the watch, telling him he wanted something to eat. Soon after two bags of rice arrived which supplemented fruit from the nearby orange trees. 'I lived on oranges and rice for quite a while and we used to get an occasional chook when some native from the interior came down and handed over a chook for money.'

Several weeks passed before the Japanese consul appeared again, this time with a proposition. He wanted Ross to go inland and make contact with the Australian soldiers there. 'He said because the East Indies had surrendered and Singapore had surrendered, the soldiers too must surrender. If they don't they will be treated as bandits and executed.' Ross, however, wasn't fooled, as it was common knowledge in Dili that the Australian commandos' hit and run ambushes were causing high casualties among the Japanese.

The next morning, although none too happy at the prospect, Ross headed towards Liquissa, a settlement about thirty kilometres along the coast from Dili. It was a nerve-racking trip, sitting in the front of the first of a convoy of six trucks and several captured Australian Bren gun carriers, a Japanese soldier with a British-made Tommy gun beside him, fearful that at any moment the Australians he was going to meet might ambush the vehicles. If that happened, he'd be the first hit.

When they eventually stopped on the edge of the jungle, some of the Japanese went out on patrol and the others sat down for lunch, although they didn't have any for him. A bizarre discussion followed when, for some reason he couldn't understand, the Japanese officer in charge wanted to take him back, but Ross argued that if they wished the Australians to surrender then he should complete the mission. 'I wanted to get out and see how the troops were going.' So astride a Timor pony and accompanied by a local guide called Salvadore, he set off into the mountains in an attempt to find the Australians.

It was a day's walk and tough going through rugged mountain terrain, but it was another opportunity for Ross to later demonstrate his earthy Australian sense of humour: 'A woman's saddle and haemorrhoids and you can't beat that on a wet Sunday and an empty stomach.'

Given their active watch and loyal assistance from the local Timorese, there's little doubt the men of the 2nd would have been following his approach for some time, so his arrival in their area was no surprise. Having been told by the Japanese the Australians were in poor condition and had suffered many casualties, Ross was relieved to find the opposite. Not only did they have adequate food but their morale was high, to a large extent due to the damage they knew they were causing the Japanese.

It took several days for their two commanders, Major Alex Spence and Captain Bernard Callinan, to call their troops together to meet Ross and hear what he had to say. Their answer was immediate and has since entered Australian military folklore: 'Surrender? Surrender be fucked!'

If the Japanese needed any further elaboration, Ross was to tell them that being a special unit of the Australian Army, it took its orders from headquarters in Melbourne and as far as Spence and Callinan knew there had been no surrender there. 'This was placing an exceedingly liberal interpretation on our role, but it had some germs of truth in it,' Callinan would later write in an account of the Timor campaign.

His men did, however, have a monetary problem, needing funds to purchase food and other essentials from the local population, and here Ross was able to help, providing them with a note from the British and

Australian governments written over his signature that any such help would be honoured at the end of the war.

Ross stayed two more days, during which he was able to tell the commandos all he knew about Japanese installations in Dili, particularly around the aerodrome, which the commandos told him they planned to attack. He then set off again to the coast, this time to be the bearer of news not well received by the Japanese.

More weeks went by, the ambushes continued and the Japanese became more and more frustrated and agitated until finally, in June, the Japanese commander, a colonel, called for Ross and demanded he repeat the performance. This time he would carry a letter under the colonel's signature offering a guarantee of safe passage as prisoners of war, something Ross knew would have little effect on the commandos given the Japanese reputation for executing POWs. Ross, by now his own health deteriorating from poor food and extended confinement, was quick to seize this as his chance to get away from Dili. This time he wasn't coming back.

By the time he had reached part of the way at Aileu he was thoroughly exhausted and was cared for by Portuguese until he was fit enough to meet the Australians further inland. Even then he had to be carried for the final part of his journey to the commandos' position in the mountains. Once there, and as if they had no idea of his circumstances, the Australian authorities in Darwin suggested by radio he return to Dili so they could arrange for him to be part of a prisoner exchange. Far from impressed and convinced that if the Japanese ever saw him again they would execute him, Ross instead sat down and wrote what he would later describe as an 'awful rude letter' to the Japanese telling them he hadn't enjoyed their company, 'and they were a lot of bastards anyway.'

Years later he would also take out his anger on External Affairs: 'As to whether I should go back on reciprocal arrangements and all that sort of rubbish, sitting on their tails, typical in Canberra. Imagine them sitting in the mountains.' Unsurprisingly he also heard later from Timorese refugees the Japanese were angry at his failure to return: 'I had about nine hundred quid in my hands and they were very upset. Here was this man and we sent him off on a mission and he does this to us.'

Ignoring the suggestion from Australia that Ross return to Dili, Callinan insisted that, even if he did avoid being executed, as virtually a prisoner in Dili he would no longer be able to achieve anything and should be sent home.

Before then, however, the radio that Civil Aviation's Ivan Hodder had provided for the Qantas services would see service of its own, eventually smuggled to the commandos to replace their own makeshift radio, known as 'Winnie the War Winner', and help improve their communications with Darwin.

Ross would finally leave the island in July 1942 aboard an Australian naval vessel under the noses of the Japanese. Until their eventual withdrawal from Timor, the 2nd would remain in combat longer than any other AIF fighting force during the Allied retreat through the Netherlands East Indies.

It would probably not be drawing too long a bow to suggest that David Ross could be regarded as the only Qantas representative ever to play an important part in tying down an entire enemy army for almost twelve months. His subsequent wartime role as the senior officer of RAAF air transport command must have seemed a somewhat benign assignment after his Timor experience.

Chapter 15

THE RAT TRAP: TJILATJAP

While Timor took its first steps into a guerrilla war, many miles away to the west the Netherlands East Indies was reaching the point of collapse. Indeed, Japanese progress across the archipelago was happening so fast that route changes for flying boats often had to be made on a daily basis.

With Batavia and Surabaya no longer tenable as evacuee points and Darwin largely neutralised, Tjilatjap on Java's south coast had fast become the last remaining link in the escape chain to Australia. As Lew Ambrose's survey in December had shown, Tjilatjap was hardly an ideal choice for such a vital mission, but as the only port of any substance anywhere on the south coast of Java and the only suitable alighting area for flying boats, there were no other options. Unfortunately, Ambrose's earlier reservations about its suitability for flying boats were more than matched by Tjilatjap's shortcomings as a shipping port. Not a natural harbour, its narrow entrance was made even more dangerous by rocks, shallows and fast currents.

To their credit, however, in 1940 Dutch maritime authorities began urgent work to improve handling facilities at Tjilatjap, prompted by the increasing possibility of war and concerns that enemy control of the Java Sea to the north of Java would leave the ports of Batavia and Surabaya vulnerable to any resupply. The harbour was dredged, navigation lights and mooring buoys laid and new piers constructed, although most of the cargo routed through still had to be moved from ship to shore by lighters. Adding even more difficulty to the task, the Netherlands East Indies had few industries of its own and the war in Europe had long ago severed any chance of supplies from a motherland now occupied by the Germans.

Efficient movement of goods on land presented an additional complication. Any stores arriving at or leaving the port had to be transferred inland by a single railway line on which inbound trainloads were frequently blocked by empty wagons returning to the port. The Dutch might have done their best, but nothing could have made Tjilatjap capable of handling the chaos that was about to descend on it through January and February of 1942. As for defending itself, protection against a seaborne invasion amounted to three 75-millimetre and two 150-millimetre guns, with nothing to protect it against air attack.

On 18 February Russell Tapp flew what would be the second-last flight out of Batavia for Broome, leaving at dawn to avoid Japanese air patrols. His overnight stop aboard *Clifton* at Tjilatjap was anything but comfortable as he nervously watched while a constant stream of shipping of all shapes and sizes, some without lights, brushed close by in the darkness, bringing an ever-present danger of collision. His troubles didn't stop there. *Clifton*, unlike some of the other flying boats, had not been fitted with extra fuel tanks and didn't have the range to get to Broome, so he scrounged a batch of four-gallon tins of petrol and stacked them behind the flight deck. Since you could walk inside the wings to get to the fuel tanks, it was a relatively simple matter to run a pipe up into the tanks and hand pump the petrol up, one tin at a time. Even then, packed with refugees, he just made it to Broome.

The following day, *Coriolanus*, with Ambrose and Bill Purton at the controls, flew the last service out of Batavia.

While Tapp and Ambrose were flying east, plans were being put in place for a series of shuttles to operate between Broome and Tjilatjap. Engineer Charlie Short had already joined Mansfield's Malcolm Millar in Tjilatjap, while Eric Kydd, David Thomson and Jim Lamb were on their way there overland from Surabaya, as were a small group of BOAC Batavia staff, including several engineers. Those BOAC staff remaining in Batavia were put aboard ship for India. Lester Brain would take charge of the Broome operations, with any spares and equipment available in Darwin to be rushed there, along with a spare engine from Sydney.

In Tjilatjap itself, Malcom Millar found himself in the middle of a serious logistical problem as he searched for someone in authority to help him establish the priority guidelines for the shuttles to Broome. No one among the Dutch or American authorities at Tjilatjap seemed to be in overall command, and any decisions appeared haphazard and based on little knowledge of what was happening with the fighting itself.

With the Qantas flying boats and other aircraft still flying in with equipment including machine guns and ammunition, presumably to continue the defence of Java, Millar set off by road to military headquarters in Bandoeng in the hope of getting clarification about what was required for the return flights to Australia. What he learned there left him in no doubt that it was only a matter of time: Java was doomed.

Military headquarters in Bandoeng announced a large Japanese convoy was approaching Surabaya or Bali, adding the gloomy admission that it could 'not be satisfactorily dealt with'. Still anxious to establish priorities, Millar was staggered to find that the first list of passengers he was given were female secretaries of senior military officers.

His primary concern, however, was the conflicting estimates of how much longer it would be safe to operate the shuttles he was being asked to plan. The answer was depressing: the best estimate he could get was that an attack could be expected within seven to ten days as by that time any air defence would be gone, the whole fighter force consisting of a total of forty and their average losses running at four a day. Such a loss rate, he was told, would mean a capitulation after a token resistance and the whole thing might be over by 27 February. Any shuttle operation continuing beyond that date would rely almost entirely on the actions of the enemy.

Millar immediately cabled the news to Sydney, expressing doubts he'd be able to get any reliable information as the situation deteriorated further. In a secret reply, Fysh cabled he would leave it to his judgement, explaining the Australian government considered it important that the Java evacuation flights continue so long as it was reasonably safe and Millar's judgement would be relied on to weigh up when the situation deteriorated to the point where they should cease.

It was a heavy responsibility to place on Millar, already hampered by communication difficulties between Tjilatjap and Broome, and with Fysh also reminding him of the operational difficulties presented by the two thousand kilometres between the towns:

> The long ocean crossing with no alternative alighting areas must be considered hazardous and you should visualise the possibility of ocean search should flying boats be forced down through engine trouble. In event cessation of service due to complete evacuation of Java you and staff must proceed Australia by last service, bringing all possible spares.

It is hard to imagine the nightmare of Tjilatjap through the period of the Qantas shuttles between 22 and 28 February. The one saving grace appears to be that there were no air attacks, a factor which may be put down to a plan by the Japanese fleet to lure Allied warships towards Tjilatjap and expose them to attack, or that the Japanese, now supremely confident the end was in sight, simply wanted to limit the damage there before they occupied it themselves.

The port itself was now packed to capacity, everything from large freighters to small passenger ships and naval vessels, as they loaded their human cargo of military and civilian evacuees, many of whom had made the torturous overland journey from as far away as Sumatra to finally set off on the perilous journey to Australia.

The desperation of it all was summed up by a Dutch seaman aboard the freighter MS *Abbekerk*, who would recall how his transport had just arrived full of ammunition. The lethal cargo was only partly unloaded when orders arrived to leave what ammunition remained on board and take on evacuees to Australia instead:

> The hatches could just be closed without divulging what was underneath. During the day the men came aboard, a more diverse lot I have never seen. Aircraft crews still wearing their thick woollen jackets, a few high and a lot more lower officers, soldiers and sailors both with and without weapons and then some civilians, many with worried and tired faces.

When all were aboard 1500 people were spread over the entire length of the *Abbekerk*, crowded onto the deck and into part of the hold. That day he watched more than twenty ships leave, each captain deciding his own course to steer, until the *Abbekerk*'s turn came and they set off, not knowing how many submarines of enemy warships lay in wait for them on their way to Australia. 'None of the passengers knew that in the bottom hold there were a couple of thousand tons of ammunition. I believe that every member of the crew found it better not to speak about it.' Neither, he noted, would anyone talk about the number of SOS signals they were receiving from ships sailing in their vicinity, all under attack from surface ships or submarines.

Lester Brain would later aptly describe the Tjilatjap–Broome operation as 'something of a Dunkirk', and Lew Ambrose would recall seeing Japanese submarines lying in wait outside the harbour as he climbed out towards Broome. How many were lost in those terrible days will never be known.

Orm Denny flew the first of the shuttles to Tjilatjap on 20 February, taking in medical supplies and other stores. That night he and his crew slept four to a room with a mattress and a pillow, bread and jam the only meal available. Denny did two return trips, strangely his last taking in a cargo of machine guns, although he recalled wondering whether they would ever be used.

It took the flying boats nine hours to cover the 1200-mile distance, but at least the four-engine Empires had a range advantage not available to the Dutch and American twin-engine Lockheed Lodestars and DC-3s taking part in the uplift. Even with limited numbers on board they were stretched to the limit to make it to Broome.

One advantage the Qantas Empires had over the assortment of American Flying Fortresses, Liberators, DC-3s and Lockheed Lodestars flying evacuees both ways through increasingly dangerous skies was their ability to carry up to twenty-five passengers per flight. For the flying boats, though, arrival at Tjilatjap brought its own hazards. The vulnerability of their hulls meant there was always the risk of striking debris on the alighting area with disastrous results. Luck had to be on their side.

Overnights at Tjilatjap carried their own hardships for crews. Although the Dutch army had provided some accommodation ashore, crews often chose to load the flying boats before dark and remain aboard for the night, passengers sleeping in seats or spread throughout the aircraft. Ambrose made it a habit to sleep with his life jacket on in the hull's centre section.

Despite such discomfort there could be little doubt of the dedication of the Qantas crews, Brain at one stage cabling Fysh that his pilots were arguing with each other for the 'privilege of doing the next trip'. Such a comment would have been welcome news for Fysh and others in

Sydney, now concerned at the damage to morale following the shock of the Darwin raid.

While some of those on board the shuttles were people of high rank, one flight by Ambrose would add its own footnote to one of the most bizarre incidents in Australia's war against Japan: the final stage of the AIF commander in Singapore General Gordon Bennett's journey to Australia following his controversial escape hours before the fall of Singapore.

According to his later biographer, Frank Legg, Bennett's journey from Singapore shortly before it surrendered had been an adventurous one, first escaping by boat to Sumatra, then by air to Batavia and then overland to military headquarters in Bandoeng to report to ABDA force commander General Wavell, only to learn Wavell had already left for India. Unable to find any other transport to Australia from there, he hitchhiked to Tjilatjap. It was here that Bennett's account of what happened next differed markedly from that of Lew Ambrose.

Bennett recounted how at Tjilatjap he was 'able to find a Qantas plane', going on to claim: 'The pilot was unable to give me passage as he was under charter. So I stowed away on the plane that night. We left for Broome at dawn on 27 February.'

Interviewed many years later, Ambrose would tell a very different story:

> It was my second trip and I was concerned that General Gordon Bennett was to be one of my passengers. I must say from a commander point of view I found it most difficult to believe that a general could run away and leave his men and it followed that our first contact was rather stilted and wondered whether I should do anything about it, but it was beyond my control.
>
> I was to discover later he was brusquely treated by Canberra along with my own line of thought, although he was to explain that there was no one who had any awareness of the Japanese guerrilla tactics and therefore it was important for him to get back and teach us.

According to Ambrose, Bennett had been processed normally as a passenger and certainly it hadn't been necessary to 'smuggle' himself aboard. Whether Bennett was simply over-dramatising that portion of his escape is unknown, but Ambrose would put his own tongue-in-cheek spin on it long after the war:

> I went through many experiences through my flying career but carrying generals as 'stowaways' was not one of them. In war it is always difficult to get the facts right. I saw General Gordon many times after his return to Australia and at no time did he believe it was necessary to stow away on my aircraft.

Military historians differ on whether Bennett's decision to leave his troops was right or wrong, but he would certainly suffer greatly for what was to become one of the most controversial issues of Australia's military command in the Second World War. Although his courage was never doubted, he was harshly dealt with by the AIF's commander General Sir Thomas Blamey and was never to be given further opportunity to command Australian troops in battle for the remainder of the war.

While Bennett, travelling as a passenger, was probably unaware of it, Ambrose had other more pressing things on his mind as he left Tjilatjap that morning, climbed *Coriolanus* to eight thousand feet and set course for Broome. He was flying under what he would later describe as 'extremely pleasant flying conditions' when he noticed ahead and above him a Japanese Kawanishi flying boat.

The Kawanishi was not just any flying boat. Widely used by the Japanese navy, the four-engine Kawanishi was a heavily armed reconnaissance aircraft with a range of well over 2000 miles and was to gain an impressive combat reputation throughout the war. It was more than capable of shooting down an unarmed civilian flying boat.

Ambrose knew unless he did something very quickly he was in serious trouble and immediately sought refuge in a large cumulous cloud off to one side. While hidden there he lost height to gain speed and at the same time changed course to throw the Kawanishi off. As the cloud thinned at this level he climbed further until he estimated he was high enough above the Kawanishi to break cloud and have a look around. With the plane nowhere in sight he again set course for Broome.

It was at this point he became concerned that Bill Purton, flying *Circe*, would be on his way from Broome, and by the time he approached Tjilatjap might run into the Kawanishi which by that afternoon would be hidden from him by the western sun. Ambrose decided to break radio silence, knowing Purton would be listening and warning him in morse of the possible danger ahead. The fact there was no reply didn't concern Ambrose too much, given the possibility of the Japanese listening in. It would be the last communication Ambrose would have with Purton, whose flight would be partly doomed by other communications difficulties.

Despite last-minute attempts to hold off the Japanese, things were falling apart on Java. In a final blow, the USS *Langley*, carrying thirty-two desperately needed P-40 Warhawk fighters from Perth, was attacked by Japanese bombers and so badly damaged it subsequently had to be sunk by its accompanying warships. Although another vessel carrying more fighters got through the Japanese blockade, they arrived too late to have any effect on the situation.

The shuttles had been running for five days when Java military headquarters, acknowledging that Java could not be held much longer, told Millar that the last service should leave the next day. Acting on his earlier instructions from Fysh, on the night of 26 February Millar sent a request to Sydney for two flying boats to clear stores and staff from Tjilatjap. When Java headquarters repeated the instruction twenty-four hours later Miller confirmed the final departure date with Sydney but, unknown to him at the time, the message never reached Australia.

Such communications problems had plagued Millar and the Qantas Tjilatjap operation generally since the very start of the shuttles. Radio contact between Broome and Tjilatjap was irregular and even Darwin Aeradio had suffered in the Japanese attacks on Darwin. Without a regular direct radio link, Millar often had to rely on the latest Broome input from the captains who arrived there with the shuttle aircraft.

So, when Ambrose arrived on *Coriolanus* on the night of 26 February with information that Civil Aviation in Australia had ordered a continuation of the service until further instructions were received, Millar was confronted by two completely conflicting orders. The flights would now continue until further notice.

Thus, on the evening of 27 February, *Corinthian* under the command of Stephen Howard and Bill Purton's *Circe* arrived at Tjilatjap from Broome. Now the mix-up in communications, which had effectively extended the shuttles for an extra day, would have tragic results.

Chapter 16

'ONE OF OUR AIRCRAFT IS MISSING': THE LOSS OF *CIRCE*

Although everyone in Sydney from Hudson Fysh down knew the risks their crews were taking, the cable from Lester Brain in Broome on the evening of 28 February 1942 must have come as a shock:

> *Corinthian* arrived stop *Circe* failed to arrive and feared lost stop Last heard on radio two hundred miles out from Java stop Crew Purton Oates Hogan and sixteen passengers.

Howard and his *Corinthian* crew had gone ashore to spend the Friday night at a Javanese rest house while Bill Purton had elected to stay on board *Circe*. Both aircraft were due to depart early the following morning, bringing out a mixed load of government officials, service personnel, several diplomats and as many of the remaining Qantas staff and stores as they could get aboard. Malcolm Millar and engineer Charlie Short would see the aircraft off and head for Djogjakarta (now Yogyakarta) to make their own way home.

Circe's first officer Mervyn Bateman was already at the Tjilatjap wharf when Howard arrived after breakfast next morning and the two boarded a launch to take them out to their aircraft, across a harbour now eerily devoid of shipping, most having left over the previous two days. Bateman, a New Zealander, married with a baby daughter and already a qualified pilot, had joined Qantas as a flight clerk in 1938 and served a brief period in the RAAF before rejoining Qantas as aircrew in September 1940.

As they dropped Bateman off, Howard had a brief chat to Purton before the launch headed towards *Corinthian*.

Bill Purton's youthful good looks could be misleading. Twenty-nine years old and due to marry within weeks, he was held in high regard by his peers, not only for his flying ability but the high standard of his meticulously detailed after-mission captain's reports.

Along with Purton and Bateman was radio officer Herbert Oates, who had received his radio ticket from the Marconi School in Melbourne before joining Qantas in December 1938. A few days before on an overnight at Tjilatjap, Oates had rescued the master of a refuelling barge during his aircraft's refuelling operations. The barge had started to back away from the flying boat when someone committed the cardinal sin of striking a match and the barge burst into flames. The master had immediately jumped overboard but then shouted he couldn't swim. Without hesitating, Oates, who was on the wing of the aircraft, dived in and rescued him.

Purser Lionel Hogan had been with Qantas nine months. Others aboard were officers, staff and family members from the consulate for the Netherlands in Malaya, including Consul-General Hendrik Fein along with a US Navy commander and a representative of the Sarawak government in the Netherlands East Indies. Also on board were six BOAC staff, engineer 'Shinty' Colvin and Malcolm Millar's secretary Lim Kim Swee.

Already aboard Howard's *Corinthian* with civilian evacuees were Qantas engineers Kydd, Thomson and Lamb, among the last of the Qantas staff still in Netherlands East Indies.

Perhaps the luckiest of them all that morning was Qantas steward Tom Low who, in a last-minute decision, had been transferred to *Corinthian* from *Circe*. Originally a purser on P & O vessels, Low would often tell the story how, while serving Prime Minister Menzies on the way to London, Menzies had suggested he would make an ideal steward on Qantas and had given him a note to pass on to Hudson Fysh.

Low's good fortune in impressing Bob Menzies appears to have followed him through his Qantas career. He'd already managed to survive the first attacks on Darwin to be flown to safety with the injured Aub Koch by Crowther and Hussey on *Camilla* the next morning. For whatever the reason, this latest decision to switch him from *Circe* to *Corinthian* would save his life.

Their pre-flights checks completed, Howard and first officer John Connolly got *Corinthian*'s engines running and after a short taxi across the water were soon in the air. As they climbed away Connolly could see *Circe* starting to taxi for take-off across the harbour below.

Having watched daily Japanese reconnaissance flights over Tjilatjap and to reduce the risk of running into any prowling Japanese fighters, Howard headed due south from Java for the first part of the flight, anxious to put as much distance between him and the mainland as rapidly as possible, before turning east to set course for Broome. It was a procedure he was sure Purton would also follow.

A little under two hours out from Java, Howard overheard a brief message in code from *Circe*'s radio officer Oates advising Broome of the number of passengers they had on board. Purton gave his position in code as about two hundred miles from Java. When Howard heard Broome sounding unsure of the message's content and trying unsuccessfully to confirm it, he had his own radio officer repeatedly try to contact Purton, but there was no answer.

While every pilot appreciates clear skies, this fine Saturday morning with only a slight haze over the Java mainland but otherwise visibility for miles was hardly ideal for an unarmed civilian aircraft flying through Japanese-controlled airspace. Connolly, Howard's first officer, recalls some tense moments about three hundred miles into their journey when the purser came into the cockpit to report that several passengers saw what might be aircraft in the distance. Both pilots searched the sky in the direction of the 'sighting' but could see nothing, putting it down to an outline of thin dark clouds in the distance.

The remainder of their journey was uneventful. When *Circe* didn't arrive soon after them Lester Brain began to fear the worst, and the time came when he knew *Circe*, even if had escaped the Japanese, would be out of fuel anyway.

Despite long hours of searching by other Qantas flying boats over the next several days, no sign of *Circe* was found and there was every reason to accept Purton had fallen prey to the Japanese. Amid the shock and sadness, tributes would quickly follow, including one from BOAC chief Walter Runciman that Fysh would pass on to his crews in a message of his own, expressing the company's appreciation for the 'hardships and inconveniences during the adventurous last three months':

> All this has been done willingly and cheerfully in the spirit of service to your country and your Company. You have shown that fighting spirit which is so essential to victory.
>
> The Qantas services were the last Commercial Services to cease operations to Singapore and to Java. May the splendid work of the Q.E.A. crews be an inspiration to the rest of us during the difficult days to come, and in which we must never admit defeat. Qantas will stand firm and play its part.

John Connolly, who had often shared the cockpit with Bill Purton in the difficult early months of the Pacific war, would write his own tribute:

It was a real pleasure to number oneself among Captain Purton's crew. His never-failing good humour and wit were a big help when the going was a bit difficult.

His handling of *Corinna* during the most incredibly violent storm I had ever seen was, in my opinion, a masterpiece of flying. We ran into it near Benkulen in Sumatra and it was a disturbance known as a Sumatran—a small concentrated cyclone, notorious for its extreme violence.

As Howard and Connolly flew east unaware of Purton's fate that morning, Orm Denny was already well on his way towards Tjilatjap, only to be ordered to return to Broome a short time later. The last Qantas link with Java had been severed.

As Qantas in Sydney and Broome were now coming to terms with the loss of the *Circe*, back in a now almost deserted Tjilatjap, the irrepressible Malcolm Millar and ground engineer Charlie Short destroyed all codes and confidential papers and, feeling a little more confident after arming themselves with two Tommy guns and a copious supply of ammunition from the departing troops, headed for Djogjakarta, their arrival coinciding with a series of air raids. Millar was surprised to learn that some of those at RAF headquarters and even the Dutch authorities believed they could still hold Djogjakarta. Events over the following few days showed otherwise as they watched Japanese bombers and fighters attack unopposed while defensive anti-aircraft guns were being towed away from the airport, and preparations made to sabotage the runway after the last aircraft left.

Several nights later they handed over their Tommy guns and ammunition to the RAF, along with the company car and typewriter, and boarded a US Air Force B-17 Flying Fortress to a Broome that was about to experience the full force of the war.

Chapter 17

DEATH AND DISASTER AT BROOME

Like most other casualties of the war, Broome, far from ideal as an Australian landfall, had its importance thrust upon it. The Japanese leapfrog towards Timor had brought their aircraft within easy reach of Australia's northern coastline, and the attacks on Darwin had demolished any hope of it continuing as a link with the Netherlands East Indies.

Before the Darwin attacks, however, Broome, a relatively isolated pearl-fishing town on the north-west coast, had been considered far enough south to keep it out of range of marauding Japanese aircraft.

Fiercely independent in its remoteness, peacetime Broome consisted of a population of around four hundred Europeans, themselves well outnumbered by a mix of Chinese, Japanese and islanders mostly associated with a fleet of pearling luggers which, although owned by local traders, were largely in the hands of Japanese divers. At the outbreak of war the navy took control of the pearling luggers and any Japanese in the town were interned and eventually moved south.

Broome's initial strategic value as far as the war was concerned was as an exit point for the supply of men and military supplies in the defence of the Netherlands East Indies. But as the early weeks of February 1942 passed and that defence crumbled, its primary role became a clearing station for the hundreds of troops and civilian refugees, many of the latter women and children, streaming out of Java.

The rapid collapse of Java left little time to adequately prepare Broome for what was to come, a situation not helped by the confused organisational control of the evacuation itself. Although the Qantas flying boats were nominally under the control of the Department of Civil Aviation, the aircraft themselves were under charter to the US military, a factor which would lead to further complications as Broome's main role switched from an exit to an inbound evacuation point.

In terms of the incoming airlift about to be forced upon it, even Broome's established airport was barely capable of handling the heavy US military aircraft like the Flying Fortress and Liberator bombers that would begin to pound its runway as the evacuation gained momentum, but an even worse situation faced those responsible for flying boats. Again, like any such stretch of coastal water in this part of Australia, the tides dictated all.

Early in February, when Bert Hussey flew in Civil Aviation's inspector of flying boat bases, Robert Kennedy, from Darwin for a first inspection, the challenges became immediately obvious. Not only were there no facilities for flying boats but tide ranges of ten metres meant that the aircraft would need to be moored well out into the bay. At low tide passengers and crew would have to wade ashore upwards of half a kilometre through the mud to reach the town's jetty. Even when the tide was favourable it meant transport by dinghy from the aircraft to a lugger and finally from another dinghy to the wharf. It was hardly an ideal situation but a reconnaissance by Hussey and Kennedy along the north-west coast plainly showed there was no alternative. Broome would have to do.

Two of the first in after Hussey's visit and charged with making it work for Qantas were engineers Doug Laurie and Bill Bennett. As if Laurie didn't have enough to contend with, he found communications with the outside world almost non-existent. The telegraph lines to the town had been down, meaning some of the telegrams head office in Sydney were sending him had been five days in transit: 'Today's batch were sent air mail by MacRobertson Miller from Port Hedland,' he explained despairingly in a letter to Sydney on 17 February. The good news, though, was that he had obtained a five-metre motorboat with a Chapman Pup inboard engine, albeit the latter needing an overhaul, while repairs were underway on a seven-metre motor launch that would do away with the cumbersome lugger.

Finding accommodation was another struggle but he managed to obtain some rudimentary beds for himself, Bennett and other engineers who were to join him from Darwin: 'The bathroom and lavatory facilities at each of the three hotels is exceedingly primitive and insanitary, and so far, our request for improvement there-in has been ignored. There is no sewerage in Broome.'

Such was the situation that met Lester Brain when he arrived in Broome on 21 February to take control of the organisation of the outbound loads to Java and what would soon turn into a massive evacuation from Tjilatjap.

Perhaps more so than any of the aviators Fysh had chosen to help him establish his airline, Brain was an inspired choice. Quietly spoken and a person of high principles, as a wing commander in the RAAF Reserve his diplomatic and organisational skills in the delivery of the nineteen Catalinas from the United States to the RAAF had won him high praise in aviation circles. Broome would once again put these attributes to the supreme test.

Broome was already overflowing with refugees by the time Brain arrived and he soon received a quick introduction to the state of morale of some of its occupants, noting in his diary that first day:

> The place is hot and sweaty whilst mosquitoes are thick and vicious. All the evacuees are anxious to push on from Broome as quickly as possible and have brought with them an atmosphere as though the Japs were close behind them.

As for the state of local morale, Brain saw it as parlous perhaps, but still laced with outback humour:

> Most of the locals are very jittery and drinking heavily.
>
> My room mate is one Farrell who belongs to the local defence volunteers and has in his custody one of the only sub-machine guns available. He tells me that instructions have been issued that the aerodome is to be defended to the last man but assures me that it will have to be the second last man since he is not waiting.

Later on that first day he received word that a general order had been received for the evacuation of all of Broome's women and children aboard *Koolinda*, a state-owned 4000-tonne combined cargo and passenger vessel that would take them to Fremantle. Brain noted the locals' state of mind was hardly improved by gloomy predictions that *Koolinda* would be torpedoed before it had covered the first fifty miles! Despite such forebodings, in the end the *Koolinda* made it through safely to Fremantle.

With the aircraft moorings necessarily located out in the deepwater channel, tackling the refuelling issue was Brain's first priority. The natural deficiencies of the jetty added to the problem: it might be eight hundred metres long but the fact it was ten metres out of water at low tide meant the refuelling lugger could only be loaded with 44-gallon (200-litre) drums from the jetty at high tide. Since a lugger was capable of carrying only enough fuel for one flying boat, the ability to be able to return to the jetty to load more drums required a delicate balance of tidal timing.

As for the town of Broome itself, estimates differ widely as to the number of evacuees who would pass through the town in those desperate February weeks. Some historians have cited up to seven thousand and although others query that figure, there is little doubt the town's accommodation and other facilities were overwhelmed by what began as a trickle and increased dramatically. At the height of the crisis fifty-four aircraft would arrive at the airfield and onto the waters of Roebuck Bay in one day alone.

Brain rented a furnished cottage and installed Mr Hong, the BOAC cook, as the catering clerk who would provide meals for staff mostly from the tinned food they'd managed to accumulate. He split the crew accommodation between the three hotels, but when he discovered their bags were being pilfered during their absence he instructed them to leave any surplus luggage at the cottage.

Neither was acquiring essentials for the Qantas operation easy. Brain found the Americans were purchasing or commandeering anything they required for large amounts of cash. Even the car he hired when he first arrived was soon taken from him when the owner received a cash offer from the Americans, forcing Brain to buy a second-hand one, but he at least managed to purchase another dinghy and a motorboat with a 'dodgy' engine.

It wasn't long before his first clash with the Americans. The day after Brain's arrival, the United States Army Air Forces' Lieutenant Colonel Ed Perrin arrived in a B-24 Liberator to assume overall control of the evacuation. When Perrin announced he considered himself in charge of all Broome operations, including those of Qantas, Brain would have none of it, telling the American that while he was prepared to co-operate wherever he could, his directions would not come from the US Army but from Civil Aviation and the Australian government.

Brain's main concern was that he considered it impossible to try to merge the handling of the flying boats on the water at Roebuck Bay with the landplane movements at the aerodrome. The two were mutually exclusive and any handover of his own authority would run the risk of robbing Qantas of the facilities it had put in place to operate from the bay. He was particularly concerned that any outside interference with the 56-tonne ketch *Nicol Bay*, used to refuel all the flying boats now arriving daily into Broome, would place the whole Qantas Java shuttle in jeopardy.

Indeed, the general harbour operation itself was already something of a shambles. Insufficient moorings meant the American and Dutch Catalinas and three-engine Dutch Dornier flying boats had to rely on their own small anchors to hold against a raging tide while they refuelled. As for the process of refuelling itself, beyond that required for the Qantas flying boats it was entirely hit and miss. 'There was no organisation in regard to refuelling. If the pilots didn't come and ask for juice, I didn't know whether they wanted any, and there was no central authority on shore to advise me of their particular wants,' skipper of the *Nicol Bay* Harold Mathieson would later explain. Added to Mathieson's task were the differing requirements of the aircraft themselves. 'Dorniers were the biggest job to fill; it was very slow work as they had plenty of tanks. Their pilots were pretty hungry too. They carried spare tins and asked for these to be filled also.'

Then there were the local conditions. The mosquitoes and the heat were taking a toll and four of Brain's staff were soon down with dengue fever. Within days Brain himself would be running a high temperature, the first signs of dengue fever on its way.

Three days after his arrival Brain sat down in his stuffy hotel room to write to Fysh of his assessment of Broome. The letter, written in pencil, still exists in its original form in the Qantas files and is a poignant summary not only of the difficulties he confronted but also of his ability to put a very human face on Broome as he saw it:

Dear Hudson,

This base is not bad in normal good weather. The tide difficulty is enormously aggravated by lack of suitable motor boats and proper large capacity refuelling barge. Had we been able to get the proper fuel barge and our own motor boat from Darwin all would have been well, but unfortunately the ship Koolama which was to have brought these boats to us was bombed and driven ashore before it got to Darwin to load them.

In the circumstances the only way to improve matters is to scrounge around locally and be prepared to pay freely.

With one exception, the boats suitable here comprise large pearling luggers and small dinghies. The exception is an old 24 foot boat in a dilapidated condition to which a second-hand Dodge car engine is in process of being fitted. It was necessary to buy this outright at 120 pounds and put our engineers on to complete the job. We expect to have it working by tomorrow night. This is the only boat on to which we can unload or load an engine from the flying boat in case of engine failure.

Meantime this place is becoming one of the busiest air centres in Australia and is completely jammed out with U.S. Army Air Force, U.S. Navy Air Service, Dutch and others besides numbers of evacuees brought in by air and awaiting on carriage. American and Dutch Catalinas use our moorings and hose pumps more than we do. I have also done all possible to co-operate and assist, but the Americans are impressing or buying up everything and are inclined to regard us as a private commercial concern, which we definitely are not in present circumstances. Yesterday the Australian Naval Officer here, Lieut Davis, who works with them, advised me that they wished to impress the 24 foot boat and place it aboard a destroyer to be taken away. I have offered to provide the motor boat with crew for their use here but refused to surrender it to be taken away unless instructed to do so by Minister for Air or D.G.C.A. It would leave us unable to change an engine and might result in a boat being stranded here—I have wired Corbett requesting some protection and official status.

All the women and children were evacuated from here some days ago and there was much beer drinking and local jitters. Many of the locals are ready to go bush at the first loud noise—some have gone already.

I am now able to establish radio communication from here with our own machine sitting on the water in Java—each night and early morning.

This is of the greatest value and eases the anxiety. I am satisfied that the urgent National job of the moment is to take arms and munitions to Java and bring personnel back here. It may only be possible to continue operating over to Java for a few more days but I think the National service rendered justifies some risks. I shall watch position as closely as possible and shall try and break off operations when risk appears too great unless definitely instructed to cease sooner.

Your telegram dated 24th, of 54 groups not yet decoded owing numerous apparent mutilations largely due to overworked and sleepy postal officers. They are not staffed here to cope with rush of work. In future, instruct all concerned to code only words necessary. It does not matter how many letters are in a code group but there should not be more than 5—long words can be split in half.

I have rented a furnished house at 30/- per week and shall do all possible to care for our staff. Have got good supply of tinned foods etc in case arrangements collapse. Have been obliged to buy a car at 150 pounds since the Americans started to impress and buy cars and have almost cornered transport. The car we hired has been bought from the owner by Uncle Sam for 300 pounds. New arrivals here can't even get a bed to sleep in.

Very sorry to hear of the DH 86 accident. Have no indication of cause yet. I know that you must be having a bad time in Sydney also.
With all good wishes,
Lester Brain.

The attack on the vessel *Koolama* Brain referred to, along with the rescue of the survivors of a crashed American DC-3 north of Broome, would once again demonstrate the versatility of the Qantas flying boats in their wartime role.

The *Koolama* had been attacked by Japanese flying boats as it rounded Cape Londonderry, six hundred kilometres north of Broome and the northernmost tip of Western Australia, on 20 February, the day after the first raid on Darwin.

Badly damaged at the stern, *Koolama*'s captain decided the best way to save his passengers and crew was to run his ship aground. Once on shore most of the passengers set up camp a safe distance away from the ship while *Koolama*'s crew managed to reorganise the decks of the ship to make it appear abandoned, a subterfuge which appeared to work as despite several more visits by the flying boats, the Japanese eventually lost interest. Over the following days *Koolama*'s captain and his crew managed to repair enough of the damage to get underway again, finally struggling into Wyndham by furiously pumping water pouring through her damaged bulkheads.

Meanwhile, the survivors at the campsite separated. One group, guided by Aborigines, set off inland to Drysdale Mission, while twenty-five remained at the camp awaiting rescue. It would be eight days before it came.

The DC-3, from the US 21st Troop Carrier Squadron, had left Perth on the afternoon of 26 February for Darwin. Due to refuel at Broome, the aircraft had missed the town during the night and flown on until it ran out of fuel and made a wheels-up landing a few hundred metres from a beach. Luckily for those on board the radio was still working, which enabled the crew to send out distress signals confirming no one was injured, but they had no idea where they were. Its only passengers were two young Australian Postmaster General telegraphists Dave Campbell and Jack Lyons, members of the army reserve on their way to postings in Darwin.

Next morning Perrin sent American bombers out to look for them, covering an area up to around 150 miles north without result; in fact the DC-3 was miles away from where the bombers were searching. Brain suggested that two of his flying boats were on their way from Sydney and might be able to join the search but the American showed little interest, a response Brain put down to Perrin's concentration on the developing crisis in Java.

It would be a further two days before Orm Denny left Broome for Darwin and Sydney with instructions to carry out a further search for the downed DC-3. Denny, meanwhile, had been doing his homework and after studying the distances covered, their timings and the search patterns the bombers had used, along with the DC-3 crew's description of their surroundings, he was convinced the DC-3 was in fact much further north than first thought. Starting his search as he approached Vansittart Bay, these calculations proved correct when his radio operator picked up an emergency signal from the DC-3 confirming all on board were still alive.

The signal was brief and weak but allowed the radio operator to get a bearing on the crash site. Following the bearing Denny finally sighted the DC-3 in low scrub and, after advising Broome of his find, told them he intended to attempt to get them aboard.

As soon as he was on the water Denny discovered getting the survivors off wasn't to be an easy task. The shoreline was pitted with reefs and sandbanks, and strong ocean currents prevented him from taking the flying boat any closer than 400 metres from the beach.

After dropping anchor, Denny's first officer and one of the troops on board set out for shore in a rubber raft carrying food and water, but the closer the raft got to shore the more the current and the strong surf took over. It took two exhausting hours before all four of the downed party was aboard.

Then, just as Denny prepared to take off, he caught sight of a small formation of aircraft approaching from the north. Assuming they were friendly and also searching, Denny was about to signal he had found the DC-3 when he hesitated. It was as well he did. As they got closer he realised they were Japanese but they slipped past without spotting the flying boat.

Now heavily loaded with around forty passengers and in an unknown and open sea, it took some time before the flying boat finally lifted off the water and resumed its journey to Darwin.

Telegraphist Campbell told his rescuers they ate small crabs and ripped pipes from the DC-3 and used them to distil drinking water from salt water to keep them going.

Within a few days of the loss of *Circe* and the end of the Tjilatjap shuttles, the US commander Ed Perrin would leave for Perth, to be replaced by another American. It wouldn't be long before some in Broome were regretting Perrin's departure. Despite their early differences, Brain seems to have developed a co-operative relationship with Perrin, who many believed had done an efficient job in handling the primary evacuation task.

His replacement, US Air Force Lieutenant Colonel Richard Legg by contrast, would show signs of paranoia, once suggesting flashlights seen at night were fifth columnists signalling the enemy. Indeed his general demeanour was hardly conducive to settling the nerves of an already jittery Broome.

Brain's focus too was on the enemy but had nothing to do with random flashlights, as he began to show increasing concern that the large number of aircraft movements from Java and their associated radio traffic had increased the risk of Broome to Japanese attack, noting in his diary on 28 February:

> This place is becoming busier than ever. There are as many as twenty–thirty aircraft here at one time. I shall be surprised if all this activity does not bring an enemy raid. *Corinna* and *Camilla* are due to arrive from Sydney today and tomorrow. I shall arrange to get our machines out of here as quickly as possible.

Before he began to plan a Qantas withdrawal, however, he insisted on one last attempt to find some trace of Purton, and early on 2 March he despatched Frank Thomas and Lew Ambrose in *Corinna* for what would be the final extended search for the missing *Circe*. Ambrose and Thomas ranged across five hundred miles of ocean for ten hours, sweeping wide across the course Purton would have been expected to follow, but found no trace of *Circe*.

Later that day Captain Eric Sims took off in *Camilla* towards Wyndham to rescue the twenty-five passengers from the beached *Koolama* and return them to Broome. Brain instructed Sims not to return to Broome before 11 a.m. next day, by which time Ambrose would have refuelled *Corinna* at high tide and be on his way from Broome to Sydney. Thus, as was Brain's policy, there would be no more than one machine at Broome at any one time.

As events were to play out, Sims would have his own difficulties working even to that schedule. Arriving over the section of Joseph Bonaparte Gulf where the *Koolama* was reported to have been beached, Sims' plan was to drop a note to those below and tell them to prepare to embark on the flying boat at dawn next morning. *Koolama*, however, was now nowhere to be seen, the only sign of life a wisp of smoke from a fire amid trees some distance inland. It wasn't until he arrived at Wyndham at dusk to find the battered *Koolama* tied up at the Wyndham wharf that he learned the full story.

At dawn on 3 March, Sims returned and those of the party who had remained near the beach, mostly waterside workers on their way to Darwin, were loaded aboard *Camilla* and set off for Broome, planning to follow Brain's instructions and arrive later in the morning. Sims would return, however, to a very different Broome.

While Sims was on his way to Cape Londonderry that morning to rescue *Koolama*'s passengers, nine Japanese Zero fighters were taking off from their base at Koepang, setting course for Broome, six hundred miles away.

Their commander, 26-year-old Lieutenant Zenjiro Miyano, and his fellow pilots would stretch their fighters to the extent of their range on this two hour and twenty minute flight to the Western Australian coast, but were confident their aircraft were up to the task.

At this early stage of the war the Japanese Mitsubishi Type O, armed with both cannon and machine guns, was the unassailable master of the skies in the South-West Pacific and had swept away all before it in the brief weeks since Pearl Harbor. Already having the advantage of being extremely light and manoeuvrable, Miyano's Zeros had an innovation which had already come as a surprise to the retreating Allies: fuel drop tanks which enabled them to cover distances far beyond that of normal fighter aircraft.

Miyano's pilots also had another advantage. They knew from reconnaissance flights that their target this morning was lightly defended, with the probability that no other fighter aircraft would rise to meet them. In fact, had they known there was not one Allied fighter aircraft within hundreds of miles of Broome they would have been even more confident. Neither, for that matter, did the entire north-west Australian coastline have any ground-based defensive installations, largely the result of its isolation and the speed of the Japanese advance through the Netherlands East Indies.

As Brain had predicted, Broome was now a tempting target, but Miyano's men were also in for another pleasant surprise.

Around mid-afternoon on the previous day, 2 March, a Japanese reconnaissance aircraft circled the town from around nine thousand feet then flew off. That same night another aircraft appeared overhead, this time circling much lower and further heightening the tension in the town and leaving many unable to sleep. The Japanese reconnaissance pilots had confirmed the presence of Allied aircraft on Broome's airfield, which would be the main target for Miyano's Zeros.

As they now dived towards Broome, however, one could imagine their surprise when met with the tempting sight of all the Dutch and

American flying boats that had arrived during the night and were now lying defenceless on the waters of Roebuck Bay.

On Roebuck itself, the *Nicol Bay*'s skipper Mathieson and his crew had worked late into the previous evening refuelling three Dutch Dorniers so they could leave on the right tide next morning. For some unknown reason the pilots had delayed their departure, a fact that would cost them dearly. Mathieson and his crew then spent several hours loading more drums of fuel from the jetty to enable them to start fuelling *Corinna* first thing in the morning. They slept aboard that night so they could get an early start, conscious of Brain's desire not to have his aircraft on the water any longer than necessary.

Early in the morning darkness, two American, two RAF and four Dutch Catalinas had arrived carrying mostly military personnel to join the gaggle of other flying boats, a few of which had been there for several days. Apart from the activity surrounding their arrival it had been a quiet night, the silence broken only once by shouts of instructions as one of the American Catalinas dragged its anchor and drifted into *Corinna*, causing minor damage to both aircraft.

By dawn, however, *Corinna* and its identical twin, *Centaurus*, one of the two Empires which Qantas had handed over to the RAAF eighteen months before, were moored close to each other amid a cluster of fifteen flying boats, all rocking gently on the incoming tide. *Centaurus* had been busy flying support and evacuation missions out of Koepang, Ambon and Buru and was standing by in case it was needed for further evacuations. Both the RAAF Empire's pilots, Captain Keith Caldwell and his first officer Fred Derham, were former Qantas employees.

The morning started early for Harold Mathieson and the *Nicol Bay*. None of the flying boats arriving overnight had been refuelled and his first task had been to take the crews of two of the Dorniers to shore.

Lester Brain at the controls of an Empire flying boat.

Lester Brain, Scotty Allan and P.G. Taylor in San Diego for the RAAF Catalina delivery.

Hudson Fysh's shrapnel-damaged book purchased as a souvenir from a bookshop near the Raffles Hotel the morning after the first air raid on Singapore on 8 December 1941.

Ern Aldis's 'home built' muffler system used to reduce the noise from engine test runs at the Qantas Randwick factory after complaints from neighbours.

Engineering staff gather beside the nose of a Liberator at Archerfield. One of the most important tasks of the Qantas teams was to install the nose gun turret on these aircraft after Japanese Zero pilots discovered their vulnerability to head-on attacks.

A US Air Force Liberator bomber undergoing work outside the Qantas hangar at Archerfield. Much of the heavy work on these aircraft was done here.

A B-24 engine overhaul, Archerfield.

A line up of B-24 Liberators during a busy time at Qantas's Archerfield facility. The B-24, along with the B-17 Flying Fortress, fulfilled the primary Allied bombing role in the South-West Pacific.

Captain John Connolly was among the Qantas airmen who had narrow escapes in the early days of the war.

Qantas captain, Russell Tapp.

A busy engine overhaul line at Qantas's Randwick facility.

A somewhat rakish photo of Qantas engineer Norm Roberts who survived the Japanese raid on Darwin and later played a key role in the establishment of the secret Indian Ocean service.

Dave Ross, civil aviation and Qantas representative in Dili when the Japanese attacked in early 1942. He was confined by Japanese authorities but later escaped with Australian commandos.

A rare photo of legendary Qantas captain Aub Koch, giving the appearance of a man not to be reckoned with, during his days flying with Guinea Airways before the war.

Qantas station engineer Doug Lawrie watches Timorese local, Pat Luz, operate the Qantas radio at Dili. It would later be smuggled out from under the nose of the Japanese to help Australian commandos communicate with Australia.

The landing jetty at the Qantas flying boat base in Surabaya. The base was abandoned and engineer Eric Kydd and his team had to race to safety as the Japanese captured Java.

Empire flying boats at the Rose Bay flying boat base in Sydney. Aircraft left from here on the long flight to London along the Empire route until the fall of Singapore in 1942.

Lew Ambrose, John Oram and crew were at the far end of this jetty when the Japanese attacked Broome. Oram raced along the jetty and commandeered the jetty train to bring the injured to safety.

Burning flying boats in Broome's Roebuck Bay after the Japanese attack in February 1942. This photo was taken by a Japanese reconnaissance aircraft that accompanied the Zeros on the mission.

Qantas publicity man Ben Bennett-Bremner kitted out for the New Guinea campaign. He served on the Kokoda Track.

Eric Kydd (left) and Jim Lamb (right) make a leisurely diversion to visit Borobudur despite being on the run from the Japanese after the enemy attack on the Qantas base at Surbaya.

Coriolanus being refuelled at Broome. *Corinna* was being refuelled by the same tender when the Zeros attacked aircraft on Roebuck Bay.

A rare photograph of the four men responsible for the formation of Qantas, from left Hudson Fysh, Fergus McMaster, Arthur Baird and Paul McGinness.

Perth-based meteorologist John (Doc) Hogan (left), who with his British counterpart in Ceylon Wing Commander Arthur Grimes were responsible for the exceptional weather forecasts that contributed greatly to the success of the Indian Ocean Service.

The remote Department of Civil Avition base on Groote Eylandt was an essential fuelling stop for Qantas flying boats operating between Brisbane and Darwin during the war.

Engineers Eric Kydd, Dave Thomson and A. Beck relax atop *Camilla*, Townsville, in November 1942.

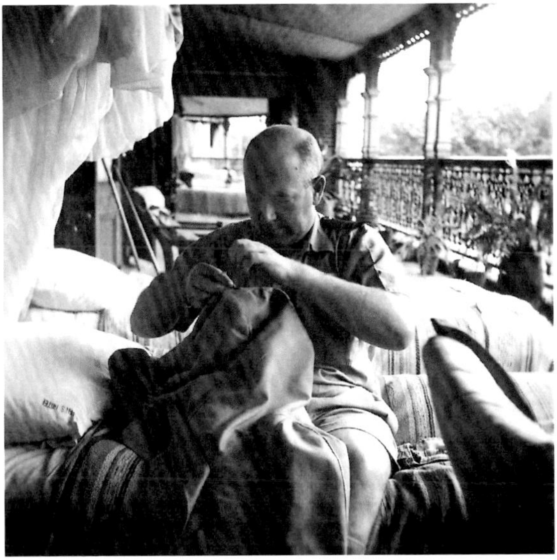

Captain Lew Ambrose finds some time to make clothing repairs during a stopover.

The legendary flying missionary, Father John Glover, whose epic flight across Papua New Guinea in early 1942 led to the Qantas rescue of soldiers and civilians stranded at Mt Hagen.

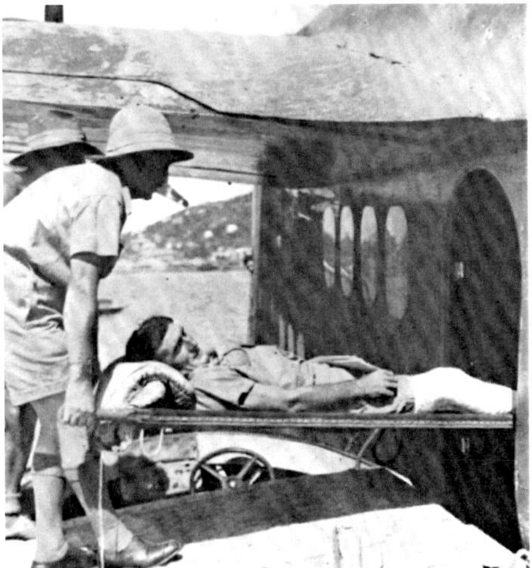

A wounded Australian serviceman is loaded aboard QEA's *Camilla* at Port Morseby in 1942.

Orm Denny used the hundreds of stamping feet of a local sing-sing to harden the rain soaked grass surface so aircraft could keep operating on the Mt Hagen airstrip in May 1942.

Orm Denny's DH-86s at Mt Hagen during the daring rescue mission in May 1942.

Coriolanus at Milne Bay during the height of the struggle for Papua New Guinea. Qantas captain Lew Ambrose, in white cap in the middle, can be seen standing on the tender.

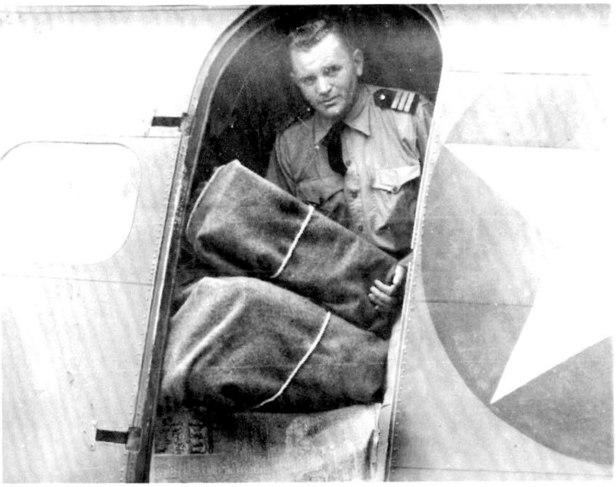

Orm Denny at the door of one of the Qantas Lockheeds during the Buna airlift.

Several of the crew and their injured gunner from a B-17 approach Bert Hussey's *Coriolanus* off Eurasi Island in August 1943.

Bert Hussey can be seen leaning out the cockpit window as the B-17 raft approaches.

Cooee's captain, Bill Crowther, looks on as radio officer Glen Mumford casts off from a mooring.

The Double Sunrise Catalinas being serviced on the ramp at Nedlands on the Swan River, with *Vega Star* in the foreground.

Lew Ambrose and his crew at Cocos Island after achieving pinpoint navigation to deliver two meteorological officers to the island in September 1943.

Rugged-up for the cold, Captain Russell Tapp operates an astro compass to take a quick position fix from a Qantas Catalina over the Indian Ocean in 1943.

Baroness Dr Edith Summerskill was one of the few women VIPs ever to travel on the Double Sunrise long hop over the Indian Ocean from Perth to Ceylon.

Women played a key role in the maintenance of Qantas and other Allied aircraft during the war, typified by this photo of a fabric worker at the Rose Bay flying boat base.

Connie Jordan, Qantas's first female engineer at work.

Hudson Fysh (second from right) pictured during the loading of Qantas aircraft at Port Moresby.

Aircrew who formed the basis of the RAAF's No 11 Squadron after two of Qantas's Empire flying boats were taken over following the declaration of war in Europe. Qantas captain Goff Hemsworth is third from right. Captain Bob Gurney, sixth from right, would be later lost on operation with the RAAF in the South-West Pacific. Bill Purton, fourth from right, would return to Qantas and be lost with *Circe* off Java in early 1942.

The Double Sunrise Certificate earned by Hudson Fysh in August 1943 when he flew home on the Catalina service after a visit to the United Kingdom. The flight took 32 hours, the longest ever recorded for the crossing.

Coorong being dismantled at Darwin after running aground in a storm in 1941. The aircraft had to be shipped back to the UK for repair.

Cooee being refuelled en route to Singapore.

Aub Koch among aircraft wreckage in Singapore post war. The aircraft in the background is a Japanese flying boat.

While there he had taken extra fuel on board for *Corinna*, scheduled to be first on his list that morning. Lew Ambrose and twenty-five of *Corinna*'s passengers and crew would wait on the jetty until refuelling was completed before going aboard.

Around 9 a.m. Mathieson had attached a line to the front of the big flying boat and was passing the hose aboard when he heard the roar of approaching aeroplane engines and the crackle of machine-gun fire as the first of Miyano's Zeros attacked. Fortunately, *Nicol Bay*'s main engine was still running, which allowed Mathieson to cut the line with *Corinna* and throw his vessel into reverse until he was about forty metres away.

Brain, still suffering the onset of dengue fever, was in his hotel room writing another update of the situation in Broome to Fysh when he heard the unmistakable sound of machine-gun fire. Running outside he reached the harbour to see six bright silver Zeros with red spots under their wings take it in turns to dive low across the water, the sound of their machine guns mingled with the slower bursts of cannon fire. High above them three other fighters providing top cover circled, waiting to intercept any Allied fighters that might rise against them.

Already three of the flying boats were burning fiercely and Brain could hear shouts and screams coming from people in the water. Spotting a rowing boat sitting in the mud some distance from the tideline, he first tried to drag it towards the water himself but, weakened by the effects of his fever, he found it impossible. A group of locals standing nearby panicked and ran when he asked them for help, and he was wondering what to do next when Malcolm Millar arrived. The two finally got the rowing boat into the water and headed towards the heads bobbing in the bay.

Further out, Qantas engineer Bob Jenkins, dangerously exposed atop *Corinna*'s wing, watched the Japanese choose the nearby *Centaurus* as their first target, RAAF servicemen aboard clambering into their dinghy as *Centaurus* burst into flames.

Then Jenkins saw a second Zero turn in towards *Corinna* and start firing, its bullets hitting the wing all around him as he dived headfirst into the water. By the time he resurfaced *Corinna* too was well alight and already sinking. After some minutes in the water Jenkins saw a dinghy which had been cut loose from one of the luggers, pulled himself on board and used it to pick up others in the water and row them to shore.

Two other Qantas engineers inside the flying boat had scrambled aboard the dinghy they had been using with the *Nicol Bay* and began to row away, but when bullets started to slam into the bay around them they abandoned their craft and took to the water. Later the dinghy was found riddled with bullet holes.

Engineers Dave Thomson and Jim Lamb were aboard a lugger just off the jetty about to leave for *Corinna* when their vessel attracted the attention of a Zero. They abandoned the lugger and sought shelter under the jetty until the attack was over.

Above them at the end of the jetty, waiting with his passengers, several Dutch naval officers and others to be taken out to their aircraft, was Lew Ambrose. It took him only seconds to realise that not only were they dangerously exposed metres above the waterline, but around forty 44-gallon drums full of fuel were stacked on the wooden jetty only a few metres away.

Ambrose's first thoughts were to hide his passengers. 'It soon became noted that as far as gold braid was concerned I was to be looked at as the senior officer on the jetty, and therefore direct matters,' he would comment wryly over forty years later. Herding his charges to a set of wooden steps used to board craft from the jetty, he settled the group on the decking below the wharf, out of sight of the fighters but still acutely aware that if the Japs decided to target the fuel drums they might all still be blown to kingdom come.

By now Brain and Millar had made it several hundred metres out into the bay where seven Dutchmen, two supporting a woman in the water, were in a state of collapse. Another Dutchman was swimming on his back nearby supporting a baby and keeping its face above the water. A further few metres away others were keeping company with a young Dutch boy about eight years old who was at least able to swim and support himself.

After Brain and Millar had dragged the woman, the baby, the boy and three of the more exhausted men aboard, the dinghy had little more than ten centimetres of freeboard, so the remaining four men clung to its side as they made for the beach.

Mathieson meanwhile might have managed to create a bit of distance between his *Nicol Bay* and the sinking *Corinna* but he was still dangerously exposed, the deck of his boat lined with bright red fuel drums. He would later describe one of the Zeros flashing past him at mast height:

> I could have shot the pilot from the deck with a rifle. I could see the expression on his face. They didn't waste a shot. They commenced firing about fifty yards before reaching the boats—with the cannon they were deadly accurate, never missed.

He saw six men jammed into a dinghy nearby, but when he went to rescue them he was waved off with an abusive burst describing how his fuel-laden boat was too much of a target. Mathieson didn't give up on them, though, sending the lugger's launch to tow them in.

All of those at Broome that day would be amazed at the devastation caused by the Zeros in such a short time. Within the space of twenty minutes all the flying boats on the water had been destroyed, the sound of burning and explosions from them mixing with the terrified screams of those in the water.

One of the largely untold Qantas stories of the raid, however, was played out on Broome's jetty.

Fred Derham, a former Qantas auditor and Keith Caldwell's first officer on the RAAF flying boat *Centaurus*, and *Corinna*'s steward John

Oram were among those with Ambrose on the jetty when the attack began. Derham shouted at an islander crew on a lugger near the jetty to start their engine and bring people in, but when they took no notice Derham dived in, swam to the lugger and took charge, sailing off through the flames towards those burnt and injured and still in the water. Oram, meanwhile, sprinted the length of the jetty and returned at the controls of the jetty's small cargo train, and soon the badly injured were being placed on the carriages for the long journey back along the wharf to the hospital.

So impressed was Ambrose by Oram's actions that he made a note to bring it to the attention of Qantas in Sydney. 'Regrettably I wasn't to know until sometime later that Qantas had decided they could no longer retain stewards and he was fired,' Ambrose would recall. Ambrose's sentiment, though understandable at the time, perhaps needed to take into account that Darwin, Broome and subsequent events would so denude Qantas of its fleet that it became necessary to reduce steward numbers. Within weeks of the raid on Broome, however, New Zealand–born Oram would graduate as a pilot in the RAAF, winning a Distinguished Flying Cross and Bar before the war ended.

With the Zeros now concentrating on the aircraft on Broome's airfield, Thomson and Lamb climbed onto the jetty to help. A lugger carrying survivors, some badly burnt, pulled alongside and the two Qantas engineers jumped aboard and tried to revive several people who appeared to have drowned, then assisted getting the injured onto the jetty's train.

It took only a further few minutes for Miyano's Zeros to repeat their devastating performance at Broome's airfield, their bullets and cannon shells ripping through the gaggle of Flying Fortresses, Liberators and smaller aircraft parked there. Several of those watching the attack noted the Zero pilots seemed to be enjoying themselves, hedgehopping their aircraft over and around obstacles between attacks as if performing at an air show.

Suddenly it was all over and Brain watched as the nine Zeros gathered together in loose formation and flew away to the north, leading Brain to contemplate somewhat ruefully: 'You little blighters. If I was on your side I'd say you've done a very efficient job. They just formed up, as if to say—"Kiss my Tail"—and off they went.'

They left a Broome in a severe state of shock. Screams were still coming from people struggling in the water as the few luggers moved to pull them aboard, with ammunition from the flying boats still exploding in short bursts and the dark pall of smoke from the burning oil shrouding the scene. If there was one saving grace it was that Miyano's pilots had not made any attempt to strafe those in the water. Neither had they attacked the town itself, perhaps because their long overwater flight to reach Broome meant the amount of ammunition they carried was limited and therefore to be used to maximum effect.

The actual death toll that day remains unknown. Indeed figures range up to eighty and beyond a hundred according to some historians, but any definitive figure is difficult to arrive at because the number of people on individual flying boats was unknown. Still others would have drowned or been swept out to sea before rescuers could reach them. Brain's diary entry that day describes the aftermath:

> There are very distressing scenes as the dead and wounded are brought up from the jetty. Many of them are frightfully burned. Others have seen their wives and children killed or burned. All these women and children were Dutch. One cannot really blame the Japanese for this. It was unfortunate that women and children were aboard military aircraft at the time.
>
> The dead have been buried and the wounded, after treatment at the local hospital, have been evacuated by air to Port Hedland.

Brain's meeting with the US commander Legg that afternoon must have been a tense one, as his diary goes on:

> Colonel Legg is peeved. He has said 'Give us twenty-four hours to get out of this God-damn place and you can have it.' This pronouncement has not improved the morale of the local non-combatants.

Already aware that all fifteen flying boats on the bay had been destroyed—the only exception a small US Navy float plane that had managed to leave only minutes before the raid—it would be at this meeting that Brain would learn what had occurred at the airfield.

Six landplanes had been lost, one a B-24 Liberator called *Arabian Nights* which had been taking off with wounded bound for Perth and had barely left the ground when a Zero pounced and it was shot down into the sea. The Zero which shot down the B-24 was itself shot down, although arguments have raged since as to whether it was a victim of the B-24's guns or the remarkable efforts of Dutch pilot Lieutenant Gus Winckel, who was servicing one of the machine guns from his Lockheed Lodestar at the airfield when the attack began. Without a stand to cradle the weapon, Winckel rested the barrel on his arm and blazed away at the Zero, the hot barrel badly burning his arm in the process. One experienced Western Australian historian Dion Marinis, who has closely researched the actual B-24s that were lost at Broome, insists credit for the 'kill' most likely belonged to Winckel as his research indicates the *Arabian Nights* didn't have an active weapon in its rear turret. Whatever the true story, Winckel offered the only resistance of any significance in Broome that morning beyond a few army men and pilots at the airfield who fired on the Zeros with pistols and rifles as they watched their aircraft ripped apart by cannon shells.

Eric Sims was returning to Broome with *Camilla* and his rescued extras when he received a radio message the attack was on, so he immediately turned inland to avoid flying along the coast. By the time he arrived the smoke from the burning flying boats had cleared and Sims was able to find a clear patch of water on which to light, but his problems were far from over.

Fearful of another attack catching *Camilla* on the water, Ambrose and Brain wanted to move her on as soon as possible, but Sims was so low on fuel by now he was unable to go anywhere at all unless he refilled his tanks. With every available lugger engaged in rescuing those in the water and the harbour's fuel barge now nowhere to be seen, their only option was to reach the fuel tanks on the bank of a creek which ran into the bay. With Ambrose and engineer Bill Bennett aboard to assist, Sims began a delicate operation up the narrow creek, at one point slightly damaging the wing of *Camilla* as it slammed into the mast of a moored lugger. On reaching the tanks they ran a line ashore and Ambrose and Bennett hand-pumped enough fuel on board for Sims, having now added wounded and other evacuees to his load, to soon be on his way to Port Hedland, with instructions from Brain to return as soon as possible. Brain desperately wanted to get Qantas staff out.

When *Camilla* returned just after 6 a.m. next day Broome was virtually a ghost town. Within an hour the flying boat was on its way south again, carrying nineteen US Navy personnel and seventeen of Broome's Qantas staff. One of those on board was Mansfield and Company's Malcolm Millar, now on the final stage of a remarkable journey supporting his 'adopted' airline. Brain wrote in his diary:

> Broome is almost deserted this morning.
>
> Many people have packed their belongings and moved out permanently, heading south in a so-called 'land convoy'. Actually, their convoy is a nervous rabble and includes a number of American deserters who would not even wait in Broome for an extra day.
>
> Many other townsfolk, particularly those with official or semi-official positions in Broome, have evacuated themselves from the town area for the day and have located themselves a few miles away and will, I understand, return to their jobs about 4 or 5 o'clock this afternoon.
>
> I have always credited the man outback with possessing more moral courage than city folk. The result was that the town was undefended

at its most vital points and practically deserted, except for American troops awaiting evacuation by air.

Several days later, in a telegram to Fysh in Sydney detailing plans to withdraw Qantas, he would be even more scathing: 'After seeing firsthand the high priority given to evacuating people who won't stand and fight I consider our duty to get our staff back to their base where they can do useful work.'

After the passing of many years, perhaps Brain's comments need to be seen as coming from a man who had been involved in the sharp end of the war since 1939, while the people of Broome had it thrust upon them out of nowhere. From their perspective there was every chance that bombing raids and a landing of Japanese ground forces would follow at any time.

Brain did, however, record contrasting examples of courage.

The US freighter *Admiral Halstead* had been on its way to Broome several days after the raid with a cargo of urgently needed aviation fuel, but with no moorings or any ability to offload the fuel and the ever-present danger of another attack, frantic efforts were made to warn her captain to avoid Broome and head south out of danger. Unfortunately no one in Broome had the US Navy code book so the only way *Admiral Halstead* could be contacted was to radio a general alert of the situation in Broome, hoping the captain would bypass Broome for his own ship's safety.

The *Admiral Halstead*'s captain, however, wasn't to be distracted from his mission, and Brain and the Australian navy man in Broome watched as she anchored in deep water about a mile out, running up a string of flag signals to communicate with those on the jetty. What followed was a mini pantomime. Those on shore knew any attempt to take their small dinghy out to meet him would have seen it rapidly swept out to sea on the fast-running tide, but they had no way of telling him so. They didn't even possess a code book to enable them to read the meaning of the *Halstead*'s flags. Eventually realising the problem, the captain moved again and steamed the final distance to the jetty.

The first question they asked the captain as he leaned over the ship's bridge above them was whether he had received their radio message to avoid Broome. 'He replied that he was already in the danger area at the time and since his instructions were to come in and unload fuel at Broome he was carrying them out!' Brain would recount. 'One cannot but admire the tenacity with which these mariners stick to their duty and instructions under dangerous conditions.'

At a meeting with Legg that afternoon the American told him that an unidentified aircraft, which he presumed was a Japanese reconnaissance plane, had flown over Broome at 4.10 that morning and that he expected to complete the evacuation of all American personnel that night.

As the day wore on a drama unfolded which would not only produce one of the most remarkable human survival stores to come out of Broome, but would involve Brain in yet another risky exercise.

Around 9 p.m. that night a solidly built, bare-footed American, his face badly sunburnt, walked into the hangar at Broome's aerodrome. It was US Army Air Forces Sergeant Melvin Donoho, who had been aboard the doomed *Arabian Nights*. Donoho told how *Arabian Nights* had broken in two as it hit the water and, losing contact with other survivors, he and Sergeant Willard Beatty began swimming towards land. It was exhausting work: the more they gained, the more the current swept them back. For much of the twenty-four hours that followed, Donoho had to support a weakening Beatty until it was decided he would attempt to reach shore himself to bring help.

After hearing Donoho's story Legg called another meeting with Brain late that night and announced that he planned to cancel *Camilla*'s return flight to Broome next day to collect the remainder of Qantas staff and stores and divert it to search for the Liberator.

Here once again came the clash of orders and authority between Qantas, its Civil Aviation masters and the complications of the charter arrangement with the US Army. Much of this would be traced back to Harold Gatty, an influential Australian aviation executive who had been employed by the Americans to oversee their Australian charter operations. Gatty's involvement would turn out to be of continuing concern for Hudson Fysh and his plans to keep Qantas flying after the war.

Brain told Legg he couldn't see any benefit in using *Camilla*, arguing she was fulfilling a useful role, and such a search would expose his unarmed flying boat to danger if the Japanese returned. And anyway, Legg could delay and divert any of the numerous armed Flying Fortresses or Liberators that were lining up hour by hour at Broome airport to fly evacuees south. Brain suggested the best alternative would be to search by boat, volunteering to take part himself, an offer he would regret.

At 4 a.m. the next day, Brain, Bill Bennett and an RAAF doctor left Broome jetty in an American refuelling launch in search of *Arabian Nights*. For Brain, still recovering from dengue fever, it was to be a harrowing experience. As they reached the harbour entrance it immediately became apparent the refuelling cutter was not designed for the open sea. Running against a rapid tidal rip and a strong wind, the low freeboard soon saw them bailing as a nasty swell brought water over the bow, until eventually a large wave broke over them and completely swamped the front of the boat, lifting the stern out of the water. Then the engine stopped. As the cutter began to founder, and now standing waist-deep in water, they lifted the three heavy drums of fuel it was carrying over the side and bailed furiously until the cutter righted itself. By dawn they had the engine going again and finally made it to the spot of where the Liberator had gone down, about fifteen kilometres off shore. There they found numerous items of wreckage including life jackets, charred cushions, pieces of uniform and other clothing, but no sign of survivors.

The following day, 6 March, those Qantas staff remaining packed their stores while they waited for transport south to Perth and then on to Sydney. During the day, as Brain walked the still deserted streets of the town, he met a Dutch Catalina crew and invited them to his Qantas cottage for tea. There Brain learned one of his guests was Captain H.V.B. Burgerhout, the pilot who had rescued Aub Koch and his party off Timor only weeks before.

After receiving news that *Camilla* would be back for them next day, Brain sat down at his diary again, this time complimenting some of those who had remained in Broome:

> Despite the general panic and evacuation there have been several notable cases of local people remaining on the job and sticking to their duty throughout, working colossal hours and doing everything possible in the circumstances.

He adding a note of regret: 'I don't like the idea of running off and leaving the place at this time but our job here is finished and there is more work for us to do elsewhere.'

His final departure would, however, have one ironic twist. Having souvenired a Very pistol and some parachute flares from the American supplies, Brain was out to meet *Camilla* as she came into view just after 4 p.m. the next day. To give Sims the all clear to land he fired a green flare into the air, only to see the flare explode not green but red! *Camilla* instantly sheared off and flew out of sight on the far side of the harbour. Inspecting the cartridge case Brain confirmed it was definitely branded 'green'. When he studied the package further however he was in for a surprise: it was marked 'Made in Japan'.

On 8 March, fully loaded with twenty-seven passengers, spares and stores, Brain left on *Camilla* for Perth where he offloaded his Qantas cargo for carriage to Sydney by ship. While in Perth he received a request from Civil Aviation to send *Camilla* north to Port Hedland with a load of dynamite and foodstuffs. The dynamite was to be used to destroy

Port Hedland's airstrip in anticipation of a Japanese landing. Brain once again argued his case against using valuable, unarmed flying boats for such missions when there were no satisfactory mooring or refuelling facilities in place and there were numerous aerodromes and land-planes available. He lost the argument and Frank Thomas took *Camilla* north, although the plan to destroy Port Hedland airfield was not to take place.

Over the following days the last of the Qantas Broome staff left Perth for the east, some by rail, others aboard *Camilla* after her Port Hedland assignment. Brain hitched a ride to Sydney on an Australian National Airways DC-3.

Although Qantas had miraculously survived Broome without any staff casualties, as far as their aircraft were concerned, the first three months of 1942 had been little short of disastrous.

Of the flying boats caught east of Karachi when the Empire route was cut, a mix of BOAC and QEA machines, two, *Centaurus* and *Calypso*, had already been pressed into RAAF service at the start of the war with Germany and a further two, *Coogee* and *Coolangatta*, joined them, only to have *Coogee* lost in a landing accident at Townsville in February.

Now, of the remaining aircraft, *Corio* had been shot down off Koepang, *Circe* was missing off Java and *Corinna* had been sunk at her mooring in Broome. Unfortunately, for an airline already struggling to provide military service from day to day, before March was out another disaster was to come.

On 21 March *Corinthian*, with Ambrose in command, left Sydney for Darwin with a large anti-aircraft gun, ammunition and personnel from the United States 102nd Coastal Artillery Battalion. Crewing the aircraft with Ambrose were Russell Tapp, who had volunteered for the trip as first officer, and relieving pilot Vic Lyne, now back flying almost exactly eight weeks after being shot down with Aub Koch off Koepang. Unfortunately for Lyne he was about to end up in the water again!

Due to the urgency of the assignment, Ambrose and Tapp agreed to forego spending the night in Townsville but to refuel there and at Groote Eylandt before pressing on for Darwin, each of the three taking turns at the controls. It was 1 a.m. by the time they arrived over what Ambrose would later describe as 'jumpy people who were still expecting more raids'. Taking this into account, Ambrose, who was flying the sector, had switched on all *Corinthian*'s navigation lights to let everyone below know he was 'friendly'. He was turning past the RAAF aerodrome to line up to land in the harbour when suddenly a searchlight lit up the flying boat. Sitting in a darkened cockpit, both Tapp and Ambrose were immediately blinded by the glare, forcing Ambrose to fly *Corinthian* with one hand while shielding his eyes with the other.

Tapp estimated the searchlight kept on them for almost a minute as they approached under what Ambrose would later describe as the worst possible circumstances. Night landings are inherently hazardous for flying boats and one needs to keep a sharp eye out for what hazards may be floating or out of sight just below the water.

As Ambrose turned towards the gently lit flare path on Darwin Harbour, Tapp began calling his altitude and later estimated that the *Corinthian* touched down a little short of the last marker. 'I was about to look over at Russell and say "Well, that's that" when all of a sudden the world exploded around me,' Ambrose would recall. In an instant he was propelled headfirst through the hardened glass cockpit windows, feeling flesh being torn off his body as he went. 'I was grateful it had always been my custom when alighting to wear my cap which prevented me from getting my head fairly badly gashed.'

At first surprised he felt no pain, he suddenly realised he was being dragged down into deeper water by part of the wreckage but managed to struggle free and swim a few metres away from the aircraft. The next thing he saw was a member of the US artillery crew, standing on the still floating wing, 'who was determined to drown himself as he had been struck on the head and was hysterical.' Ambrose swam over and with the help of another man managed to restrain the soldier.

Tapp remembered calling out their airspeed at 110 miles per hour when there was a loud crash. He first thought they had hit the mast of a submerged ship but the next thing he remembered was seeing a bright light and wondering what it was, until the realisation struck him that he was underwater looking at one of the landing lights still shining on the flying boat.

When he broke the surface he was alone and kept shouting as he swam around the wing but received no answer. *Corinthian* was upside down and the wing closest to Tapp was breaking away, but he could hear voices coming from the hull. Just then the launch arrived and he was pulled aboard, along with several others in the water. But just as *Corinthian*'s hull was starting to sink someone on the launch shouted there was another man inside the hull, so Tapp dived overboard and into the aircraft. With the only light to aid him coming from the spotlight on the launch, he groped around in the darkness but he could see no one, and with the hull continuing to sink he returned to the launch.

With Tapp back on board the launch headed for the rear of the flying boat where Ambrose, Lyne and several others were hanging on to the tail. Soon an RAAF launch arrived to continue the search while their own launch headed for shore and those injured were taken to hospital.

Two of the sixteen armed forces personnel on *Corinthian* died in the accident and it would be eight months before Ambrose's injuries would be healed enough to allow him to return to flying duties. Two members of the US 102nd Coastal Artillery Battalion would receive medals for saving others in the crash and Tapp would receive a civilian award.

The subsequent inquiry into the crash absolved both Ambrose and Tapp from any blame, with the probable cause put down to the hull being split open by a partly submerged object in a harbour that still contained a considerable amount of wreckage from the Japanese air raids. For his part, Tapp considered much of the blame for the crash rested with the vagrant searchlight that had half blinded him and probably Ambrose as well, along with a loading error allowing the heavy equipment in the forward lower compartment of the hull to shift as the aircraft hit the water, splitting it in two.

Chapter 18

THE LAST STAND: PAPUA NEW GUINEA

The day after the attack on Broome, Fysh was called to a conference in Melbourne with Arthur Corbett, director-general of the Department of Civil Aviation, the RAAF's Air Marshal Sir Charles Burnett and Air Vice Marshal William Bostock, and BOAC's John Brancker. There Fysh was met with the alarming news that the RAAF wanted another of his flying boats to replace *Coogee*, which had been lost in the landing accident at Townsville the previous week. Fysh was in no position to reject the demand but, as it would turn out, other events appear to have caught up with it and the swap never took place.

The second item on the agenda was even more alarming. With the Japanese landings at Rabaul on New Britain in late January 1942 and attacks on other parts of Papua New Guinea, the US Command was now starting to concentrate on New Guinea and northern Australia as the last line of defence and the jumping-off point for any Allied attempt to drive back the Japanese. With vast numbers of troops and support material preparing to descend on Australia, the Americans now wanted control over all Qantas and civilian aircraft. But the Australian government was inclined to take another view, primarily because it would make it impossible for the RAAF, which had virtually no transport aircraft of its own, to acquire civil aircraft to meet its own requirements.

The request itself, however, was not unusual and in fact had something of a precedent in the evacuation of Java, where Qantas had played a prominent part under charter to the US while itself under the control of Civil Aviation. On that occasion Brain had been forced to stand his ground when actual control of the Qantas flights by the US had been threatened. Now the pressure for such control by the Americans was coming once again from Harold Gatty, with whom Fysh had earlier crossed swords when Pan American attempted to introduce a Pacific service to New Zealand before the war, a move which Fysh and his chairman, Fergus McMaster, believed would threaten Qantas's own international ambitions.

Born in Tasmania, Gatty had an impressive background as an aviation pioneer, having acted as navigator for American Wiley Post on Post's record-breaking aerial circumnavigation of the world in 1931. He would be strongly identified with the Americans through Pan American in the prewar years and later during the war when given the honorary RAAF rank of group captain while working for the US Army in the South-West Pacific, eventually appointed director of air transport under MacArthur.

Both Fysh and McMaster appear to have regarded Gatty as something of a shadowy character, often wary of what his control of civil operations in Australia during the war might mean for the ambitions of Pan American when the war was over. This issue of the Qantas role in Australia's postwar international aviation was of great concern to both Fysh and McMaster as American influence increased during 1942 and 1943, not only because of the Gatty factor but also other influential high-ranking officers in the US Transport Command who might attempt to directly influence Australia's civil aviation policy.

The very structure of United States war work meant much of it was in the hands of civil airlines such as Pan American and other US carriers, a situation which Fysh and others in Australian civil aviation feared would leave them in an unassailable position in terms of modern equipment and experienced personnel once the war was over. Pan American was already running five services a week for the US government into Sydney and there were plans for United Airlines to follow.

On this occasion, however, Australia and therefore Qantas and other operators such as Australian National Airways (ANA) and Guinea Airways won the day, and it was decided that the civil operations would remain under departmental control while still meeting the demands of the United States Command.

By now with only two of its flying boats remaining and another two and several of its DH 86s still in RAAF service, Qantas's work as a commercial operation was on the edge of collapse. While its remaining DH 86s continued their inland service between Brisbane and Darwin, the airline was now much reduced in size, a situation which had forced cuts in staff, mainly within the traffic and administration areas. An attempt to have its trained crews undertake aircraft ferry work for the RAAF fell on deaf ears. As it would turn out, the perilous situation to Australia's north would, in Qantas's case at least, save it to fly another day.

Through January and February 1942 there was little good war news for Australia as a series of Japanese landings in Papua New Guinea led to further retreats by Australian forces. Following the fall of Rabaul the focus was now squarely on the New Guinea side of the island, while the urgent build-up of American forces took place on the Australian mainland.

There's little doubt that if you set out to fight a war, Papua New Guinea would be the last place you'd choose. The sheer size of the island and its dense jungle combined with peaks reaching towards 4500 metres made it one of the most challenging countries on earth. In all there were around five thousand Europeans, mostly Australians, in the country running businesses and plantations when the war threatened, but due to a well-organised evacuation plan, most women and children had been moved south to Australia. The achievement was even more commendable given many of the communities were isolated and the only way out was often by sea or air. In a co-ordinated air and sea evacuation effort, people were gathered in the main centres of Rabaul, Port Moresby, Wau, Lae and Salamaua to be eventually repatriated to Cairns.

The major task fell to ANA and Guinea Airways, although the RAAF too played a role, several of their missions flown by former Qantas captains Mick Mather and Len Grey now operating the two Empires in RAAF service. Qantas played little part in this, fully occupied with its commitments in the Netherlands East Indies and to Australia's west.

Not everyone had gone, however. Scattered across the Owen Stanley Range inland from Port Moresby were even more remote communities, situated in valleys many hundreds of metres above sea level. Centres like Mt Hagen in the Western Highlands or the even smaller settlement of Kainantu, in the hills above the Markham Valley inland from Lae, had no road links to either the north or south coasts and, like most other such outposts, relied solely on the aeroplane for the transport of people and goods.

With the fall of Rabaul on 23 January 1942 came a whole new level of urgency as word spread of the fate of some of those who had been captured by the Japanese, particularly when reports came in that many of the defenders of Rabaul, who had surrendered at Tol Plantation on New Britain, had been massacred. The fate of still others captured in smaller groups was as yet unknown.

Through March and into April, some of those who did make it across Vitiaz Strait separating New Britain from the New Guinea mainland, along with others from as far afield as Manus Island off New Guinea's north coast, had walked hundreds of kilometres through some of the world's most difficult terrain to reach Mt Hagen. There, trapped due to the enemy landings at Lae and Salamaua, they waited in hope for someone to come and get them.

So far it had been the flying boats that had undertaken most of Qantas's commitment to the war effort. Now, however, it would be the airline's land-based workhorse, the DH 86 biplane, which would be used in a daring operation to pluck stranded soldiers and civilians from under the very nose of the Japanese.

The story of Qantas's Mt Hagen rescue really begins with the efforts of a remarkable Catholic missionary, Father John Glover, for without Glover's determination and courage the plight of the eighty people who had by now gathered at Mt Hagen would have not been known.

Glover, ordained at Albury, New South Wales in 1932, learned to fly while a parish priest at Cootamundra, but had precious few hours in the air before he was posted to the Divine Word Mission near Madang on New Guinea's north coast. In New Guinea in 1940, missionaries either walked or flew as there were few other ways to tend their 'flock'. It would be to help those at other missions that would see Glover embark on his rescue plan.

Glover and his tiny two-seater Simmonds Spartan aeroplane arrived unannounced at Kainantu in the foothills inland from Lae one April morning in 1942, much to the surprise of Alex Campbell, the Seventh Day Adventist missionary there. Campbell and his people had witnessed Japanese aircraft flying overhead from Lae for some weeks now but had little other knowledge of what was going on with the war beyond the alarming tales brought to them by some of the soldiers who had trickled into Kainantu from New Britain. Unfortunately, unaware of any orders to leave, Campbell and several other missionaries had been left behind when the earlier general evacuation of coastal areas to their south had taken place.

As the biplane circled and they confirmed it was not Japanese, Campbell's people unhooked the trip-wire that had been stretched across their grass airstrip to prevent any enemy aircraft attempting to land and ran to meet their new arrival. Glover was anxious to explain the plan he had concocted but first he wanted Campbell's help. He needed to hide his aeroplane.

That problem was quickly fixed by pushing the Spartan into a patch of corn and tall banana trees on the fringe of the mission, but when Campbell heard Glover's plan was to take them all out to safety by air he tried to talk him out of it, considering the risks too great. But Glover would have none of it, instead explaining that he knew where a slightly larger Moth aircraft had been hidden at the Catholic Mission headquarters on Sek Island off the north coast of New Guinea.

Within a day or so Glover was on his way again, this time overland towards Sek Island accompanied by Hungarian Karl Nagy, who had worked as an aircraft engineer with Guinea Airways. It was a nine-day walk, then by boat to reach the Moth, which to their delight was reasonably intact and, after constructing a makeshift raft supported by empty fuel drums, they floated the aircraft twenty-two kilometres down the coast to Madang, gambling on the hope that the Japanese air patrols were engaged elsewhere.

There, in a cleared area near Madang airfield, Nagy worked to get it airborne, although when the Moth was ready to fly back to Kainantu Nagy must have harboured some doubts about it and declined the offer to accompany Glover. He decided to walk instead.

Back in Kainantu, Glover, Nagy and Campbell worked on the next stage of Glover's plan, to use his own mini air transport arm to fly as many of those who had now gathered in Kainantu to Mt Hagen and attempt to organise an evacuation from there. In mid-March he set out first in the Spartan, but its tiny, tired Gypsy engine couldn't get him high enough to clear the Purari Gap through the mountain range so he was forced to return to Kainantu, only to smash the Spartan's propeller on landing. It was now up to the Moth, but still with its severe passenger limitation of only one passenger seat there would need to be another change of plan. He would head for Australia and raise the alarm.

Constructing a crude petrol tank out of some sheet metal to give the Moth added range, he and Nagy decided to set off for Mt Hagen and from there fly direct across the Owen Stanley Range to Horn Island off the northern tip of Queensland to alert authorities to the plight of those stranded. In the meantime, Campbell and his group would walk to Mt Hagen, a distance of some 250 kilometres, in the hope they could be rescued from there. Once again Campbell, who considered the attempt to reach Australia in such a flimsy machine impossible, tried to talk Glover out of the idea but to no avail.

At their first attempt late in March, the Moth, like the Spartan, proved too heavy to gain enough height over the mountains and, despite jettisoning everything they could, Glover and Nagy were soon back at Kainantu. Success, however, came at the second attempt, and at Mt Hagen they did more work on the Moth engine to increase their chances.

In aviation terms the whole exercise was primitive in the extreme. Nagy, sitting in the rear cockpit, would cradle a lavatory pan full of oil which he would feed into the engine to stop it from overheating. His courage is even more commendable when one considers his pilot had little more than twenty hours' experience and their only navigation aid was a page torn from a school atlas. Despite such handicaps, they made it the 150 miles over the mountains to the Papuan coast with the intention of pressing on to Horn Island but then their luck ran out. By now Nagy had used all of his oil supplies for the Moth's overheating engine, and bad weather closed in reducing visibility to the point where Nagy, a worried look on his face, passed a note back to Glover.

'Do you know where we are?'

'No, I don't,' Glover scribbled back.

'Never shall I forget his face,' Glover would recount. 'Even through the oil I could see the pallor of his skin and his brown eyes were gleaming pools of helpless rage. There was no need for him to tell me later that his consuming desire was to sock me with a spanner.'

With fuel also running low Glover banked the Moth and sought out the nearest beach and although the aircraft was slightly damaged he managed to land safely. From there he persuaded local villagers to take him by canoe towards the Australian mainland until they came across a passing vessel, which took him to Thursday Island. Hitchhiking aboard southbound aircraft, after an epic journey lasting several weeks, Glover finally walked into military headquarters in Melbourne and told his story.

Back at Kainantu and with no further word from Glover, Campbell was at first reluctant to leave for Mt Hagen. It wasn't until he received a radio report that missionaries in the Solomon Islands had been imprisoned by the Japanese that he reached the conclusion that the enemy obviously wasn't regarding missionaries as neutral so far as the war was concerned. Campbell and his party set off through the mountains but by the time they reached Mt Hagen, a nine-day walk away, there was still no further word of Glover.

Meanwhile, those in Melbourne pulling plans together faced a dilemma. There were no military aircraft available or capable of doing the job so the only suitable aircraft, two unarmed Qantas DH 86s, would have to do. Lester Brain chose Orm Denny, not long returned from the Tjilatjap charters, to lead the mission.

The choice of Denny was an obvious one. Years flying for Guinea Airways in Papua New Guinea before joining Qantas in the mid-1930s meant Denny well knew the dangers the country presented to an aviator. Pilots there either treated the harsh New Guinea terrain with respect or died, but even Denny's experience had its limitations. Most of his flying had been carried out in the eastern regions of Papua New Guinea, leaving him with very limited experience flying around the mountains in the western area.

Denny knew, however, that the golden rules of flying anywhere in Papua New Guinea were always the same: head for the gaps in the mountains and never take the risk of flying through cloud. No matter how sure you were of your position, clouds often hid mountain peaks with 'hard centres' and fatal results.

The team to gather with Denny and Father Glover would be Qantas pilots Eric Sims and Rex Nicholl, another experienced former Guinea Airways pilot Tommy O'Dea, three radio operators Frank Furniss, R. Anderson and L. Louttit, and engineers Doug Chambers and Robert Carswell. Denny would have welcomed O'Dea's addition to his Qantas team. A pilot of wide experience in New Guinea, he would have offered invaluable knowledge of operations beyond the mountains and into the New Guinea Highlands.

Denny decided to use Horn Island as the base with the idea of running a shuttle between there and Mt Hagen, and while the pilots worked on their own flight plans the Qantas engineers started work on fitting auxiliary fuel tanks on the cabins of the DH 86s. This would enable the aircraft to return to Horn Island if weather closed in on them as they approached Mt Hagen as there were no alternative landing fields in that part of the world.

To add to their difficulties, because the Japanese had captured most of the main coastal towns on the New Guinea side and were carrying out bombing attacks on Port Moresby in Papua, their control of the skies over the island meant that any rescue flights would have to be under radio silence, a factor which robbed Denny's pilots of any accurate update of weather conditions between Horn Island and Mt Hagen.

On 13 May 1942, with extra fuel tanks fitted, the two DH 86s finally left Horn Island; it had been almost six weeks since those at Mt Hagen watched Glover and Nagy disappear towards the mountains to the south. Denny's New Guinea experience told him that an early morning departure would give them the best chance of arriving over the mountains before the customary build up of cloud in the late morning and early afternoon.

Mt Hagen, itself in a valley 1500 metres above sea level, was on the far side of the Bismarck Range, with peaks as high as four thousand metres. Denny knew there was a gap in the range at around two thousand metres they could slip through, but if that was blocked by clouds they would have to climb high enough to clear the mountains, something the DH 86s were not designed to do.

With Denny, Nicholl, Anderson and Carswell in one machine and Sims, O'Dea and Father Glover flying close by in the other, Denny picked his way through the cloud around the range to arrive in Mt Hagen to a hero's welcome from the more than eighty now gathered there.

Amid the joy and relief, however, there were serious difficulties to overcome. Firstly, it had taken them three hours to reach Mt Hagen so it was apparent the original plan to fly two flights a day with each aircraft would have to be changed. Any second flights might expose them unnecessarily to late afternoon enemy air patrols in the Horn Island area, not to mention the vagaries of the weather in between.

Taking off in a DH 86 in the high altitude of Mt Hagen was another consideration. In the thin air at 1500 metres above sea level there was no chance of the twelve-seater DH 86s taking a full load, so Denny decided to try the first trip with seven passengers and cut that to six if it proved too much for the DH 86.

That concept appeared to work during the first two days of operations, but then another unexpected complication came their way when the grassed surface of Mt Hagen's airstrip began to show the first signs of deteriorating into a bog, threatening to put the whole airlift at risk.

It was here that Denny's prior experience led to an old New Guinea airman's trick which would save the day. The next morning at Mt Hagen, knowing that local New Guineans relished any excuse to hold a 'sing-sing', he gathered several hundred from surrounding villages onto the airfield. There, plumed in their warrior finery, they spent that night and into the following day stamping their feet on the airport's grass in a traditional celebration, and by late afternoon they had transformed the soggy ground into a rock-hard surface. From then on, despite further bad weather, there was little difficulty with take-offs and landings.

One morning, however, Rex Nicholl was to experience what every pilot flying in New Guinea dreads. Heading towards Mt Hagen, Nicholl's DH 86 was suddenly caught in an updraught which within seconds shot the aircraft up to five thousand metres. Struggling to breathe and handle the aircraft at the same time as loose drums of fuel cascaded around him, Nicholl fought to right his aircraft. With its outside control surfaces now icing up at this altitude, the DH 86 flicked into a spin and plummeted earthwards through the clouds. Even for experienced pilots the DH 86 could be a difficult aircraft to handle under such circumstances, but Nicholl finally regained control as the machine broke through the cloud and into a valley. How fortunate he had been became immediately apparent: he had broken through into a valley. A short distance either to his left or right and the DH 86 would have slammed into a mountain.

It took eighteen flights before all those at Mt Hagen were safely flown to Horn Island, two of them having to turn back when approaching Mt Hagen due to bad weather. Father Glover meantime had remained at Mt Hagen, acting as ground controller and load master until coming out on the last flight. Qantas flew many of those saved on to Cairns while others completed the journey by ship.

Shortly after it was over a telegram arrived for Denny from the Department of Civil Aviation:

> Congratulations to you and all members of your party on successful conclusion your important and dangerous task that it should have been completed without hitch demonstrates sound organisation and high courage and ability of all personnel concerned.

The words contained in that departmental cable must have been particularly gratifying for Tommy O'Dea. Four months earlier, Director-General Corbett had suspended the licences of O'Dea and four other New Guinea pilots after accusing them of little short of cowardice by flying several Guinea Airways aircraft out of Port Moresby to Australia 'without permission'. It would later transpire that the RAAF had in fact ordered the aircraft out to save them from being damaged by Japanese air raids. Presumably when the true story was revealed O'Dea's licence was re-issued prior to the Mt Hagen rescue, but there is little doubt Corbett's accusation hardly took into account that someone with O'Dea's long history of flying the dangerous skies of New Guinea lacked courage.

Denny and others involved would also receive a commendation from the Australian government for their efforts.

Two years after the war was over, missionary Alex Campbell and Father John Glover would meet again in Lae and reminisce about their experience, with Glover promising to fly into Kainantu again soon 'for old times' sake'. But it was not to be. Shortly after, while approaching to land at the Catholic Mission at Mengendi, Glover's aircraft was caught in a downdraught and crashed, killing him instantly. He is buried near a New Guinea Highlands highway, which in 1942 was part of the primitive track Campbell's party used to walk to Mt Hagen.

While May 1942 had marked a commendable achievement with the Mt Hagen rescue, that same month brought the distressing news of the loss of two of Qantas's most experienced pilots, Bob Gurney and Goff Hemsworth, within days of each other in the South-West Pacific theatre.

Born in the New South Wales town of Corowa, Charles Raymond 'Bob' Gurney had, like Denny, flown with Guinea Airways in Papua New Guinea before joining Qantas in 1936 and had been one of the commanders on the Empire route through to Singapore and Karachi.

Sydney-born Godfrey Ellard 'Goff' Hemsworth, son of a well-known mariner, had also flown in New Guinea in the thirties and taken part in the 1934 MacRobertson Air Race from England to Australia with another pioneer Australian aviator, Ray Parer. Although an engine failure put them out of contention on the first day, they pressed on to Australia, arriving 117 days after leaving England. Hemsworth joined Qantas as a first officer on the Empire flying boats in 1936.

Along with Eric Sims and Bill Purton, Gurney and Hemsworth were part of the small group of Qantas pilots seconded to the RAAF when two Qantas flying boats were handed over to the service at the outbreak of the European war in 1939 to form the nucleus of No. 11 Squadron. As its war commitments increased and BOAC struggled to provide enough aircrew to man its Empire route, Sims and Purton were returned to Qantas to help with the extra flying required of the Qantas crews. Gurney and Hemsworth were still in the RAAF when the Pacific war broke out.

Regular RAAF officer (and later air commodore) Gordon Steege joined the small former Qantas band in the early days of No. 11 Squadron as its two Empire flying boats were fitted with guns at Qantas's Rose Bay base and prepared for war. Steege would later recall that neither Hemsworth or Gurney, who had enjoyed flying on the international route, were particularly pleased when told that the squadron's first posting would see them both back in Papua New Guinea.

By mid-1942 Gurney, now a squadron leader, was commanding a Catalina squadron out of Port Moresby but had been chosen to operate on some missions with the US Army Air Forces' 22nd Bomb Group flying twin-engine B-26 Marauder bombers. Many of the American crews had been rushed into the war with only rudimentary training and the intention was to regularly inject experienced Australian pilots who knew the area well into the American squadrons to act as navigators and assist them in handling local conditions.

Gurney appears to have enjoyed his brief sojourn with the Americans, once volunteering for an attack on Lae as it gave him the opportunity to bomb the house he lived in during his time there before the war. His argument was that no one in the squadron had more right to bomb his house than he did!

During a night attack on Rabaul on 2 May, Gurney's aircraft was badly damaged when hit over the target and, with one engine out and little chance of making it back to Port Moresby, limped south towards the Trobriand Islands, five hundred kilometres away. With the B-26 gradually losing height, the crew jettisoned every loose item they could. On reaching the Trobriands, to ensure the Japanese couldn't identify their location they sent a coded radio message advising Port Moresby of their chosen landing point on Owi Island in the Trobrian Group. By the time their next message was sent their code book must have been jettisoned as the second message was in plain English and, given his New Guinea background, must have been transmitted by Gurney himself. He told Port Moresby they were landing at the 'place where Francine used to live'. Francine was a former resident of the island known to both Gurney and members of the operations staff in Port Moresby.

The aircraft's captain, American Chris Herron, ordered the rest of the crew to move to the rear of the aircraft and prepare for a crash landing on what appeared to be a flat area of land. While no one will ever know what went on in the cockpit in the darkness of early that morning, Herron's decision to attempt a landing with his wheels down appears strange, particularly with an experienced pilot like Gurney on board. Under such circumstances actual ground conditions are difficult to judge from the air, and although the ground may have appeared firm the safer option probably would have been to drop the aircraft onto its belly.

In fact they had landed in a swamp and seconds after they touched down the B-26's nose wheel dug into the mud and the bomber flipped onto its back. The five crewmen down the back survived the crash but when they reached the cockpit they found Gurney had been killed instantly. Despite their efforts to drag Herron from the cockpit, he drowned as the aircraft sank deeper into the water.

By then Gurney, aged thirty-five, had been awarded the Air Force

Cross. As a tribute, a few months later the main airfield at Milne Bay was named Gurney Field in his honour.

Goff Hemsworth, who had also won the Air Force Cross, transferred from the original No. 11 Squadron and its Empire boats to Catalinas operating out of Port Moresby and was destined to play a part in the discovery of the Japanese fleet that would meet the US Navy in the Battle of the Coral Sea.

Hemsworth's story is made all the more interesting by comments made about him by his RAAF squadron commander Charles Pearce, quoted in Mark Johnston's *Whispering Death: Australian Airmen in the Pacific War*, and perhaps provide an insight into how regular RAAF officers may have regarded members of their squadron with a civil flying background. While describing Hemsworth as a 'competent pilot', Pearce suggests he is 'marked by his Quantas [*sic*] outlook . . . will not take the slightest risk in flying in case it will jeopardise his position with Quantas Airways after the war'. Johnston describes the comment as a 'slur' on Hemsworth and, given Hemsworth's record with the squadron and his promotion to squadron leader within months of joining, we are left to wonder what Pearce could have based his comments on, perhaps beyond the fact that the very nature of his Qantas training would have made Hemsworth particularly fastidious in trying to eliminate any unnecessary risks in operational flying.

There are perhaps several missions undertaken by Hemsworth that would seem to put Pearce's opinion at odds with the facts. In February 1942, after an attack on shipping at Rabaul a RAAF Hudson bomber under the command of Flight Lieutenant Bob Green was damaged and forced to ditch in the sea off the northern New Guinea coast. When word was received that Green and his crew had survived, and had reached the tiny settlement of Ioma, seventy miles inland, plans were made to rescue them. Given Ioma's small landing field limited the use of larger aircraft, a small Fox Moth biplane was used to lift some of Hudson's crew out, but when Hemsworth went back in the Fox Moth to bring Green out they crashed on take-off. Green and Hemsworth then set off on a four day walk overland to Kokoda, where they were lifted to safety. That same month, another Hemsworth mission would amply demonstrate his courage and airmanship.

With its long-range capability the Catalina would prove to be one of the most effective Allied aircraft of the war in the Pacific, but its slow speed made it particularly vulnerable to fighter attacks. On a night bombing mission to Rabaul early in February 1942, Hemsworth's aircraft, one of two Catalinas bombing shipping in Rabaul's Simpson Harbour, was 'jumped' by a night fighter, and although Hemsworth's gunner shot the fighter down, the Cat had crippling damage to its tail, both wings and one engine. Turning for home with fuel streaming from his ruptured tanks, Hemsworth struggled to keep the aircraft aloft on one engine, all the while realising that unless he had both engines working he had little hope of lifting the aircraft over the Owen Stanley Range to his base at Port Moresby.

After jettisoning his bombload and every loose item on the aircraft, Hemsworth coaxed the Catalina for five hours over hundreds of kilometres through the night to land on the water off Salamaua on the New Guinea north coast but, realising that Salamaua was frequently attacked, he remained there only long enough to make temporary repairs to the damaged engine to allow him to take off again.

Still unable to get enough power to cross the mountains, he decided to fly the long way around the coast, keeping low to the sea and feathering the damaged engine until he eventually reached Port Moresby twenty-five hours after setting out on the mission, fourteen of them on one engine. Maintenance crews counted more than a hundred bullet holes in the Catalina.

These were hardly the actions of a pilot averse to taking risks when absolutely necessary to survive, but perhaps another extract from Pearce's original report might provide a clue to the reason for his negative comments on Hemsworth. Pearce notes that Hemsworth 'Lacks the right service outlook' and 'Is inclined to be argumentative with his seniors'. With more than five thousand hours flying experience before he joined the RAAF, Hemsworth probably felt he knew a lot more than some of those over him.

Neither did he lack courage, an attribute he would demonstrate in the mission that would cost him his life.

Thanks to the breaking of the Japanese codes early in the war the Allies often knew the enemy's plans in advance, but finding an enemy invasion fleet, its aircraft carriers and protective destroyer screen in the vast seas of the South-West Pacific came down to long-range patrols by Catalina squadrons.

Early in May intelligence reports told of large Japanese naval forces leaving Rabaul and Buin on Bougainville believed to be headed for Port Moresby. On 6 May while patrolling the Solomon Sea, Hemsworth spotted two enemy destroyers to the south-east of Misima Island and while shadowing them he reported being attacked by Zeros. No further word was heard from him.

After the war, captured enemy documents indicated that Hemsworth and his crew had survived the attack and were taken aboard a Japanese vessel, one account suggesting they were later transferred to land as prisoners of war, another suggesting they were executed and thrown overboard.

The true story will probably never be known. Detailed research by the author for an earlier book on postwar searches for missing RAAF airmen in the South-West Pacific would reveal that most of the airmen captured at the time were taken to Rabaul, but few survived the war. They were either executed there or lost when the Japanese prisoner freighter *Montevideo Maru* was torpedoed by a US submarine off the Philippines later in the war.

Many of those POWs executed at Rabaul, including all nine of the crew of another Catalina, were found in a mass grave at the foot of Matupi

Volcano, but Hemsworth and his crew were not among them, leading to the probable conclusion that he and his crew met their fate aboard the Japanese war ship.

The Battle of the Coral Sea, which followed the discovery of the Japanese task force by Hemsworth and other Catalina units, ended in victory for the Allies, the withdrawal of the Japanese fleet and a turning point in the war.

Gordon Steege, who had been closely associated with Gurney, Hemsworth, Purton and Sims in those formative days of No. 11 Squadron, would become an 'ace' Kittyhawk fighter pilot, with eight Zeros to his credit. Later in the war, while in command of a fighter wing operating out of Kiriwina, Steege visited the site of Gurney's crashed B-26. In his memoirs of his own war service he would note that of the nine aircrew in the original No. 11 Squadron, only himself, Eric Sims and one other survived the war.

The compromise reached with the Americans for the Department of Civil Aviation to retain control of Qantas operations for the coming New Guinea campaign would come to mark a watershed for the Australian carrier, although it still faced the dismal prospect of being an airline running out of aeroplanes. Now, as the war's emphasis switched from Australia's north-west to its immediate north, the remaining Qantas Empires were to act as troop and supply transports to the front line, initially to Darwin and then fully engaged in support for MacArthur's New Guinea campaign.

The Darwin flying boat charters were part of the general reinforcement of Darwin in the weeks following the first attack on Australia's northern outpost. As the Japanese raids continued, crews operating between Townsville and Darwin had to be very aware that the enemy was dangerously close, so close Russell Tapp heard a Japanese radio station replying to his own position reports: 'Whether he is being quietly sarcastic and telling us he knows all our movements or is hoping for some reply to be sent which will give him information, is not known.' Tapp suggested his company's own radio procedures be altered to cut the enemy operator out of the loop.

Such instances caused Fysh to question the dangerous exposure of his still unarmed flying boats and soon after the start of the Darwin assignment in March he expressed his doubts to Corbett on the wisdom of the government's decision to use flying boats instead of the safer overland air route:

> ... we can only express our reluctance to do these trips unless it is quite out of the question to undertake by landplane.
>
> Flying boats leaving Brisbane on a trip to Darwin enter a dangerous area in approaching Townsville and remain in it right across the North of Australia to Darwin, which is a grave risk compared with the landplane journey.
>
> We urge consideration of the best utilisation of the three Empire boats remaining to us, with the view of reasonable conservation, and trust this can be done.

(Within eleven days of his letter his reference to 'three Empire boats remaining to us' would be relevant. *Corinthian* would be wrecked during Ambrose's night landing at Darwin and although not due to direct enemy action, war wreckage in Darwin Harbour was almost certainly to blame.)

Such a concern for what he considered to be the unnecessary exposure of the flying boats would be an issue Fysh would return to for much of Qantas's involvement in the war. Indeed, from as far back as the outbreak of the war in Europe Fysh had conducted a relentless campaign with the government in an effort to protect his crews by arming his flying boats, even to the point of clashing repeatedly, and occasionally acrimoniously, with Corbett and his director-general's political masters in Canberra. Both Fysh and McMaster saw no difference in the missions being carried out by the fully armed former Qantas Empire boats taken over by the

RAAF and their own aircraft. Both were running the same risks as they flew into the same dangerous airspace.

The issue would rise to the forefront again as the New Guinea campaign developed, particularly in the case of the battle for Milne Bay.

The Darwin charters began on a regular basis of several flights a week but could be alternated with other ad hoc requirements such as to Noumea and Port Moresby as well as the increasing demands from the south into Townsville itself, which was now the primary base for operations to and from Papua New Guinea. Depending on your luck, even transiting Townsville during this period could be something of a lottery as far as being subjected to the attention of the enemy was concerned.

On one three-day trip to Darwin in late July, Orm Denny and his crew hardly got any sleep, their night in Townsville coinciding with a Japanese raid on the town. The first alarm was sounded about 11.50 p.m. but high cloud prevented the searchlights from gaining a hold on the aircraft. 'Two aircraft were all that were seen by anyone although the opinion is that there were four of them. It was forty to forty-five minutes after they were first sighted before they dropped their bombs,' Denny said later.

In fact there were three Japanese flying boats above Townsville that night and although, along with Denny's Empire, there were other flying boats in the harbour, the bombs dropped harmlessly out to sea.

Three days later they were back in Townsville in time for another raid at around 2 a.m. by a single Japanese aircraft, which dropped its bombs in bushland on the edge of town.

With experience of air raids in quick succession at both Townville and Darwin, Denny suggested that to safeguard the remaining two precious flying boats consideration be given to dropping passengers off at Townsville and flying empty to Bowen for the night, returning next morning for the passengers. The same procedure could be implemented at Darwin by overnighting the boats at Groote Eylandt to restrict their exposure to continuing attacks there.

Events, however, would overtake such precautionary measures as the value of the flying boats with their ability to quickly reach the war zone with personnel and supplies started to move them towards more urgent tasks. While Townsville had increased in importance as the primary New Guinea–Australia transit point, Noumea, more than 1400 kilometres from Brisbane, had also achieved its own strategic importance.

The Allies recognised that Noumea sat at a strategic point in the Pacific and any Japanese occupation would allow them to interdict the crucial sea lanes between the United States and Australia, but that concern would fade with the US Navy's victory at Midway in June. Noumea meanwhile became an important base in the battle for Guadalcanal in the Solomons.

Orm Denny and Bert Hussey made four of the thirteen flights to Noumea between June and September 1942, with one of Denny's flights carrying a tonne of gold bullion, presumably on its way to a safer haven further across the Pacific but nonetheless proving moments of humour still existed during a bitter war.

Denny had no idea what was in the bags when they were loaded aboard at Brisbane but when he inspected the manifest before take-off he noticed they were listed as 'change'. Misreading the entry as 'chains' and concerned that his aircraft was going to be overloaded, he casually remarked to one of the load supervisors that at least if he ran into trouble he could jettison a few bags of 'chains' overboard and 'nobody would be any the wiser'.

After a stunned silence the loadmaster countered, 'Holy smoke, you can't do that. That's real money!'

Regular Qantas charters to Port Moresby began in earnest in August. It was the time of the Kokoda campaign and the war had now reached a critical stage. Midway and the Coral Sea battles may have shattered Japanese naval plans for the Pacific, but their control of Rabaul and its importance as a key base for their assaults on the Solomon Islands and Papua New Guinea meant Port Moresby was under threat.

Until American air power began to arrive its early defence relied on RAAF fighters and army anti-aircraft batteries to repel the constant attacks on the town's airfields, military installations and shipping in Fairfax Harbour. In the early months most of the fighting for Port Moresby was in the air and the intensity of the battle was such that in seven days in March the RAAF's No. 75 Squadron had lost eleven aircraft and were struggling to get their ten remaining aircraft into the air.

Japanese forces landed on New Guinea's north coast in July and immediately set out across the Owen Stanleys towards Port Moresby, figuring what they couldn't take by sea they would achieve by land. The fate of Papua New Guinea now hung in the balance and depended on the decisive battles of Kokoda and Milne Bay.

The Qantas charters started out as regular supply missions carrying troops and equipment ranging from anti-aircraft weapons, other armaments, aircraft parts, ammunition and mail to Port Moresby and flying wounded out. But it wasn't long before the deteriorating war situation changed the game plan and once again Qantas would find itself caught between a willingness to do the job it was asked to do while at the same time doing all it could to minimise the risk to its last remaining assets.

The charters themselves were under the control of both the Allied Air Transport Command and the RAAF. Add to that Qantas's responsibility to its own Department of Civil Aviation and it was a structure that was anything but clear-cut, with the result that it wasn't long before the rapidly changing war situation led to disagreements over the use of the unarmed aircraft. The establishment of a secret base at Milne Bay would bring it to a head and once again Lester Brain would be in the thick of it.

By now Brain was spending a great deal of his time directing the Qantas involvement from Queensland, but still, as he would describe it, 'keeping his hand in' by flying some of the charters to provide rest for his overworked crews.

Substituting for an exhausted Eric Sims late in July Brain took *Coriolanus* from Brisbane to Port Moresby carrying, as he quaintly put it, 'three and a half tons of empty sacks for some urgent Army purposes.' The sacks may have been for air dropping supplies into places like Myola in the Owen Stanleys in support of the hard-pressed diggers fighting on the Kokoda Track.

Brain's *Coriolanus* arrived in Port Moresby late on the afternoon of 31 July. Brain planned to leave at 1.30 a.m. next morning to enable the aircraft to stick to its tight Brisbane–Townsville–Port Moresby schedule, only to be told by the RAAF they required him to fly on to Milne Bay.

Such a demand must have struck Brain as deja vu, reminiscent of his Broome experience when conflicts had developed between him and the United States commanders over the use of his aircraft. He refused, unless the instruction came from Civil Aviation in Melbourne.

While Brain was willing to undertake just about anything in support of the war effort, his argument in this case was relatively straightforward: he required more than simply an order to fly somewhere he'd never been before to convince him to risk his boat.

Milne Bay itself, operating under the code name of 'Fall River', was on the extreme south-east tip of Papua New Guinea and had been chosen by MacArthur as an air base to cover any Japanese attempt to move again by sea or land towards Port Moresby. It was virtually unknown to Qantas crews.

The impasse finally reached MacArthur's air force commander in Port Moresby, General George Brett, who agreed to accept responsibility for the flight. Brain appears to have considered Brett an appropriate authority, later commenting drily: 'In these circumstances I considered it would be most undiplomatic to refuse General Brett.'

By 4 a.m. Brain was in the air heading for Milne Bay, arriving at daybreak. He spent three hours on the water while five stretcher cases, a critically wounded air gunner and twenty other American service personnel were loaded for Townsville. It was a tense wait. While on the water he learned Port Moresby had been attacked a few hours after their departure that morning.

Milne Bay, and its strategic importance to both the Allies and the enemy, would present Qantas crews with more anxious moments in the coming weeks as it became a regular calling point for the Qantas Port Moresby charters. The Milne Bay extension would also require an adjustment to the regular Townsville to Port Moresby and return schedule, now impossible to achieve in the time available. Thus the boats would operate on a triangular routing from Townsville to Cairns, Port Moresby and Milne Bay, then return direct from Milne Bay to Townsville.

These were long, arduous missions for the crews over two days, first 176 miles from Townsville to Cairns, 540 to Port Moresby for an overnight rest, an early morning departure for the 230 miles to Milne Bay and finally the longest stage, 580 miles direct to Townsville.

Had it not been for its wartime background the charters could be looked at as similar to a regular airline schedule. The flying boats, often laden with troops, would leave Townsville early in the morning on the first relatively easy stage to Cairns, arriving there in time for the troops to go ashore for lunch and their last chance to order from a menu and be served by waitresses. From now on for many of them it would be only hard rations and an allocation of ammunition. At Cairns the boats would take on enough fuel to allow them to increase their freight uplift by upwards of an extra 450 kilograms out of there for Port Moresby.

Although most arrivals and departures from Port Moresby were in darkness, the overnights there were hardly comfortable due to the frequent visits by Japanese bombers. If alarms came while the flying boats were loading or unloading the crews would head for shore and the slit trenches. Even the rare opportunity to relax had its moments.

One crew was watching an open-air picture show for the troops being screened on the fairway of a golf course when the air-raid alarm sounded. Once the all clear was given there was a frantic rush of troops back onto the fairway to get better seats.

But it would be at Milne Bay where the danger levels increased to the point where Fysh once again took on the battle to have his flying boats armed.

Immediately on receiving Brain's report of his initial flight into Milne Bay, Fysh wrote to Corbett suggesting something should be done about arming the flying boats as soon as possible, at the same time pointing out that the Qantas machines were carrying twice the load of the equivalent RAAF Empires on their supply runs.

Corbett's patience with Fysh's persistence, however, was running out. While promising to place the matter before his boss, Minister for Air Arthur Drakeford, he added testily, 'Don't you know you cannot have guns and butter!'

Despite such an obvious putdown, in an accompanying note to Drakeford, Corbett did take the opportunity to outline the Qantas argument: 'The flying boats are all alike. Those under Civil control carry 8,000 lbs to Moresby. Those under Allied Command (the former Qantas Empires) carry 4,000 lbs on same trip.'

His eventual reply to Fysh a few days later, however, would be dismissive of the idea: 'We cannot arm all the aircraft operating in the combat area, and Civil Aviation cannot be an armed force. That is the job of the RAAF.' Then, in a reference that must have sent a shiver down Fysh's spine: 'If you push this idea of arming flying boats, there is only one logical answer, and that is—hand them over to the RAAF. Better think about it.'

But Hudson Fysh hadn't built an airline from scratch by giving in easily and a week later another letter was on its way to Corbett, providing him with a blunt comparison between the civil and RAAF boats when it came to arming. 'By arming we do not mean eight guns, eight crew, plus parachutes, spares and extra equipment as carried on the RAAF Empire Flying Boats. Arming in our case should not run into more than 1,000 lbs at the outside.' Cheekily he drew another comparison:

> Merchant ships are armed but are not fitted with 16 inch guns, nor does it take 2000 men to work those guns and the ship as on a battleship. Neither have I noticed that arming merchantmen has meant any change in command.

Still pressing his case, Fysh followed up a few days later by attaching a report by Brain on how any arming requirement could be managed.

Brain accepted that in some areas the airline's aircraft could operate unarmed, even into dangerous airspace around Katherine and Batchelor in Australia's north, by timing their arrivals and departures in the late afternoon and early morning. He even acknowledged Darwin, still subject to air raids, was 'a borderline case' provided arrivals were made near dusk and departures at dawn. But if arrivals and departures at Darwin were made during various daylight hours then there might be a case for armament.

Brain harboured no such reservations when it came to operations into Milne Bay. 'Flights into advanced areas in New Guinea are a definite case for defensive armament,' he wrote. 'There certainly appeared occasions when the problem took on farcical proportions. In one instance Denny had left Townsville with a full load for Port Moresby at the same time as an armed RAAF Empire left with a half load for Port Moresby and a half load for Milne Bay. At Port Moresby the half load was taken off the RAAF boat and loaded onto Denny's aircraft and Denny was sent off to the front line at Milne Bay while the RAAF boat returned to Townsville.'

'He has guns and we have nothing,' was Denny's terse comment to Fysh.

The enemy wasn't the only problem at Milne Bay. Its deep, protected harbour was often covered in cloud, had an annual rainfall of more than 250 centimetres, debilitating humidity and a reputation for the most concentrated infestation of mosquitoes anywhere in Papua New Guinea.

Pilots flying in New Guinea rarely welcomed low cloud and poor visibility but Milne Bay could be an exception, realising this would help hide them from patrolling Japanese aircraft, although such conditions made the flights from Port Moresby to Milne Bay no less dangerous.

Parts of the coast, particularly around the Milne Bay area, were dotted with headlands and islands, and without any radio navigations aids or even adequate charts just finding Milne Bay under such conditions could be difficult, even to experienced New Guinea hands like Denny.

Once, gingerly picking his way a metre above the waves, Denny had not seen the coast for two hours but, calculating he should now be somewhere in its vicinity, he sighted through a break in the clouds what he thought was Milne Bay. Pulling a tight circle in the limited space, he landed, spotted a motor launch and taxied up to it, only to be informed by its skipper he was actually in a place called Mullins Bay.

'You're only a few miles from your base,' the boatman shouted. 'It's straight through there,' pointing towards a blanket of rain and clouds. Applying his hard-earned lessons from his New Guinea flying days, Denny decided to wait until the weather improved and he was able to slip across a gap in the mountains and into Milne Bay.

In all, over two weeks in August in 1942, Denny, Bert Hussey, Frank Thomas and Eric Sims made sixteen trips to Port Moresby, six of them on to Milne Bay, carrying 450 troops and thirty-one tonnes of freight to Port Moresby, and a hundred troops and nine tonnes of freight on to Milne Bay.

Several of Denny's Milne Bay trips consisted of units of special aerodrome defence troops, their light anti-aircraft guns and ammunition. When one officer in the group noticed the flying boat wasn't armed he told Denny he would be only too happy to rig their guns and 'have a crack at any hostile aircraft'. 'Little did he dream that he would only just have time to mount his guns at Milne Bay before being in action,' Denny would recall.

Late in August, while Denny and his team were battling the elements along Papua's treacherous south coast and the Fysh and Corbett letters were crisscrossing each other between Canberra and Sydney, the question of arming the Qantas flying boats, at least as far as Milne Bay was concerned, became academic.

Flying in on 25 August, Denny would describe weather conditions as the worst he had ever encountered as an intertropical front pounded the coast. Several hours after his departure for Townsville the Japanese launched their first attack on Milne Bay, and it was here again the weather proved Denny's ally as it's likely he flew close to the invading Japanese vessels without sighting them.

Over the following twenty hours the Japanese landed in force in an attempt to capture Milne Bay's airfields, precipitating a struggle fought under appalling conditions both on the rain-sodden ground and in the air. The fighting was at such close quarters that at one stage the Japanese reached the edge of one of the airstrips before finally being beaten back. So close were they that the defending Australian Kittyhawk pilots were opening fire on enemy positions immediately after take-off.

Twelve days after landing the Japanese accepted defeat and withdrew, and although the battle area and the numbers of troops involved would be relatively small, victory for the Australians at Milne Bay would mark the first defeat of the Japanese army on land in the Second World War.

As for the part played by the Qantas crews, it appears they considered they were simply doing their job and were wary of any public acknowledgement, a fact underlined by Bert Hussey when he read a newspaper report headed 'Value Contribution to Milne Bay Success', quoting Minister Drakeford paying tribute to the work of the civil aircrews at Milne Bay, describing how they had been flying 'unarmed aircraft running considerable risk'. Attaching the newspaper clipping to one of his reports, Hussey took the minister to task:

> The enclosed cutting shows that the details of the operations of civil aircraft are made public even while operations are taking place. Surely this is not in the interests of the safety of the aircrew concerned.

As for Orm Denny's view, he would likely have preferred efforts by the minister to arm his flying boat rather than making public statements about it, although another of his comments summed up the feelings of the Qantas crews to the Allied victory at Milne Bay: 'What a glorious day it proved to be for our RAAF. They found the invaders and gave them what oh!'

Chapter 19

THE STRUGGLE FOR AIRCRAFT AND THE BULLY BEEF BOMBERS

As the war moved inexorably towards its tipping point in Papua New Guinea in mid-1942, back in Australia Fysh and McMaster were fighting their own battles for the very survival of their airline, fearful that its future rested on its ability to find a useful place for itself in the months ahead. With no international route remaining and reduced to two flying boats and a handful of landplanes, Qantas desperately needed more aircraft, not only to fulfil its wartime role but to assure its place in postwar aviation.

In some respects Fysh felt they had been let down. They had passed over their flying boats to the RAAF with the assurance they would be handed back on the delivery of the nineteen Catalinas in late 1940. Not only hadn't this happened but they had lost the bulk of the rest of their fleet on active service, and moves were afoot for the RAAF to take over their DH 86s for use as air ambulances, leaving them with a surplus of pilots and the necessity to stand down other staff. Behind much of their pleadings for aircraft to replace their losses was a desire to obtain Catalinas of their own to enable a resumption of the UK route, this time across the Indian Ocean to Ceylon (Sri Lanka).

As the debate rolled on from May through to August, by now frustrated with Corbett's responses and a fruitless attempt by McMaster to personally convince Prime Minister Curtin of Qantas's needs, Fysh committed the cardinal sin of going directly over Corbett's head to his boss, Minister Drakeford.

He then added to that diplomatic gaffe by approaching the governor-general, Lord Gowrie, who informed him somewhat dismissively it was 'entirely one of Government policy'. The Gowrie approach was too much for Corbett, however, who took Fysh to task in no uncertain terms in 'seeking assistance which appears to me improper'. Suitably chastened, Fysh wrote an abject apology to Corbett but it would not be the end of the matter. Both he and McMaster would continue to take every opportunity to press their case, particularly in relation to their postwar concerns.

Then, in October, help suddenly arrived from an unexpected quarter. In the retreat from Java a small fleet of Dutch civil aircraft comprising Lockheed Lodestars, Lockheed 14s, and Douglas DC-3s, DC-5s and DC-2s had made it to Broome and were later purchased by the United States Army Air Forces for use by Harold Gatty as wartime transport aircraft. Gatty now approached Qantas, Australian National Airways and Guinea Airways with a proposal that each of the companies would operate some of these aircraft on transport duties on loan from the Air Force.

Under the arrangement, Qantas was allocated three twin-engine Lodestars painted in USAAC colours but bearing the civil registrations VH-CAA, VH-CAB and VH-CAK, and would be responsible for their engineering and servicing. Fysh's relief was palpable, telling his board: 'From a company point of view this move is of the greatest importance and appears to remove the previous fear of having no aircraft to operate in the event of further losses.'

All three aircraft were destined to play a pivotal role in the bloody finale to the Japanese assault on the mainland of New Guinea and aftermath of the Kokoda campaign.

The ferocious battle to dislodge the Japanese from the beachheads at Buna, Gona and Sananada on New Guinea's northern coast has, to some extent at least, been historically overshadowed by the Kokoda campaign which marked its origins. Within days of their original landing on the coast in late July 1942 the Japanese had advanced one hundred kilometres into the Owen Stanley Range and captured the vital airstrip at Kokoda, a key staging point in their plan to attack Port Moresby by an overland route.

The difficulties presented by the Kokoda Track in wartime are difficult to comprehend by anyone who has not experienced it. Perhaps the most graphic description was offered in September 1942 by Colonel (later Major General) Frank Kingsley Norris, then attached to the Australian 7th Division and quoted in Raymond Paull's notable account of the Kokoda campaign, *Retreat from Kokoda*:

> Imagine an area approximately one hundred miles long. Crumple and fold this into a series of ridges, each rising higher and higher until seven thousand feet is reached, then declining in ridges to three thousand feet. Cover this thickly with jungle, short trees and tall trees, tangled with great, entwining savage vines. Through an oppression of this density, cut a little native track, two or three feet wide, up the ridges, over the spurs, round gorges and down across swiftly flowing, happy mountain streams. Where the track clambers up the mountain sides, cut steps—big steps, little steps, steep steps—or clear the soil from the tree roots.

Kingsley goes on to describe drenching tropical downpours turning the steps into mud and concludes with a note of sarcasm: 'Such is the track which a prominent politician publicly described as "being almost impassable for motor vehicles". Along that track in those first days the unblooded Australian 39th Battalion was sent to hold back a jungle-trained Japanese army flush with victory.

Kingsley stopped short of naming the politician but much the same might have been said of Douglas MacArthur, headquartered hundreds of kilometres south in Brisbane and with no concept of what conditions on the track were like, and yet would describe the initial Australian retreat to his American superior, General George Marshall, in early September: 'The Australians have proven themselves unable to match the enemy in jungle fighting.' Several historians have suggested MacArthur's comment might have been prompted by his acute awareness that he could ill afford another defeat after being caught unprepared by the Japanese attack in the Philippines.

Ironically, on the same day MacArthur cabled his opinion to Marshall, Australians forced a Japanese retreat from Milne Bay and the tide was already beginning to turn in favour of the Australians on the Kokoda Track as they prepared to stand and fight at Imita Ridge, almost within sight of Port Moresby. There the Japanese offensive petered out. In their rush to obtain their objective they had carried little with them beyond ammunition and the bare necessities and had outrun their supply lines. So dire was their situation that in the withdrawal back down through the mountains towards the coast the advancing Australians would witness many examples of starvation and even cannibalism. But the Japanese occupation of Buna and Gona would prove they were far from finished, and it would take all the resources the Allies could muster to dislodge them from their coastal redoubts. A major part of those resources would become known as the 'Bully Beef Bombers'.

In October 1942 MacArthur had finally moved his headquarters to Port Moresby and by early November the stage was set for the battle for the beachheads. Because adequate shipping was unavailable, the main support for both the Americans and the Australians engaged would be by air across the Owen Stanleys via air drops where necessary but mainly concentrated on two primitive landing strips at Popondetta and Dobodura, both within reach of Japanese guns for the duration of the campaign.

Once again MacArthur, and to some extent Australia's Thomas Blamey, had underestimated the strength and tenacity of the Japanese who had brought in fresh troops and now numbered around nine thousand on the coastal fringe. Their fortified bunkers, camouflaged and well defended and extremely difficult to penetrate with small arms and mortar fire, would become a feature of Japanese defence for the remainder of the war, and added to that the preparedness of the Japanese to fight to the death would mean the Allies would pay a high price.

The battle opened on 19 November in co-ordinated attacks on three fronts by the Americans and Australians against Buna, Gona and Sananda.

Two days after the attacks were launched Orm Denny arrived in Port Moresby to be told he was to remain there for 'special work to the Buna area', which would turn out to be the movement of three million pounds of food, troops, ammunition and equipment into the battle zone as quickly as possible. Allied Air Transport Command would run the overall operation and Qantas, with Denny in charge, would be responsible for the civil aircraft contribution to the airlift, which would involve two Qantas Lockheed Lodestars, a Lockheed 10A and two DH 86s. These would soon be joined by four aircraft from Australian National Airways and two from Guinea Airways.

The Qantas crews would eventually comprise Denny and captains Thomas, Howard, Ashley and MacMaster, acting captains Connolly, Mills and Doug Tennent, first officers Elphingstone, Reeve and Johnston, and radio officers Furniss and Louttit. RAAF pilots and radio officers would make up the numbers as required.

The first stage involved air drops into troop positions at Jimburu and Soputa, and while both outposts were within twelve kilometres of the Japanese lines, the landing strips being prepared at Popondetta and Dobodura would be even closer—five kilometres, well within range of Japanese anti-aircraft guns.

Both latter airfields were primitive in the extreme, hacked out of bush and kunai grass, 1000 to 1500 metres long and barely double the width of the aircrafts' wingspan. Basically all the army engineers had done was cut the grass and take out any large stones which littered the strips, leaving a surface that would rapidly deteriorate as the airlift reached its peak and more than twenty heavily loaded aircraft, each averaging three trips a day, pounded it.

All the Air Transport Command aircraft, military and civil, were unarmed, but they were provided with a fighter cover of Kittyhawks and P-39 Airacobras over a battlefield within easy reach of Japanese Zero fighters from their base at Lae, directly across Huon Gulf from Buna and Gona, a situation which naturally led to some close calls.

Denny, who did much of the early flying, was once skipping across the top of a cloud when three Zeros zoomed up in front of him. 'I could have touched them, but thank goodness they did not have eyes in the back of their head, for another three seconds and they would have been behind me instead of in front.'

Australian National Airways pilot Jim Turner would describe another hair-raising experience. Turner was approaching to land at Dobodura when he saw bombs falling on it:

> I had my wheels down, flaps down, everything. I looked around and there was another Jap on my tail. It looked as if he was waiting for me to climb and then he would shoot me off at his leisure.
>
> Instead, I did a sideslip, which you're not supposed to do anyway in a Lodestar, certainly not with your flaps down. I twisted away into

> the kunai and made a landing. The Zero had taken it just a bit too easy, for I pulled up within four hundred yards and he went past in a flash. All he did was shoot away the hydraulic lines on my port wing.

Turner's Lodestar was a write-off and when he filed his own report for that day's flying, Qantas's Frank Thomas commented wryly: 'Now Jim Turner drinks his whisky neat.'

Steve Howard's first two days on the job involved air dropping supplies at Soputa. Two AIF soldiers had the risky job of throwing the load out through the open door as the aircraft bucked around at low level, but Howard found there was no shortage of volunteers:

> There were so many offering my difficulty was to decide who was to go. They were all new to the job, enjoyed the ride over and worked like hell when they got there.
>
> Some were better than others at it and it took three to five circuits of the dropping ground to get it all out.

One can understand their problem when Howard goes on to describe the dropping zone as a small open patch, close to Soputa village and surrounded by jungle. To ensure the supplies hit their mark Howard had to bring his aircraft down below treetop level with barely a few metres to spare on either side of his wingtips. Even to get to that point he had to pull the aircraft around in a low, tight circuit: 'The ground is so close to the front line and a wide circuit would give "Nippo" a chance to shoot the machine up.'

Then there were the clouds and the 4000-metre-high mountains of the Owen Stanleys separating Port Moresby from the battlefield.

The first trips in the early morning were usually the easiest as these took place before the regular build-up of clouds covered the mountains as the day wore on. Under these early conditions pilots were able to 'feel' their way through a gap in the range at about 7500 feet. Once through there it was a steep descent down a gorge past Kokoda to either Popondetta or Dobodura. The moment the goods were delivered it was a quick take-off, a sharp turn to avoid Japanese positions and a high-speed getaway back through the peaks. On a good morning the return trip could be achieved in one and a half hours.

As the clouds built up later in the morning it was often necessary to climb above them, then look for a 'hole' to dive through, a procedure according to Howard that offered its own hazards:

> The business of diving through the 'hole' was alright providing you were sure that no one else was coming out through the 'hole' from the other side, and with thirty transports in the air at a time one could never be sure of this.

On a flight to Buna Howard had struggled to 12,000 feet to top the clouds only to spend thirty minutes trying to find an appropriate 'hole', finally deciding to chance his arm by returning to another entry via the Kokoda Gap, a route he had originally turned down because of the number of aircraft in front of him. By now, however, he could see the Kokoda Gap looked relatively clear so decided to give it a go. He was halfway down the gorge when a Douglas DC-3 in front of him suddenly turned, giving him no option in the limited airspace but to turn away himself. At the same time Howard's radio operator shouted: 'George wants to see us!'

'George' was part of a signal system developed for the Buna operation which allocated all aircraft operating into the area with a daily call sign, such as 'Chicago', while the radio ground station would be identified as 'Omaha'. Under the code scheme, 'George wants to see us' meant either the weather had closed in over the beachhead or Japanese aircraft were in the area, a warning for all inbound aircraft to return to base. 'Transports came out of that hole like ants,' recalled Howard:

> It appears that they had all got down through this hole into the valley and the weather had closed down completely on the other side sending them all back up through the same hole. This was apparently the reason for the machine in front of me suddenly deciding to turn back.

Such was the intensity of the airlift that Denny once likened the stream of transports as resembling a city suburban railway.

The weather too played havoc with the landing strips themselves as tropical downpours regularly reduced them to mud. Under such conditions aircraft skidding off the runway or their undercarriage collapsing was a common occurrence, although few fatalities appear to have occurred. Unfortunately, due to limited communications, pilots had no way of knowing before leaving Port Moresby what condition the strips might be in beyond word of mouth by other crews as the day went on. The general instructions were that as there were several strips over there you could take your pick, recalled Howard, a type of Russian roulette which could lead to some bizarre experiences:

> When you arrived you selected the one which looked rather best and with the least aircraft 'piled' up on it and down you went only to find that it was as rough as bags with lots of holes in it about the centre, just where you didn't want them to be.

Or you could be told by an American officer on the strip that: 'You shouldn't have come to this strip and the one you should be using is further over.'

With their backloads to Port Moresby mainly wounded and sick troops, the Qantas crews saw firsthand the toll the men had suffered through the appalling conditions of the Kokoda campaign and now at Buna and Gona. 'Our troops were full of hope but I am afraid their looks gave them away, they were tired, worn and hungry,' Denny would note, adding that many were too ill to even look out the window at the country below them on the way back, even though it may have been their first aeroplane ride. 'It is an inspiration to all of us to work and work more when you see what our troops in this area have gone through.'

Occasionally, too, that particular brand of Australian humour surfaced. As Steve Howard taxied to a stop at Port Moresby after a flight of wounded, one of the diggers commented: 'Well Skipper that beats hell. It took us three months to get over there and thirty five bloody minutes to get back!'

'Back', as the digger described it, was Wards Strip, part of a complex of runways, taxiways and revetments which had transformed Port Moresby into one of the busiest airports in the world. Wards Strip was 'not all beer and skittles'. Howard would note: 'The dust was terrific as the day went on and "Kelly's" rules prevailed in taking off and landing. You got in and out when you could and how you could, chased your own loading and petrol supplies more often than not.'

For the Qantas crews and their ground staff, Wards Strip had few comforts after long hours in the air or toiling through the oppressive heat and dust on the ground. From his first days there Denny had to struggle to get the bare necessities he needed to service the aircraft on the ground, often forced to hitch rides on passing vehicles to get from one part of the vast airfield to another. Finally he scrounged two trucks, a utility and a jeep, but in the early days had to rely on help from the RAAF's No. 6 Squadron whose Hudson bombers were based nearby.

The No. 6 also extended a welcome Australian hand when it came to use of their mess, which at least gave the crews some respite from the heat and dust. Accommodation was also an early problem, particularly as manpower increased with the arrival of the ANA and Guinea Airways aircraft and their crews.

Along with the regular Qantas courier service operating from Australia, Denny often had to find accommodation for around thirty people but once again No. 6 Squadron came to the rescue, allowing Denny to establish three large tents on their area and another smaller one and some stretchers to sleep on. Before that one of his engineers spent his first five nights at Wards sleeping in one of the aircraft.

Meanwhile the battle raged across the Owen Stanleys. With little hope of resupply, bombed from the air, shelled by artillery and many of them starving, the Japanese held on, forcing the Americans and Australian troops to take their fortifications out one at a time and at a great cost in lives. Disease, mostly malaria from swarms of mosquitoes amid the coastal swamps, also took its toll on both sides.

On 9 December 1942, the day the Australians, taking heavy casualties, finally captured Gona and joined the Americans at Buna, Hudson Fysh set out for Port Moresby to visit his own 'troops' on the front line. Fysh arrived aboard *Camilla* and, as was his habit while flying, took time during the trip to note the stark difference between flying on his boats on the Empire route and this journey. 'Before the war, it was said that if a passenger sneezed the steward would be sure to hear, and would immediately produce an Aspro,' he would write. Things had certainly changed.

Now stripped of its upholstery and surplus furnishings and with the seats long removed from the main cabin, service for the fourteen passengers, including an American colonel sitting on a pile of blankets and a mattress and three Australian Army doctors stretched out on the floor, was at a wartime minimum. Lunch between Sydney and Brisbane came in a cardboard box, and even that was missing between Townsville and Port Moresby.

One of Fysh's first meetings in Port Moresby was with US General George Kenney, who complimented him on the contribution his regular Empire flying boat courier service was making. The service, under captains Crowther, Hussey, Tapp, Sims and Ambrose, had operated more than a hundred uninterrupted round trips between Townsville and Port Moresby since September.

It must have been music to Fysh's ears when Kenney asked how he was able to operate such a regular service, Fysh explaining its success relied on a 'properly equipped' base in Sydney, adequate spares and 'because veteran crews are employed whose job is to get there safely'.

As for his first impressions of wartime Port Moresby, for Fysh it had echoes of his First World War experience: sunburnt men whose only apparel was a pair of shorts, and areas that reminded him of places in Sinai, 'though not nearly as grim as Gallipoli,' he conceded in his diary.

The next morning out at Wards Strip he was offered the choice of a ride in a DH 86 for an air drop or with Qantas's Frank Thomas on a run into Dobodura with a load of armour plating for a jeep and several Australian officers on their way to the front. He chose the latter and, reassured by the presence of several fighters above them, Fysh pondered the unforgiving nature of the territory below as they crossed the Owen Stanley Range, noting in his diary that Private Ben Bennett-Bremner, his airline's former publicity officer, was below him somewhere doing it the hard way as a member of a machine-gun unit. A brief stop to unload and be loaded again and they were in the air once more with two sick diggers on their way to hospital in Port Moresby:

> . . . one would not have been recognised by his own mother with his sallow face, dark heavy beard and dressed only in an identity disc and a pair of cut down slacks which hung in tattered rags. His constant companions were a pair of brand new army boots which he never let out of his hand.

At dinner with Kenney that evening, along with the RAAF's commander, Group Captain 'Bull' Garing, Fysh was treated to a long dissertation by the general on the success achieved by bombing highly manoeuvrable Japanese destroyers with the B-17 Flying Fortress. Fysh would recall the conversation several months later when, in company with RAAF Beaufighters, the technique would be used to telling effect, almost wiping out a Japanese convoy and its escorts in the Battle of the Bismarck Sea.

Along with the rest of Port Moresby, Fysh spent the remainder of that night going backwards and forwards to an air-raid shelter as alarms sounded and the sky lit up with searchlights and exploding ack-ack shells trying to find the Japanese bombers overhead. He was up before dawn driving through choking dust at Wards to be greeted with the news that several of Denny's aircraft had been slightly damaged during the previous night's raid. Early next morning he was on his way back to Australia, the old air warrior confessing to one regret: 'That I would dearly like an operational trip in a Fortress sitting behind a machine gun.'

It would take until the early weeks of 1943 before the Buna campaign was over, and Denny would write with pride of the reaction of the Australian troops when they saw the word *Qantas* painted on the noses of his aircraft as they arrived at the front. He'd adopted the idea after watching numerous American aircraft taxi past bearing names like *Swamp Rat, Hell's Bells* and *What's Cookin'*. 'To me QANTAS was something to be proud of,' Denny would write in his final report.

Indeed he had good reason to feel that way.

In terms of the invaluable support the Bully Beef Bombers rendered to those fighting the vicious ground campaigns at Buna and Gona, the uplift figures speak for themselves. In a single week between 22 November and 1 December 1942, one Qantas aircraft alone made thirty-five trips carrying 53,000 kilograms into the Buna area. Throughout the whole of the crucial battle period the two Qantas Lodestars made seventy-seven return trips between Port Moresby and the Buna beachhead, carrying more than three hundred passengers to the front line and evacuating almost one hundred wounded, along with more than 90,000 kilograms of freight.

The US 5th Air Force's deputy chief Brigadier-General Ennis Whitehead was high in his praise of those involved in the civil airlift:

> The extraordinary devotion to duty by operating crews of the airplanes is in my opinion an outstanding performance. These crews have operated through all kinds of weather and in the face of enemy opposition. The skill of these crews operating from the emergency strips in the Buna area indicates the high degree of flying proficiency.

Reporting to his board in December, Fysh described 1942 as an 'anxious year' for his airline, with four of its Empire boats lost and valuable lives along with them, adding: 'Warfare has changed. This is the first war in history in which air transport has been used as a major service.' In recounting to the board General Kenney's compliments on the standard of service the Qantas flying boats were providing, Fysh said the company had every reason to be proud of its contribution.

In fact for months now the two flying boats *Camilla* and *Coriolanus* had operated a daily 'airline' service between Townsville and Port Moresby with extensions to Milne Bay, albeit with a wartime overlay. Hidden among the Qantas files of those days is an account of one of these services in which its unknown author describes in a matter-of-fact way a last-minute change of plans calling for a direct flight from Townsville to Milne Bay, a distance of 1100 kilometres.

It was a Sunday morning and the crew were standing by ready to take *Camilla* from Townsville to Port Moresby when the call came from Air Transport Command that supplies of men and material were urgently required at Milne Bay. The heavy load would normally require a refuelling stop at Cairns but to do that would mean a night landing at Milne Bay, a dangerous option for a flying boat. By midday Milne Bay had been alerted, code books and recognition letter for the day (necessary to avoid being mistaken for an enemy aircraft) distributed, and weather forecasts studied, and the three-tonne load was aboard, along with enough fuel to allow for 'meteorological and war exigencies'.

Once airborne a course was set for Milne Bay, making allowance for a typical intertropical front about 400 miles ahead and plainly visible by the crew after two and a half hours into the flight. Sextant shots of the sun were taken before it disappeared into the clouds but the 'front' didn't disappoint them. With a cloud base of between five hundred and a thousand feet, they were soon flying through heavy rain and being buffeted by fierce winds as they dodged around water spouts between the sea and the clouds for a hundred miles.

Finally the weather cleared and a cruiser and two destroyers were sighted to starboard and a lamp from the cruiser flashed a challenge. These were the anxious moments where they hoped they'd given the correct reply but it was acknowledged by the cruiser. There was no time to relax, however, as the crew continued to scan the sea and the sky until landmarks were sighted ahead and the quiet satisfaction that they had 'hit it on the button'.

By now the clouds had descended on New Guinea's notoriously dangerous hills so they turned right and flew down the coast. Ahead an aircraft approached and as it came closer binoculars identified the star on its fuselage as a 'friendly', a American B-25 medium bomber.

Arriving over Milne Bay, *Camilla* circled to ensure the alighting area was clear and the mooring buoys in place then settled on the water, and before long the barges were alongside, refuelling was in progress and the soldiers and freight were being unloaded. While that took place the crew could go ashore and, carrying raincoats in case of rain and tin helmets in case of air raids, they were 'offered a glass of Christmas cheer out of a bottle kept under lock and key'. After dinner there was more 'cheer' with bottled beer before the night was spent on stretchers in tents, with tin helmets placed close by until a 4.30 a.m. wake-up call for departure.

Soon after daylight, with nineteen passengers aboard, some injured or suffering the malarial scourge of Milne Bay, *Camilla* was airborne again and, aided by favourable winds and clear skies, reached Townsville to be refuelled, serviced by the engineers and prepared for delivery of another load to Papua New Guinea that afternoon.

As such operations continued into 1943, with the Japanese defeats at Milne Bay, Buna and Gona, along with increasing American naval dominance, signs were becoming evident that the enemy had reached the extent of its advance through the islands. Along with a consolidation of its meagre fleet, the airline would see an increase in its role in maintenance and support for the massive amount of American aircraft, arms and other war materiel pouring into an Australia that was now the launch pad for the offensive against Japan. For Qantas, however, New Guinea was not without its price.

It's to the enduring credit of the civilian pilots who operated for hundreds of hours through the Papua New Guinea campaign that they came through it largely unscathed, since New Guinea's peacetime skies were dangerous enough without having the Japanese to contend with. It's a little known fact, however, that Port Moresby would be the site of one of the most serious accidents ever suffered by the company, with the loss of one of its three Lockheed Lodestars in November 1943.

It was still dark early on the morning of 26 November when the Lodestar, under the command of RAAF Squadron Leader William Campbell, took off from Port Moresby's five-mile strip carrying a crew of four and military and civilian passengers to Townsville. Two of the passengers were American war correspondents, photographer Harry H. Poague and journalist Robert E. Lewis. Both were part of a small team of correspondents sent out to Australia by the Red Cross to report on the activities of combat soldiers.

With Campbell as crew on the aircraft were three other RAAF men, Pilot Officer John Randolph Henderson, radio officer Flight Sergeant Neil Evan and purser Flying Officer Keith George Little. It's likely that the RAAF crew had been seconded to help crew the three Qantas Lodestars, which were running a frequent shuttle service between Townsville and Port Moresby. Their eleven passengers were a mix of Australian and American military personnel.

Soon after take-off the aircraft crashed into the top of a hill fifteen kilometres west of the airfield, killing all on board instantly. What actually happened that night will never be known, although detailed research by Robert Kendall Piper, one of Australia foremost authorities on Papua New Guinea wartime accidents, suggests the crew, with limited night-flying experience, may have misjudged their rate of climb in the dark with the result they hit the ground only twelve metres from the mountain top. Wartime accounts of Qantas operations make little mention of the accident, even though it marked one of the most serious in the airline's history.

The year 1943 would also bring Fysh and his team their much sought after resumption of an air link with Britain, which, in addition to providing a vital war service, would become an important step in cementing the airline's international future.

The airline's role in New Guinea and the north, however, was still far from over.

Chapter 20

EMPIRES TO THE RESCUE

New Year's Day 1943 had barely arrived for Bill Crowther and his crew on *Camilla* when they were once again tangling with the vagaries of Papua New Guinean weather and an urgent call to rescue the crew of a downed US Army Air Forces B-24 Liberator bomber.

By now Rabaul and other Japanese installations such as Gasmata on New Britain were the subject of relentless day and night attacks by Allied bombers operating from Port Moresby and from airfields in northern Queensland. Manned by more than 90,000 Japanese, Rabaul's valuable harbour and airstrips bristled with anti-aircraft gunners and fighter aircraft, resulting in heavy casualties among attacking aircraft.

Crowther's original flight plan that New Year's Day was the usual Townsville to Port Moresby shuttle, but as he approached his destination the weather at Port Moresby was so bad that he had to quickly check his fuel supplies and turn away heading for Milne Bay, several hundred miles to the east.

Milne Bay, with its even more notorious weather patterns, was not the type of place Qantas pilots liked to think about in an emergency, but on this occasion Crowther was relieved to find the sky was clear, and ninety minutes after he changed course he found himself looking down on the placid waters of the bay. There followed a few anxious moments when he realised no one knew he was coming, certainly not the best way to arrive over trigger-happy anti-aircraft gunners who had recently fought off a Japanese landing.

Fortunately there were no puffs of flak and he was soon on the water, waiting to be told the weather in Port Moresby had cleared enough for him to resume his journey, when he was told to dump the load he had for Port Moresby and fly north to rescue a Liberator bomber crew which had crashed returning from a mission over Gasmata, on New Britain. 'Ours was the only flying boat available and we were wanted in a hurry.'

But first *Camilla* had to be refuelled, which now confronted Crowther with another problem. The usual refuelling launch was being used elsewhere so refuelling had to be done by transferring petrol from drums, a time-consuming task made even more critical because daylight was running out, thus limiting their search time.

Eventually, with Crowther estimating they would have just enough daylight left to carry out the mission and return to Milne Bay, they were in the air again, heading towards a row of islands which make up the Lusancay group to the north of the Trobriand Islands and well off the New Guinea coast. All they had as a search aid was a spot marked on a map off Kiriwina Island believed to be the last position report of the Liberator's crew before they crash-landed.

By the time he saw the island ahead Crowther calculated he had just enough fuel left to collect any survivors he could find and make it back to Milne Bay. The landing itself was largely all guesswork. With no charts to work from Crowther had to risk running aground on a submerged reef, but he took the chance anyway, only to find after he landed there was no one there. Certain, however, that they were at the right rendezvous point, he decided to wait, anxiously watching the daylight fade with the setting sun.

They had been there for more than half an hour when an eight-metre lugger approached manned by an RAAF signals officer and a native crew. They turned out to be the actual rescue party, which had made the long journey from another island to the south with nine crew from the downed Liberator.

By now all the activity had attracted a gaggle of canoes carrying inhabitants from the nearby island who bobbed around in the waves, all the time keeping at a respectful distance from this strange new machine which had arrived in their waters.

The Liberator crew, led by a US air force major, were in a sorry state. One man was missing, three were seriously wounded and the rest had been injured when the Liberator crashed into the sea. Since there were no stretchers it was a difficult task transferring them to the flying boat, now becoming affected by a strong rip-tide. Wrapped in blankets, the men had to be slid across the deck of the lugger and into the aft cabin of the flying boat, with the ever-present danger of the lugger's masts slamming into *Camilla*'s wing.

When all were finally aboard and as comfortable as possible, a relieved Bill Crowther headed out into open waters and took off for Milne Bay. Once in the air the major recounted how they had successfully bombed their target and had turned for home when they were attacked by a flight of enemy Zeros. Although badly shot up, they managed to keep the Liberator aloft until they reached the Trobriand group. From there friendly natives took them to Kiriwina where they were able to radio for help.

For once the weather was kind and Crowther welcomed a gentle tailwind which helped what was left in *Camilla*'s tanks make it back to Milne Bay and hospital care for those injured, the light lasting just long enough for him to touch down and anchor. Back on land, Crowther and his crew discovered that the part of New Guinea they had just visited was the legendary Trobriands, a land where free love is not only allowed but encouraged. After the day's experiences it's likely Crowther and his crew were happy enough with a beer and a warm bed at Milne Bay.

Within forty-eight hours of Crowther's flight, Bert Hussey and *Coriolanus* were called on for another rescue mission, this time as part of the search for one of the most senior US air force officers to be reported missing in the Second World War.

Coriolanus was being loaded with thirty-three sick and wounded on Port Moresby's harbour when the call came through that a 'flying boat' had gone down into the sea somewhere off east Papua. When Hussey checked his own charts he realised that the position report for the downed aircraft was obviously inaccurate as no flying boat would be operating in that area. It was most probably a B-17 Flying Fortress or B-24 Liberator bomber returning from a mission to Rabaul. With the rescue assignment handed on to Milne Bay, Hussey continued loading, only to receive an urgent call ashore to ask if he could carry out the search.

Hussey was initially reluctant for two reasons: firstly, the doubtful accuracy of the report and secondly, it seemed unreasonable to offload thirty-three wounded soldiers and fly five hundred kilometres east if an aircraft much closer at Milne Bay could do the job.

Unable to convince the Americans who were calling for his help, Hussey decided to go over their heads and approach General Kenney with his doubts. Kenney was quick to explain this particular search was something of a special case. One of those in the B-17 was General Kenneth Walker, the commander of the V Bomber component of Kenney's 5th Air Force. Kenney was calling all available resources to be thrown into the search.

Kenney's concern was understandable. Walker was something of a maverick and renowned for disobeying orders, particularly when it came to accompanying his men on dangerous bombing missions. Despite earlier being paraded before both Kenney and even before Douglas

MacArthur for the habit, he had once again pushed his luck in a B-17 on a daylight raid on Rabaul.

Unlike the war in Europe, the South-West Pacific was not suited to strategic bombing campaigns. Japan itself, unlike Berlin, Frankfurt and other targets in Germany, was well beyond bomber range, and even closer targets were difficult to reach with the numbers of aircraft available. To attack important targets like Rabaul, any large formations often had to be mounted by flying bombers from bases like Townsville into Port Moresby to join the B-17s based there, thus exposing additional precious aircraft to Japanese bombing raids on Port Moresby itself.

Walker appears to have been a handful for Kenney in other ways. As Kenney had explained to Fysh, his own tactics were to use his bombers not only to attack Japanese shipping in Rabaul's harbour but also to bomb ships at sea from higher altitude. The accuracy and therefore the effectiveness of the latter tactic, along with other strategies, had caused some friction between Kenney and his commanders, including Walker, although some of Walker's crews would doubt Walker's own judgement when it came to attack planning.

Convinced by Kenney, Hussey and his crew offloaded their injured cargo and set course for the last position report given by the B-17, with the reassuring presence of a pair of US Air Force Airacobra fighters off each wingtip, the first time during the war a lone Qantas flying boat had received such protection. After a wide, sweeping search of the area found nothing, word came that another B-17 from the raid had crash-landed at sea off Eurasi Island in the Trobriands, so Hussey headed in that direction. Again, on first arrival over the spot there was no sign of the B-17, but after circling Eurasi several times Hussey's crew sighted a parachute spread out as a signal on a high point of the island. Setting a flying boat down in the open sea was never an easy task, but once achieved Hussey taxied close inshore to be met by one of the downed airmen in a rubber raft and soon, assisted by locals in canoes, all nine members of the B-17 crew, including an injured gunner, were on their way to Milne Bay.

During the flight the copilot of the Flying Fortress described the raid on Rabaul as little more than a suicide mission. Again, contrary to an order from Kenney forbidding daylight raids, with a relatively small force of six unprotected bombers Walker had launched the mission. By the time they reached Rabaul and started their bombing run, the Japanese ships that were to be their target had already left the harbour and the B-17s were met by a swarm of Zero fighters. Two B-17s were lost, one, believed to be Walker's, last seen streaming smoke and disappearing into a cloud as the rest of the bomber crews fought off repeated attacks by the Zeros.

With their gunner shot in an arm and leg, their B-17's fuel tanks holed and one of their four engines out of action, the pilots decided their only chance was to ditch the aircraft close to an island and were within a kilometre of what would turn out to be Eurasi Island when their fuel ran out and the aircraft crashed into the sea. Taking to rubber rafts they made it to the shore, and after spreading the parachute on the hilltop spent the night in the islanders' huts.

The next day they heard aircraft engines and watched as Hussey circled. 'Boy, were we pleased to see your flying boat,' the copilot told Hussey.

As for the Rabaul mission itself, a crew member of another of the B-17s would comment, 'Many of us believed we wouldn't come back from it.' In the case of Walker, Kenney was furious when he learned that the raid had gone ahead and Walker had disobeyed him once again by accompanying it. One wonders what some of the survivors felt when Walker, on the recommendation of MacArthur, was posthumously awarded America's highest honour, the Congressional Medal of Honor. Such are the ironies of war.

The Eurasi Island rescue wouldn't be the last time Bert Hussey would have the protection of a fighter escort in 1943. Two other fighter escorts would take place that year, the first again sitting off Hussey's wingtips as he ventured deep into inland Dutch New Guinea, and the second later in the year in a bizarre role reversal, when a Qantas Lockheed Lodestar would be assigned to 'escort' a squadron of Spitfires to Darwin.

Tanahmerah, 250 kilometres north of Merauke on the Digul River, had been established as an advance base to forestall any Japanese plans to launch attacks against Merauke and Horn Island in the Torres Strait. Since Tanahmerah's small airstrip restricted use by any large aircraft, the initial uplift of troops from Australia's 26th Battalion was by the RAAF's Empires landing on the Digul River, but when one of the RAAF aircraft was recalled for maintenance at Rose Bay, Hussey's *Clifton* was called in.

Originally the RAAF anticipated it could achieve two return trips daily into Tanahmerah, but it soon became obvious both the terrain and the weather would work against such an optimistic schedule.

Tanahmerah was not an easy place to operate into. Two and a half hours from Horn Island, its river was surrounded on both sides by dense jungle, often covered in fog and a cloud base down to four hundred feet. Worse still there were few landmarks to rely on, the only available one being two bends in two other rivers about forty miles out from the village.

Despite low cloud, Hussey and his crew had little trouble finding their target on his first flight in only to be confronted with another problem as he arrived overhead: an assortment of logs and trees being carried downstream by the fast-flowing river. Circling above, he waited until a clear patch appeared and landed safely, again forced to wait for forty minutes while a launch cleared more debris from the river, before taxiing.

Such situations became routine over the following days, with Qantas engineer Sam Ames once having to stand on the wing waiting for debris to clear while their fighter escort circled above, conscious if their delay was too long the fighters would run short of fuel and be forced to leave, hardly something to look forward to while within range of Japanese aircraft based 150 kilometres north of them.

Lloyd Hill was Hussey's flight engineer on the ninth trip when they ran out of luck in their battle with the Digul and the aircraft hit the river bottom on landing. When Hill first raised the floorboards to inspect the hull and bilge area for damage they appeared clear of water, but it would turn out that mud and debris had blocked a hole in the hull. When the river washed the hole clear during take-off the water rushed in, and by the time they reached Horn Island they were forced to man the bilge pumps to save *Clifton* from sinking. The damaged hull meant the ninth would be the last flight into Tanahmerah as *Clifton* headed back to Rose Bay for repairs.

As far as fighter escorts of Qantas aircraft go, Frank Thomas probably had the best story to tell as it's not every day a twin-engine civil aircraft, especially in wartime, got the opportunity to act as nursemaid with one of the icons of the skies, the Spitfire.

Thomas's report of his 'mission' sits alone in the Qantas archives. It has none of the usual official section headings of the reports covering engine performance, crew efficiency, base facilities and so on that Thomas and his fellow captains were required to lodge during their days of operating the Empire flying boats to and from the war zones, but merely a whimsical two-page note, headed:

> ESCORTING SPITFIRES—Being an account of a recent trip in Lodestar VH-CAK from Richmond N.S.W. to the N.T. via Mildura and the centre, playing 'nursemaid' to an Australian manned squadron of Spits.
>
> —Crew Captain O.J.Y. Thomas, Sgt. Pilot Millar, W.A.G. Evans, Engineer Schofield.

The report begins on 15 January 1943 with Thomas's arrival at Richmond air base in New South Wales to discover some of the Spitfire pilots were old friends. Although Thomas provides no background, these were the first Spitfires to arrive in Australia from the United Kingdom, on their way north to defend Darwin against the continued attacks of the Japanese.

The RAAF's No. 1 Fighter Wing had been formed under Group Captain Allan 'Wally' Walters, with one of his wing leaders the legendary Wing Commander Clive Robertson 'Killer' Caldwell, a much decorated ace from the fighting in the Western Desert, along with other combat veterans from the war in Europe. The Spitfires followed strong representations by the Australian government to Winston Churchill, who finally agreed to send two RAAF and one RAF squadron for the defence of Australia which, due to the parlous shape of adequate RAAF aircraft, had largely fallen to American Kittyhawk squadrons. The arrival of such a renowned fighting machine was to be a closely guarded secret, however, even down to the point that no reference was to be made to the word 'Spitfire', the aircraft instead given the code name 'Capstan', after a popular cigarette of the time.

The next morning, 'after much fuss and messing about', according to Thomas, they finally got airborne, led by a twin-engine Beaufighter whose role would be to make sure the Spitfire pilots 'find Mildura', their first stop on a route planned to take them via Alice Springs to Darwin. 'It certainly was a great sight seeing so many Spits milling around the "drome" eventually all tagging on behind the Beau. We got cranked up later with twelve ground crew as passengers and an assortment of bits and pieces.' Among the 'bits and pieces' aboard Thomas's Lodestar was Wally Walters' alsatian dog!

After an early start the next morning they headed over featureless terrain towards Oodnadatta, with Thomas noting that his Lodestar's 160 miles per hour ground speed was proving a bit slow for the Spitfire pilots, who were obviously showing signs of boredom. One can sense Thomas's envy as he notes: 'To weaken the monotony occasionally one would come right up close and then slide underneath and appear on the opposite side.'

By Alice Springs, however, Spits popping up either side of him must have been a welcome relief for Thomas as Walters' dog was being anything but friendly to anyone beyond his keeper: 'There was a strong movement afoot to inadvertently leave the hatch open in the event he would fall out. However, his keeper kept open a vigilant eye and he survived.'

From Alice Springs on it's a tale of attending to a series of mechanical delays to individual Spitfires while waiting to shepherd them into the air again, and then a more serious delay at Daly Waters when the propeller of one of the Spitfires accidentally wiped the tail off another while taxiing. 'That broke our 100% delivery figure,' comments a disappointed Thomas.

Then it was on to the last stage to Batchelor:

> Felt good having a Spit on each side as escort. They amused themselves by 'flicking' from one side to the other or sitting just under our wing. We arrived at Batchelor without incident and reluctantly handed over our bodies. So ended one of the most interesting jobs I have yet been entrusted.

Chapter 21

'THE JAPANESE HAVE LANDED'

It's probably fair to say that by mid-April 1943, not much fazed Qantas station superintendent at Townsville Doug Laurie. After all, he'd been instrumental in setting up the Qantas Empire route base at Dili, part of the Australian government's attempt to thwart Japanese civil aviation aims in the Pacific in the months before the war, then been on the receiving end of the Japanese raid on Broome in March 1942. But even he must have been alarmed when he picked up the phone late on the morning of 12 April and an Air Transport Command officer told him that a Japanese force had landed in the Gulf of Carpentaria.

He was to keep the alert a secret, but there wasn't much to go on beyond that a submarine was reported to have landed between forty and fifty Japanese marines at the mouth of the Nassau River, on the eastern side of the gulf about 150 kilometres north of Karumba, a key refuelling stop on the Norman River for the Qantas boats to and from Darwin.

The Japanese were reported to have moved inland and had already occupied two cattle stations, Inkerman and Galbraith Downs, and troops were being marshalled in Cairns to meet the threat. The problem was it would take days to get them there by sea as the wet season had rendered the primitive Karumba landing strip unusable. Therefore a Qantas flying boat was urgently needed.

Even allowing for the degree of paranoia which existed about the possibility of major Japanese landings on Australian soil, it's difficult to imagine an enemy force choosing such a remote, forbidding and desolate part of the Australian coastline to launch their assault.

Russell Tapp, with Laurie also aboard, left Townsville that afternoon for Cairns to meet with the army's 11th Brigade, who would be responsible for the uplift, and it was there they learned a little more about the alert.

It began when a Volunteer Defence Corps patrol spotted the 'Japanese' near Inkerman station; a Catalina had been sent to search the area and had confirmed the report. Meanwhile, for several nights locals had reported lights out at sea that could be interpreted as signals. Acting on this combination of factors, all women and children in Normanton, the main settlement about seventy kilometres inland from Karumba, had been evacuated.

But in Cairns itself confusion reigned. Orders had still not come from Brisbane but the army was insisting the mission would go ahead, so loading continued and by dawn next morning Tapp was ready to go with thirteen infantry troops, their arms and ammunition, and a signals section with two wireless sets, batteries, generators and petrol to power them.

Since the plan was for *Camilla* to unload troops at various points along the coast, Tapp had also procured a rubber dingy from a RAAF Catalina, an essential addition to get the troops and their equipment ashore but one that would prove to have substantial limitations in the circumstances under which it was to be employed.

The hours ticked by as orders were awaited and it wasn't until early afternoon that *Camilla* finally left the water at Cairns bound for Karumba.

With Tapp were first officer Rex Senior, radio officer R. Jackson and purser H. Pain, and it was a Karumba delighted to see them, now increasingly aware of their exposure to the war. Alarm heightened during the night when what appeared to be signal lights again appeared off the mouth of the Norman River. Action stations were called, the troops and the Qantas team scrambled out of bed, but nothing happened.

The next morning Tapp was in the air early and flew at low level across the river mouth just to check on any evidence of the previous night's alarm, then turned along the coastline to the north of Karumba, aiming to find a point where he could land a small party of troops as close as possible to Inkerman or Galbraith Downs stations. There was no sign of Japanese activity along the shoreline and when he chanced his arm with a low pass over the two stations there was no sign of life.

Choosing a stretch of water on the Staaten River north of Karumba, Tapp alighted, but first attempts to land the troops quickly proved the inadequacy of the rubber dingy, which was no match for the Staaten's fast-flowing current, eventually requiring the party to use every rope on board *Camilla* to rig a line to the riverbank. Adding to their woes were the crocodiles. The Staaten was alive with them and several came so close they had to be scared off by rifle fire. After agreeing to a rendezvous at the spot at noon in two days' time, Tapp returned to Karumba to await developments.

The next day passed without any flying as signals flashed back and forth between military authorities at Townsville, Brisbane and Karumba, with no one appearing to know what to do next. In the meantime Tapp busied himself trying to find a replacement dingy, sturdy but light enough and of a convenient size to carry on the aircraft; it had become obvious an attack by an aggressive crocodile could rip the Catalina's dingy apart, with the likelihood of fatal results.

By late on 15 April the troops ashore had found no sign of any Japanese and military headquarters in Brisbane signalled that *Camilla* was needed back at Townsville the next day, so Tapp returned to the Staaten River rendezvous, recovered the soldiers and returned to Townsville.

Despite the misinformation and apparent indecision which surrounded the Karumba incident, the exercise was a reminder of the vulnerability of such remote outposts as Karumba and Groote Eylandt.

In a report on the mission Tapp was fulsome in his praise of the assistance his team had received from the civil aviation staff at Karumba, a common experience for Qantas crews who passed through these isolated stations, only too aware those who manned them in this early stage of the war were within easy reach of the Japanese. One incident alone highlighted the perils they faced.

Three months before the Japanese landing scare at Karumba, HMAS *Patricia Cam*, a 300-tonne former fishing boat, now used by the navy as a general purpose vessel, left Darwin on its regular supply run to islands on the north-western edge of the Gulf of Carpentaria. One of those on board was the Reverend Leonard Kentish, chairman of the Methodist Northern Australia Mission District.

Approaching the Wessel Islands off the north-western tip of the gulf, the *Patricia Cam* was attacked by a Japanese float plane, dropping a bomb which struck the vessel amidships. The *Patricia Cam* sank almost immediately while Kentish, other passengers and crew took to the water with only one life raft between them.

Their ordeal was far from over, however, as the float plane attacked again, this time dropping another bomb onto the survivors and machine-gunning them in the water before flying off, only to return a short time later and alight nearby. Those still in the water watched as the Japanese signalled to Kentish to swim towards them and took him on board at revolver point.

Although a number of the survivors were later rescued by another naval vessel, Kentish's fate remained unknown until after the war when Japanese records showed he had been taken to the float plane's base at

Dobo in the Aru Islands. There he was interrogated and beaten for some weeks before being beheaded in May. Kentish is believed to be the only Australian taken prisoner by the Japanese in mainland Australian waters during the war. The Japanese officer who ordered his execution was later hanged for his crime.

Whether many of those who manned these lonely outposts in northern Australia were aware of the *Patricia Cam* incident is not known but it nevertheless shows they were in the front line of the war against Japan. Comprised mostly of Aeradio operators, marine launch and refuelling crews, their presence at places like Karumba and Groote Eylandt dated back to the first days of the entry of the flying boats onto the Empire route in the late 1930s. They could certainly be regarded as 'hardship' posts, with few amenities and difficult working conditions.

In contrast to large Qantas flying boat bases like Townsville and Darwin, there was no Qantas presence at these outposts beyond the arrival and departure of the flying boat when refuelling, or on the rare occasion an engine change might be required, an occurrence that fell under the responsibility of Qantas's engineering base at Townsville from where engineers would be flown in to handle the problem. Even such relatively short stays underlined the difficulties with handling a disabled flying boat at such locations.

The flying boat mooring at Karumba, for instance, was in the middle of the Norman River, which flowed quite quickly most of the time. This rapid flow wanted to 'stream' the flying boat in one direction while the large hull surface and high tailplane of the flying boat was subject to wind direction, which wanted to push the boat in another direction entirely, often even at right angles to the river current, thus creating a dangerous situation for men working from any refuelling barge or work launch.

The rapid advance of the Japanese to the islands just to the north and north-west of Australia placed the Department of Civil Aviation men who manned the Aeradio and flying boat support facilities in these areas at great risk. This was well illustrated by the department's work during the air raids on Darwin where Coxswain John Waldie was awarded the British Empire Medal for his heroic rescue of those in the harbour, and Radio Inspector Ted Betts, Officer in Charge Arthur Tarlton, Control Officer William Wake and Aeradio Officer Bruce Acland received the Commendation for Brave Conduct.

As the war edged closer, those at Groote and Karumba took their own precautions, secreting tinned food and spare wireless sets in the bush in case of enemy landings. Aboriginal scouts were positioned to report any approach of suspect vessels, although a shortage of communications equipment often meant runners had to carry the news of any suspicious activity back to the base.

Preparations, however, had begun early. Soon after war was declared in Europe, those at Karumba formed their own 'rifle' club which, under rifle club regulations, could be used for the defence of important facilities such as Aeradio stations and provided an 'excuse' for the army to issue each man with a personal Lee-Enfield .303 rifle and the base itself with a Vickers machine gun.

Such precautions were taken seriously. Rosters were established and men stood guard overnight at the wireless transmitter, an unpopular assignment for some who spent a nervous night in the total silence after the transmitter's generator was turned off.

Like Hudson Fysh in the case of Qantas, as the war went on, Director-General Corbett attempted to win some recognition from the government for their efforts but to no avail, in the meantime however, assuring them their efforts were nevertheless greatly appreciated. In a note to staff in March 1942 following the Japanese attacks on Darwin and Broome, he wrote:

> There are men engaged in Civil Aviation who are serving right up in the front lines: pilots, aeradio operators, ground staff and Base

> staffs. In the course of duty in maintaining service, or in evacuation of women and children from danger areas, some of these men have given their lives and others have been wounded by enemy action. Unarmed, without protection or means of escape, they carried on. We honour them.

Many of the Qantas personnel who had daily contact with them would be willing to honour them as well.

Chapter 22

AUB KOCH'S WAR, PART TWO

By late April 1943, northern Australia had become an armed camp of hastily built airfields and stores depots stretching the length of Queensland and, as the vast war production capacity of the United States gathered momentum, the Qantas flying boats had settled into a regular routine of operations between the Australian mainland and Port Moresby.

Of all the Queensland bases contributing to the war effort, Townsville was arguably the most important as the launch port for troops and materiel heading for the war. Here, although Qantas was responsible for its own operational control, it and other civilian aircraft flights to Port Moresby came under the jurisdiction of the Allied Directorate of Air Transport operating through the RAAF's No. 41 Squadron.

Aub Koch and Station Superintendent Doug Laurie had spent the morning of 22 April lodging flight plans and overseeing loading procedures to prepare for Koch to leave for Port Moresby on *Camilla* just after midday. On board would be twenty-two RAAF men bound for base and aircraft repair units in Port Moresby and five US Army airmen.

Aub Koch could count himself lucky he had so far survived the war. Wounded when shot down by Japanese Zeros off Timor in January the previous year, he had survived hours in the water before being rescued, only to be still recovering in Darwin when Japanese bombs fell on the hospital a few weeks later. Flown out of the still-burning town next morning for Sydney, he had spent weeks recuperating before returning to flying.

By now one of Qantas's most experienced and highly regarded captains, Koch had once been described by Qantas operations manager Lester Brain as 'one of the best and most versatile pilots and navigators of his era . . . one of the most manly, courageous and honest characters I have ever known'. In the coming hours he would once again prove the accuracy of Brain's assessment, in addition to calling on all his leadership and willpower to help others survive.

Flying with Koch as first officer today would be Sydney Peak, a 22-year-old RAAF pilot from Melbourne who had joined Qantas on loan only two weeks previously, just in time to accompany Russell Tapp on the false alarm of the Japanese landing at Karumba. It would be Peak's first trip to Port Moresby. Radio officer John Phillips and purser Walter Bartley would make up the rest of the Qantas crew.

While Allied air power had by now wrested much of the control of the air from the Japanese, operations into forward areas still carried the risk of running into stray Japanese aircraft, in addition to the ever-present unpredictability of tropical weather fronts.

The initial en route weather report provided to Koch for the flight was favourable, although he would ensure this was regularly updated by radio as the flight progressed. When it came time to leave, however, delays began to creep in, largely due to a test flight on *Camilla* to ensure engine trouble on an earlier flight had been remedied, and it was 1 p.m. before they were finally in the air. Three hours into the flight they were monitoring weather reports over the radio from other aircraft that Port Moresby was experiencing light and moderate rain showers, but the cloud ceiling was around one thousand feet and visibility was good. Normal for any operation, a weather watch was particularly essential when heading into the tropics as conditions could change rapidly, often requiring the flight to be abandoned, or in Koch's case, return to Cairns and wait it out. But noting that a frontal zone that had been mentioned in the original forecast was not there and confident that the showers were local and temporary, Koch made the decision to proceed rather than turn back As he approached the Papua coast, however, Koch could see high clouds developing ahead, and at the same time reports began to come in from Port Moresby that the weather there was deteriorating.

It was now far too late to turn back and, realising he might need an alternative alighting area if Port Moresby weather closed him out, Koch told Peak they might have to land in the open sea at Hood Point, some miles west of Port Moresby, and immediately headed in that direction, only to find the whole coastal area hidden behind cloud. So he turned again for Port Moresby, relieved to be advised by radio that the weather had improved and although light rain was falling there was a cloud ceiling of a thousand feet and visibility around six thousand feet, more than adequate for the Empire to approach.

Still flying through showers but his confidence growing, Koch, an old New Guinea hand from his prewar flying days, continued west, aiming for Basilisk Light, which marked one side of the channel into Port Moresby's harbour. Once there and with reasonable visibility he could expect to make a safe landing. But it was not to be. Both he and Peak easily spotted Basilisk Light, only to discover Port Moresby and its harbour beyond obscured by rain. The situation confronted Koch and *Camilla* with an aviator's worst nightmare: weather closing visibility out ahead, no alternative landing area and too late to turn back.

Now occurred another element of the drama which conjecture would suggest might have contributed to the tragic results that were to follow. Realising Koch's dilemma, RAAF Port Moresby advised him to hold while they laid a flare path on the waters of the harbour. Koch would later admit that had he not received that message he was seriously considering landing on the water adjacent to Basilisk Light and taxiing into the harbour on the surface. 'But in view of the fact that the flare path was being laid out for me I decided to stay up in the air.'

Now down to five hundred feet above the waves, Koch circled the light several times before realising that continually turning the big flying boat on instruments at such low altitude in poor visibility would quickly tire him, so he headed north-west along the coast in the hope of finding a clear approach to Port Moresby from that direction. Conditions there were no better and by the time he returned he could not even find Basilisk Light. Even worse, Port Moresby advised that although the flare path had been laid, visibility was now nil.

With *Camilla*'s options closing, purser Wal Bartley went back into the cabin to instruct passengers to don life jackets and brief them on the use of the life raft while Koch played what he now believed was the final card in his pack.

During his pre-Qantas years flying seaplanes in Papua New Guinea, he knew of an anchorage suitable for a flying boat between Yule Island and the Papuan mainland around a hundred miles west of Port Moresby, so he set out in that direction only to find as he approached that although the weather was relatively clear out to sea, it was so poor in the vicinity of Yule that he couldn't even find the island.

By the time he was overhead Port Moresby again he had been in the air for seven hours since leaving Townsville, and with only forty-five minutes of fuel remaining realised he had to face the inevitable: a night-time landing in stormy conditions at sea.

Advising the RAAF at Port Moresby of what they planned to do, Koch and Peak decided to use the radio beacon at Port Moresby to help calculate a landing run which would enable them to avoid any high ground and descend through the cloud and safely onto the water.

First they would fly at 2500 feet directly over the beacon, turn south to seaward, start the stopwatch and lose height for ten minutes down to 1500 feet. They would then stop the stopwatch, turn back towards Port Moresby, start the watch again and fly for eight minutes, all the time losing height until they caught sight of the waves below for landing.

The first part of the process went precisely to plan and they were soon on their final eight-minute run, Koch priming the throttles on *Camilla*'s four engines back to a quarter power as he lowered the flaps to reduce speed and began to descend at two hundred feet a minute at just over a hundred miles an hour, the wing light probing the thick cloud ahead.

Despite the tension which must have been present in the cockpit that night, some indication of Koch's coolness under pressure can be gauged by a later comment he made to the subsequent Court of Inquiry into the incident: 'I felt everything was under control and had Purser Bartley bring us all a cool drink, we were all very thirsty by this time . . .'

Koch had calculated their best chance of keeping the aircraft steady under such circumstances was to engage the automatic pilot and, if they were unable to see the water at all, let it fly the aircraft on until they felt it touch. Alternatively, if Peak could see the water during that last phase they would disengage the autopilot and Koch would put the aircraft down by hand.

In these last seconds, however, things would not go according to plan. At one hundred feet on the altimeter they were still in cloud and by the time it read zero their eight minutes was also up. Just then Peak called out that he could see the water immediately underneath. Koch instantly disengaged the autopilot and closed the engines and both pilots held the controls slightly back to ease the aircraft on to the water. *Camilla* continued to descend, its two pilots expecting to feel contact with every passing second, but the water still wasn't there. Then Peak shouted that the water was still some distance below and Koch opened the throttles to gather airspeed and regain control but it was too late. *Camilla* stalled, its nose suddenly dropped and it crashed into the waves.

Koch would later recall glancing at the altimeter as *Camilla* slammed into sea—it read minus thirty feet.

While the ultimate reason for the crash might be put down to Peak misjudging the height of *Camilla* above the waves, any subsequent criticism of him needs to take into account the appalling weather conditions *Camilla* was being subjected to and the fact that he had a split second to make his call.

Now, for the second time in fifteen months, Aub Koch found himself struggling for his life, carried under the water still strapped in his seat, his legs jammed under chunks of wreckage. When he managed to tear himself free he broke surface and was surprised to find *Camilla* still afloat, and himself not near the cockpit in the bow but behind the port wing almost level with the tail.

His first thoughts now were for Peak and Phillips, who had been in the cockpit with him, and purser Bartley who had been downstairs behind them. He shouted their names but there was no reply, so he swam to the aircraft's promenade deck door to see if he could get the life raft out only to find the door jammed half open and someone standing in the doorway helping people out one at a time through the narrow opening. When Koch tried to clamber through the door from the outside the man pushed him back into the water with his foot, yelling at him that he was 'trying to get men off not on'. 'I think he thought I was panicking and trying to get back on board,' Koch would recall.

As men came singly through the door, others were climbing out through windows as *Camilla* now began to sink, so Koch swam towards the port wing where he was pulled aboard by two men already hanging there, intending to climb on top of the hull and pull the raft out through *Camilla*'s emergency exit.

He was now feeling dizzy and realised for the first time he was bleeding from a deep gash in one arm so he sat on the wing while one of the men tied a handkerchief around it then set off along the wing towards the fuselage. But he must have fainted as the next thing he knew he was back in the water watching *Camilla*, now in her death throes, gradually sinking beneath the waves.

Men were swimming all around him. One, RAAF airman William Warhurst, grabbed Koch around the neck and begged him not to let him drown as he had no life jacket and couldn't swim. Koch now realised for the first time he hadn't inflated his own life jacket and called to another man with a life jacket near him to help the struggling airman while he inflated his own. Once that was done Koch suggested Warhurst hold onto both their shoulders for support, but when the panicking airman kept pushing Koch under, he finally gave him his own life jacket.

Koch called out once more for Peak, Phillips and Bartley but again there was no answer, and it was becoming obvious from the conversation of the men around him they considered their situation was hopeless. To calm them he now identified himself as the aircraft's captain and told them he had got a message through to Port Moresby giving their exact position and they could expect a crash launch to reach them within an hour.

(Unknown to Koch and the survivors, however, circumstances at Port Moresby itself were working against them. Not only was no radio-equipped launch available at Port Moresby that night but the first position those in Port Moresby plotted as *Camilla*'s likely crash landing was miles from where *Camilla* had actually come down. In fact it would be more than four hours before a full-scale sea and air search was mounted.)

In the meantime, Koch suggested they should remain together and keep their uniforms on because the dark clothing could protect them against sharks. Unfortunately, his first suggestion had little effect and the group began swimming, soon leaving Koch and his companion, still supporting Warhurst, well behind.

They had been in the water for little more than an hour when the weather began to clear slightly and Koch could make out Basilisk Light blinking about a mile away. Then they saw another light in the distance as a searchlight began to probe the water and heard the unmistakable sound of a launch engine. Once the searchlight passed right over the top of them but to their despair the launch then turned away towards Port Moresby. Koch would later learn this was an American launch that had been sent out after the RAAF launch had run onto the reef.

They realised there was nothing else to do but keep swimming towards the light, but no matter how hard they tried the light seemed to be getting further away.

It was during that long night that Aub Koch's fitness as a former rower and boxer paid off as he and his companion kept Warhurst afloat, encouraging him to help them by dog paddling with his arms and kicking his legs. When dawn broke they were joined by one of the US airmen, and with his arrival came one of the rare moments of humour in the aftermath of the crash when he proudly shouted he had kept himself afloat with his pants!

Intrigued, Koch swam over to find the American had turned his trousers into a pair of water wings by taking them off, knotting them at the legs and waving them about in the prevailing wind to fill them with air, then pulling them under his armpits to keep him afloat.

When Koch asked him how he had come to think of such a brilliant idea they all got a laugh out of his reply: 'It wasn't my idea. I saw it on the talkies a few days ago and thought I'd give it a try.'

Later that morning they came across Peak, whose life jacket had been punctured and was using an airman's kit bag as support.

But the sea and its offshore tide was still working against them. By mid-afternoon they had drifted well east of Port Moresby and were still five or six kilometres offshore when they sighted a small steamer towing a schooner manned by Papuans. Dragged aboard, they were soon heading for Port Moresby where, using Koch's calculations on the speed of the tidal drift, rescue launches brought thirteen other survivors into Port Moresby that afternoon, bringing the total number of survivors to eighteen of the thirty on board *Camilla*. Most had been more than eighteen hours in the water.

Of the Qantas crew, no trace was ever found of Phillips or Bartley, who now joined an increasing list of those to have died on company wartime service.

When he flew into Port Moresby a few days after the crash, Lew Ambrose visited Koch in Port Moresby hospital. Ambrose, himself only just returned to flying after five months recuperating from his own crash into Darwin Harbour, had known the somewhat shy Koch for long enough to not want to appear to embarrass him by asking too many questions about the crash itself. He thought the easiest course was to make something of a joke of it, allowing Koch, if he felt inclined, to explain the full story.

'Good Lord, Aubrey,' said Ambrose, 'you're making a bit of a habit of this, aren't you? I do hope this is not the only way you bath because we'll finish up not having enough flying boats for you to take-off!'

Koch, a serious expression on his face, glared at Ambrose: 'You know me. You know that this watch is waterproof. You know that with the knowledge we both got from incidents of this kind there are a number of things you could do.'

But he gradually relaxed and went on to explain that while he doubted all the survivors could swim ashore, he could see the mountains in the distance and, continuously watching a point on them, calculated that they were moving along at around one knot. Therefore, since he knew this part of the coastline well, he believed if they could keep their spirits up they could continue floating until they reached a promontory jutting out from the mainland.

Ambrose could see the logic but was nevertheless stunned at what Koch's calculations meant: if they could keep up that rate of drift it would be merely another *forty hours* before they would be finally washed ashore. Decades later Ambrose would comment: 'I have never quite overcome my respect for his courage and his outlook ever since.'

Camilla's loss was yet another setback in Qantas's struggle to stay in business. The dismal figures spoke for themselves: of the ten QEA and BOAC Empire flying boats caught at the Australian end when the Empire route was severed in early 1942, seven had now been lost either in service with the RAAF or the company. If there was any good news, however, it was that the RAAF, by now equipped with Catalinas, agreed to release both *Clifton* and *Coolangatta* back to Qantas to bring the fleet back up to three flying boats. Qantas was still 'alive', but only just.

Hudson Fysh was in London to discuss the very subject of QEA's future with his BOAC counterparts when the news of *Camilla* reached him, adding to what was proving to be a disappointing visit. He found British civil aviation still in chaos, increasingly weakened by the war and BOAC itself with limited influence against the dominance of the navy, army and air force, precisely the situation he and McMaster had been concerned to avoid at home given what they identified as the American commercial threat looming on the horizon.

But within days he would be heartened by a British government desire to reopen air contact with Australia via an Indian Ocean service, admittedly a development driven by the military, now anxious not only to reconnect with the Australian end but also as a midway link with the British Army's Burma–India theatre.

When the final agreement for an Indian Ocean service was reached between the two governments it would be a wartime expedient and not a return to the original Imperial–QEA prewar arrangement. This operation would be based on a combination of agreements between the British Air Ministry, BOAC—who would meet the operating costs—and QEA, under which Qantas would operate the service on their behalf for a nominal annual profit of one hundred pounds. Five RAF Catalinas would be provided by the British and painted in wartime camouflage, with the Australian government accepting part of their operating cost, payment for mails carried and responsibility for ground facilities at the Australian end.

Despite their primarily military role, the five Catalinas would carry the Qantas Empire Airways name. Bill Crowther would take it further and name each individual aircraft after the stars that would be used to navigate them through dangerous skies. *Altair Star*, *Vega Star*, *Rigel Star*, *Antares Star* and *Spica Star* were about to fly their way into world aviation history—and their superb performance and reliability into the hearts of the men who flew in them.

Chapter 23

'THE MOST FASCINATING AND ROMANTIC UNDERTAKING': IN SECRET ACROSS THE INDIAN OCEAN

'My reaction is that at present such a proposal would be little short of murder and I would strongly oppose risking crews' lives.' So wrote Department of Civil Aviation Director-General Arthur Corbett in 1942 in his first reaction to Hudson Fysh's proposal to use Catalinas to re-establish the fractured link between Australia and the United Kingdom with a service across the Indian Ocean to Ceylon.

In some respects, with the Japanese established in every landfall between Australia and Singapore and Darwin and Broome within range of their fighters and bombers, one could sympathise with Corbett's view. Even Fysh would have to concede that the concept of twin-engine Catalinas crossing more than 3500 miles through enemy-controlled skies to Ceylon would have struck Corbett, a man with virtually no prior association with the aviation industry before his appointment as director-general, as a trifle bizarre. In addition, in those days of struggle in 1942, Corbett's rejection was safe in the knowledge that there were no Catalinas available anyway, they were all urgently needed for military roles.

While such a proposal would, in one stroke, provide a vital link between the South-West Pacific campaign, Lord Louis Mountbatten's forces in the India–Burma theatre and the United Kingdom, Fysh of course had an ulterior motive. War or no war, he was determined to drive a stake in the ground on Qantas's postwar future as Australia's international airline.

Despite Corbett's misgivings, both Brain and Crowther had done their homework and had no doubt it could be done, based largely on their own pioneering experience in the delivery of the original nineteen Catalinas to the RAAF at the start of the war, along with P.G. Taylor's record-breaking long-distance flight across the Indian Ocean to Kenya in 1939.

But now, even as their earlier plans were becoming a reality, they would have to start with virtually nothing and fight a ground battle with the bureaucracy along the way.

The initial planning would fall to Qantas's Long-Range Operations Division, Lester Brain's template for the ferrying of the RAAF Catalinas from the United States between January and October 1941, an organisation which would now morph into the Western Operations Division, based in Perth under Bill Crowther.

Ironically, despite its impressive reputation, the Catalina was not Crowther's first preference. If he had his way he would have chosen the added security of the four-engine B-24 Liberator to carry a much greater payload across such a vast ocean route, but, as in the case of the early Catalinas, the B-24s were all flying off their production line directly into the war effort.

This early preference was also influenced by the logistics of the route which had originally been planned to operate between Trincomalee in Ceylon to Exmouth Gulf, five hundred miles to the north of Perth.

Subsequent studies however showed Exmouth's fickle weather patterns and rough waters presented problems for the Catalina and it was now obvious the only alternative was to accept the extra distance by operating out of the much smoother, protected waters of Nedlands on Perth's Swan River. Crowther did, however, achieve something of a trade-off at the other end. Ceylon's inland Koggala Lake offered similar conditions to the Swan and slightly shortened the distance, although over a span of over three thousand miles the difference was marginal.

At Koggala they would use already established RAF facilities, but at Perth Crowther's people would be on their own. Although the Catalinas of the US Navy's Patrol Wing 10 were based just around the corner at Nedlands on Crawley Bay, the two entities had totally different roles.

Patrol Wing 10, tasked to monitor shipping movements off the Western Australian coast, had already experienced a difficult war. Forced out of the Philippines by the Japanese, it had been engaged in a fighting retreat through the Netherlands East Indies, losing men and equipment along the way. They finally reached Australia with five of their Catalinas in March only to have two of the five destroyed during the Japanese attack on Broome on 3 March 1942. In any case, strict orders were that the top-secret Qantas operation was to have nothing to do with them, although it would not quite turn out that way.

The various components of the Western Operations Division began to converge on Perth in June 1943, the airline's first major deployment back to Western Australia since the abandonment of Broome in March the previous year. While their aircraft were being prepared in England, crews who required basic type conversion were checked out at the RAAF's Rathmines base under the watchful eye of their former colleague Scotty Allan before being sworn in as members of the RAAF Reserve and issued with RAAF uniforms and flying kits.

Crowther flew into Perth from Sydney on a scheduled Australian National Airways DC-2, while others in the group, including engineer

Norm Roberts, who would lead the team responsible for keeping the Catalinas flying, made the long journey across the continent by train.

Roberts, who had narrowly escaped death during the Japanese attack on Darwin, would later refer to those early days as the 're-birth of an airline via fifty spark plugs'. Roberts may have meant it in jest, but it was largely true. He and fellow engineer Charlie South carried with them what he described as the total 'infrastructure and parts inventory' to launch the venture: their personal toolkits along with fifty spark plugs they had collected in Melbourne on their way through, not even enough to handle a complete change on the two engines of one aircraft.

'Despite this rather quaint situation we had few doubts about our ability to cope—our previous experience with Catalinas had given us great confidence in the machine,' Roberts would later say. 'My main worry was that I didn't have a spark plug spanner with which to fit them!'

In time Roberts would resolve the plug spanner issue in his own unique way, but other engineering obstacles, largely the result of stubborn opposition to the service by the Department of Civil Aviation, would present Roberts with serious problems in the early months. With the passage of so many years it is difficult to determine just where this attitude came from; certainly Director-General Corbett had not originally supported the idea of the service and may have harboured some resentment that Fysh had finally got his way, although his departmental compatriot Assistant Director-General Edgar Johnston visited Perth to ascertain the department's commitments. Roberts' own accounts indicate that the reluctance to assist stemmed mainly from the department's local Western Australian arm, although the reasons for it are still unclear.

The first of five survey flights, with QEA crews on board for familiarisation, was carried out by the RAF in May 1943, providing important data for Crowther, who had by now been joined by Russell Tapp and Lew Ambrose.

Since Cocos Island had been ruled out as a navigational point due to the fact it was within range of Japanese aircraft, the 3000-mile journey had to ensure prevailing weather conditions worked in its favour whenever possible. Therefore the westbound flight to Koggola needed to be operated at relatively low altitudes of between 1500 and 2000 feet to keep under the stronger headwinds higher up, as any attempt to climb above them would drastically increase the amount of precious fuel burnt. But operating at such low altitude brought other penalties, not least a formidable navigational challenge, as it meant cloud cover often obscured the star shots critical for accurate navigation, necessitating crews to utilise every cloud break opportunity to check their position. By contrast, a favourable western airstream on the return journey to Perth meant the flights could be operated at much higher altitudes, often around ten thousand feet, thus improving star shot opportunities.

There was also the question of the amount of fuel needed to make the journey and it was here that the Catalina was to demonstrate one remarkable advantage: its ability to carry the equal of its own weight in fuel. The Catalina had been designed with all-up weight of 27,000 pounds (12,000 kilograms) which Crowther and his team managed to increase to 35,150 pounds (16,000 kilograms), a remarkable achievement in itself but meaning that the aircraft on take-off would be carrying seven tonnes of fuel, a total overload of four tonnes. Even the most conservative calculations showed that at such a weight they would need to fly for eleven hours to have burnt enough fuel to continue flying on one engine should the other engine fail. The alternative of landing in the open sea in such a heavy aircraft hardly bore thinking about, let alone the fact they would probably be beyond reach of rescue anyway!

Such heavy loads also required the introduction of unique take-off, climb and cruise techniques. The normal military procedure for holding the control column hard back from the start of the take-off run to eventually bring the aircraft 'on the step', or to that point where the hull has lifted enough to overcome the drag caused by the water, now had limitations.

These were overcome by centring the control column as the pilots applied full power, holding it there until they achieved enough speed for effective control, then pulling the controls back as hard as possible and the aircraft 'onto the step'. This technique, they found, shortened the take-off distance by more than ten seconds, a significant saving when they were already using a lengthy stretch of the Swan to get airborne.

Then there was the weather and all its variables. The requirement for radio silence meant that crews would have to rely on the briefest of weather information, delivered by morse at a critical point during the flight, and it was here that the weathermen at either end of the route would become the unsung heroes of the success of the service.

Their challenge was immense. Before the outbreak of war the only weather information to be gleaned from the Indian Ocean came from ships operating there, but the imposition of radio silence once war broke out presented meteorologists with a vast, empty canvas. From early in the war the only reports coming in were from naval vessels and the anti-shipping patrols of US Navy's Patrol Wing 10, but these would be of only limited assistance as the Qantas Catalina flights were venturing much further out across the Indian Ocean.

Help was at hand, however, in the form of a special weather section set up within the Australian Directorate of Meteorological Services' Perth office to specifically handle the Qantas flights. In charge was Flight Lieutenant John 'Doc' Hogan, who along with his RAF counterpart in Ceylon, Wing Commander Arthur Grimes, would become the Met service's iconic characters during the remainder of the war. Grimes had been the senior aviation meteorologist in Singapore, moving to the equivalent role in Ceylon after Singapore's fall. Qantas would be fortunate in that both Hogan and Grimes were without peer when it came to tropical weather forecasting.

Hogan, a Western Australian by birth, had earned the nickname Doc at school where he seemed to enjoy looking after the sporting injuries of schoolmates. Known as a down-to-earth character, he joined the Bureau of Meteorology in 1937 and was sent to Papua New Guinea, an experience he would later use to relate one of his favourite anecdotes about the accuracy of weather forecasting.

Based in Rabaul on New Britain, he and his elderly Tolai assistant were often at odds over predicting thunderstorms. Finally they bet each other a stick of tobacco to a paw-paw on their respective forecasting abilities. Hogan would relate how after a month the old local had two hundredweight of tobacco and Doc two paw-paws. 'Which goes to show you can't beat local knowledge,' he would admit ruefully.

Stick tobacco and paw-paw had now been replaced by the more serious business of forecasting intertropical fronts and other atmospheric disturbances which would face the Catalina crews.

The RAF survey flights ended with the delivery of the first Qantas Catalina into Perth on 25 June 1943, and the flight four days later to Ceylon would be the inaugural Qantas crossing. Under the command of the Senior Route Captain Russell Tapp, first officer Rex Senior, navigation officer Walsh, radio officer Glen Mumford and flight engineer Frank Furniss, it reached Koggala at 8.35 the next morning. Also on board were the returning RAF delivery crew and Qantas's Charlie South, who would remain as station engineer in Ceylon.

The return flight to Perth, scheduled for 7 July and the first in that direction by an all-Qantas crew, would be beset by problems from the start. Three hours out from Koggola, when they went to check their position they couldn't find the sextant, only to discover it had been left in the operations room back at Koggola. Without such a vital navigational tool they had no option but to return to Ceylon and the flight rescheduled for 10 July.

On 10 July the gremlins struck again, this time in the form of food poisoning. Again under the command of Tapp, with Crowther acting as navigator and carrying twenty-four kilograms of diplomatic and military mail, they were several hours out of Koggola when Senior, Mumford and Furniss became violently ill and had to take to the bunks. A quick decision had to made whether to return once more, but with Crowther available to fill in at the controls it was decided to continue.

Such circumstances aboard a cramped Catalina and with one tiny toilet near the blister compartment at the back of the plane hardly bore thinking about. Rex Senior would later describe heading for the toilet to find Mumford already there and demanding: 'Get off that thing fast or I'll sit on your lap!'

It's interesting to note that the official Qantas reports of this flight record that with the rest of the crew struck down with diarrhoea and incapacitated, Tapp and Crowther operated all the crew positions between them, a suggestion Senior would take some pride in disputing many years later:

> Despite our severe diarrhoea each of us continued to perform our duties to the best of our limited abilities, and as well as some hours on duty as a pilot, my log book shows that I spent seven hours and fifteen minutes as navigator on the trip.

More problems were to come when an astronavigation fix around midnight showed their ground speed at a disastrous eighty knots, presenting a serious threat to the Catalina's fuel endurance. Counting on the prevailing wind above them being predominantly northerly they gingerly coaxed the Catalina several thousand feet higher until it found the wind stream and they were relieved to see their ground speed increase to 130 knots, eventually arriving at Nedlands after twenty-seven hours and forty minutes in the air.

Contradictory official Qantas records show this return flight from Ceylon on 10 July as the commencement date of the service, presumably as this was the first purely Qantas operation, although the men of the Western Operations Division have always regarded 29 June as the start date.

Whatever records show, for those who were there at the time the service was now up and running on an initial schedule of once each week, and by October, as the remaining four Catalinas were delivered, would increase to three per fortnight.

In those earliest days in Perth Norm Roberts faced his own demons. Along with the lack of a plug spanner he had no servicing equipment, no launching ramp, no hangar as cover for servicing, no fuelling facilities and, as it would soon become obvious, no help from the Department of Civil Aviation.

Roberts partially resolved the plug spanner problem by wandering around to Crawley Bay and seeking to borrow one from the US Navy crew chief, providing the crew chief wasn't using it at the time. This arrangement continued for some weeks until Roberts on his first trip to Ceylon purchased several ivory elephants. The crew chief was so delighted to receive them he donated the plug spanner to the Qantas cause. 'It might be said that our flying at that time was often sustained by the power of an ebony elephant,' Roberts would comment years later. Despite the original warning not to approach the Americans for help, Roberts took it upon himself to foster the relationship to the point where the Americans proved invaluable in keeping the Qantas service operating in those early months.

To overcome his initial lack of facilities for a procedure like an engine change, Roberts arranged to have his aircraft towed three kilometres to the US Navy hangar where the engine could be removed using their gantry equipment, then trundle the engine around to the Qantas base while the Catalina was towed back on the water. When the engine was ready to reinstall the same cumbersome process was repeated.

Until Shell Aviation was able to establish refuelling facilities the Americans also came to the party, although the massive amount of fuel being loaded onto the Qantas Catalinas often had them wondering. When one of the Americans asked first officer Ivan Pierce what they were doing taking so much fuel on board, Pierce, pledged to secrecy, could only respond with a knowing smile: 'We're selling some of it on the black market!'

Meanwhile, Roberts and his team fought a running battle to get Civil Aviation to construct a slipway to pull the Catalinas ashore for essential land inspections. Finally, when several Department of Works trucks arrived and dumped blue metal onto the graded slope down to the water, all that remained was for enough concrete to be poured over the top of the blue metal to complete the job. But nothing happened for several weeks, and after repeated calls to the Works office Roberts was eventually told they considered the task complete as the only order from Civil Aviation was for the blue metal. Roberts improvised by spreading Marsden matting across the metal while a further four or five weeks went by until a team arrived to complete the task.

By then, though, there was an increasing confidence and the odd moment of satisfaction among the Perth group as one successful flight followed another. Bill Crowther would recall standing with Roberts midstream in their tiny dingy as they watched a heavily loaded Catalina take off and reach a hundred feet, then gradually gain height into the distance. It was the tenth service to get away and without a word passing between them, Crowther and Roberts turned to each other and shook hands 'most enthusiastically, with the great feeling that we had achieved something which was going to be of great value in maintaining vital communications which was of paramount importance,' Roberts would reflect. And to conform with the nature of their mission, and in keeping with the names inscribed on the side of the Catalinas, Roberts thereafter named their tiny dingy *Twinkle Star.*

Even today, take-off and landing are the most dangerous parts of flying, when the aircraft is at its most vulnerable close to the ground or water, but the sheer weight of fuel which had to be carried on these flights placed the Indian Ocean service in a category of its own. Crowther and his team continued to fine-tune their take off techniques, largely a combination of throttle and control column manipulation to get the Catalina onto its 'step', but even then it would take the Catalinas up to a minute before they broke free of Nedland's waters.

At Koggola also, special operational procedures were required to improve safety margins. Although its waters were relatively calm, it did not offer the generous length of the Swan at Nedlands, so the Catalinas were taxied up a creek on the far south-eastern corner of the lake to maximise their take-off distance.

To the layman, almost thirty hours non-stop through the air might suggest periods of interminable boredom, but that was far from the case. There were often hours of intense activity, working generally in four-hour shifts, as the pilots tweaked the throttle settings and monitored airspeed to coax the maximum fuel performance out of the remarkable Pratt & Whitney Wasp engines carrying them through dangerous skies. In the early months pilots like Tapp, Crowther and Ambrose, all experienced navigators, doubled in that role as well, while first and second officers kept watch in the cockpit, but as the weeks went by and RAAF-trained navigators joined their roles became easier, although even the new men confronted a steep learning curve due to the nature of such long-range flights.

There were times, too, when the elements didn't help. Typical of the aircraft of their day, the Catalinas had a tendency to 'leak' when flying through heavy rain showers, and it was common for navigators to have to cover their vital navigation charts to avoid water ruining hours of careful work.

All crew members took turns at relieving the radio officer and the flight engineer while they rested. With no outside reference points on a vast ocean, the navigator spent much time in the transparent blister compartment at the rear, hoping for a break in the clouds to provide him with a star shot to check their position, or checking their wind drift.

Since the long flights operated in what could be best described as a 'zone of silence', the most active times for the radio officer were the first hours after take-off and last hours before arrival, along with the critical mid-trip receipt of the weather forecast at the terminal end of the route, when the radio would be briefly switched on to gather the information then rapidly closed down again to minimise the amount of time available for any Japanese station to intercept the transmission.

Looking at their reports decades later, it's hard to imagine there was much idle banter among the crew, operating as they were under a naval overlay from the Empire flying boat days. The chain of command in a Qantas cockpit was an extremely formal affair; the captain was known only as 'Captain' or 'Skipper' and never by his first name, and the first officer was addressed as 'Mister' by the captain. Occasionally, though, a competitive streak surfaced when it came to navigation. While finding the vast Western Australian coastline on the eastbound trips was comparatively simple, finding the island of Ceylon westbound was a different matter, the crews vying to outdo each other on the accuracy of their navigation.

One of the most potentially dangerous aspects in the first three months was the lack of fuel dump valves on the Catalinas to lighten their load if anything went wrong. Made for lakes and rivers, landing such a heavily loaded, flat-bottomed aircraft on the Indian Ocean would be akin to crashing it, with every likelihood the aircraft's weight combined with the impact would crush its hull. Fortune favoured the brave, however, and it wasn't until after the dump valves were fitted at Rose Bay in October 1943 that any such crisis occurred, although even then Rex Senior would vividly describe the hazards of the 'dumping' procedure flying an aircraft with wing fuel tanks loaded and eight auxiliary fuel tanks alongside him in the fuselage.

They had just cleared Rottnest Island only minutes after take-off from Nedlands when one engine began to overheat, giving Russell Tapp no choice but to lower the aircraft's weight by dumping enough fuel to allow him to land. Immediately turning off the electrics to reduce the risk of a spark blowing the aircraft apart, Tapp began to fly in wide, flat circles, a manoeuvre designed to take the exiting fuel as far away from the aircraft as possible; straight and level flight would court disaster with the possibility of a spark from an engine igniting the dumping fuel streaming from the wings.

For the tense thirty minutes the procedure took, Senior stood poised in the aircraft's blister with a small extinguisher at the ready, amid the pungent aroma of aircraft fuel. 'It was a terrifying experience,' Senior remembered, as he watched thousands of litres of aviation fuel pour past him from beneath the wings, expecting any moment to be engulfed in a fireball from a wayward spark from the engines.

Their passengers of course experienced the same risks, along with similar discomforts, flying in aircraft which had been stripped of all unnecessary interior fittings, including cladding from the interior of the hull. Such passengers were a select few as travel in wartime was severely restricted, mostly to those of high military rank, from generals and admirals to government officials and other civilian VIPs. Few women were carried, although one notable exception was British MP Dame Edith Summerskill, the subject of one of the rare photographs of a Double Sunrise passenger taken just before she boarded her flight from Perth to Ceylon in 1944. Crowther took the precaution of arranging for Dame Edith to be discreetly briefed on the 'basic' toilet facilities beforehand.

It was the role of the second officer to keep a check on the welfare of the passengers, but crews found passengers generally pitched in and prepared their own meals and looked after themselves in-flight. Although there were three passenger seats on board, there were instances where they unwittingly occupied one of the crew rest bunks, but they mostly made up for it by assisting with any in-flight chores. The one concession to the appearance of an 'airline' flight appears to have come in July 1044 when the Catalinas would be replaced by the four-engine Liberator landplane and a coloured leaflet was given to passengers explaining general flight information.

Along with a flying suit and fleece-lined boots to ward off the cold, passenger meals were similar to those of the crew: cold meats, salads and hot soup, along with tea and coffee, all loaded on board in a wicker basket. Because of the fuel all around them, smoking was strictly forbidden.

Take-off from Nedlands could be a character-building experience for VIPs, their rank offering no privileges, particularly early in the service when centre-of-gravity requirements meant they had to sit or crouch in the normal bomb aimer's position, below and forward of the aircraft cockpit. During much of the long take-off run water would cascade over the front of the aircraft so they were issued with a canvas sheet to cover themselves, which at least saved them from a thorough drenching. Flying close to enemy-occupied strongholds meant that the aircraft were blacked out at night, but this would be of little hardship to the passengers who had ample reading material.

With such a large fuel requirement, aircraft cargo was restricted to important military and diplomatic documents, but thanks to a welcome innovation known as the airgraph, mail for those troops serving at both ends of the route could also be carried. Developed by the United States and British postal services, the airgraph overcame the weight and bulk factor normally related to mail by utilising a special letter sheet with a space set aside for the sender's and recipient's addresses. The letter was numbered and photographed onto light, compact microfilm, enabling more than four thousand letters to be recorded on a film weighing around half a kilogram. On arrival at the other end the original letter was printed from the film, then folded to show the address in a cut-out airgraph envelope for delivery, with no hint of it being microfilmed to make the journey.

Although close on their route, radio contact with the Cocos (Keeling) Islands was off limits for the Catalinas, but nonetheless there were times when the islands would play an important part in the Indian Ocean scheme. In all, four diversions were made there, three of them under emergency circumstances and one involving a very close call courtesy of a Japanese bomber.

The first diversion in August 1943 resulted from a call for Qantas's help after two unsuccessful attempts by the US Navy's Patrol Wing 10 to deliver two Australian meteorological officers to the Cocos. Both failures highlighted the difficulty of finding a speck in the ocean.

The fact it was so far away from anywhere probably saved the Cocos Islands from too much Japanese attention beyond a naval shelling and regular reconnaissance flight by Japanese aircraft, but its location in the vastness of the Indian Ocean was an important one. Though the Cocos may have appeared innocent to the Japanese but what they didn't know was the existence of an undersea cable linking the Cocos and Broome. To take advantage of this, two Australian meteorological officers were to be based on the Cocos to help fill the mid-Indian Ocean weather 'dead zone', and the American Catalinas of Patrol Wing 10 set out to deliver them. Their first attempt failed when their Catalina was forced to return to Perth after being unable to find the islands at all, but their second attempt several days later almost ended in disaster and must have proved a nightmare for the two weathermen.

Even though Patrol Wing 10's Catalinas were armed and radar equipped, when it came to navigation, it's probably fair to assume that their crews had nothing like the experience of the Qantas Catalina crews, most of whom had practised their 'art' long before the outbreak of war. On their second attempt after searching for the Cocos for some time without success they not only broke the cardinal rule of radio silence but misjudged their own fuel endurance. Not fitted with the long-range tanks of the Qantas aircraft, the crew of the US Catalina realised they would have no chance of returning to Perth so asked for a radio fix on Learmonth airport, their nearest point on the Western Australian coast.

One can almost imagine the trepidation of the two Met officers as they watched the crew begin to lighten the aircraft's load to conserve fuel, throwing all guns, ammunition and anything loose, including the Met men's own luggage, out through the blister and into the Indian Ocean. Luckily they were within sight of Learmonth when their Catalina ran out of fuel and landed, a coastal steamer coming to the rescue of the crew and the Met officers and the Catalina was towed the rest of the way.

When the task fell to Qantas to deliver the weathermen to the Cocos, Lew Ambrose volunteered, although he insisted on doing it his way.

Ambrose faced a series of challenges beyond those of the Americans. With no radar he would have to find the Cocos via dead reckoning, as any further break in radio silence could place the whole Qantas operation in jeopardy. There was also another problem. If he used the outbound service from Perth to deliver his human cargo it would mean his time at Cocos, while they rested and refuelled, would leave his aircraft exposed to the possibility of a daylight visit by the Japanese, a situation which would later involve a close call for another Qantas Catalina.

Ambrose therefore decided to do it the long way round, first taking the two Met men as part of his cargo to Koggola, rest and refuel and then deliver them to Cocos on the eastbound leg. By leaving Koggala at sunset he would be in a position to take an accurate star fix just before dawn and execute what was known in navigation parlance as 'flying down the sunline' to his objective.

With Ambrose that evening were Rex Senior acting as navigator, Ivan Pierce as first officer, Dick Jackson on the radio and Bill Wilcox as flight engineer. Ambrose's account, recorded many years later, offers an insight into the difficulties these men faced in the lonely skies above the Indian Ocean and the multiple factors they needed to take into account to succeed.

Early in the flight Ambrose was concerned about using extra fuel to climb quickly to the operating height he needed to ensure he was out of clouds and to acquire a star shot, but the night was a good one and shortly before dawn he was able to establish a good 'fix' on his position. It was at this point that Ambrose was to make a decision that might make the difference between the mission's success or failure. With favourable weather conditions and now with an excellent series of 'fixes', he first considered turning the aircraft at that point and flying directly towards the Cocos Islands. But he resisted the temptation in favour of continuing on their present track and then turning down the 'sunline', figuring it would give him a better chance of finding this 'dot' in the ocean. After reaching Ceylon and taking off again for the return leg, he recalled:

> From that point I handed over the navigation to my first officer and I took over control so that I could take quick sights of the rising sun and thus hand them back to him so he could calculate them and work out whether we were using the correct line to the Cocos–Keeling Group.

Worryingly, his first sightings had him twenty to thirty miles too far west of the planned track, and although he had factored in the ability to do a square search if he missed the islands on his initial attempt, it was not a prospect he relished. If that happened his options would begin to close out and would mean if he could not find the islands at all he would have insufficient fuel to return to Ceylon or make it to the Australian coast. His only alternative then would be to head for the RAF base on the island of Diego Garcia where he would be forced to land in the dark on a lagoon he had never seen. It was at this stage of the flight, as all eyes anxiously scanned the horizon, that one feels for the two Met officers aboard, doubtless wondering whether, once again, their desire to reach the Cocos was going to see them end up in the water.

Unexpectedly too they were now flying into a heavy haze which was starting to present them with visibility problems and it was then, about twenty minutes out from their predicted time of arrival, that Rex Senior remembers Ambrose asking: 'When are we due, Mister?'

Senior diligently took a quick fix, and in his haste plotted the wrong longitude, telling his captain they were around sixty miles away.

'Well, what's that down there then?' said Ambrose with a large degree of satisfaction, as the Cocos came into view through the haze out of the left cockpit window.

'It was merely a matter of doing a hand flown circuit and alighting on the lagoon to go ashore with the two Met officers who, over the last hour or so, had been watching the first officer and myself very carefully in case we made any mistakes and put them into all the problems they had been faced with in their earlier attempts to find the place,' Ambrose would comment.

In his captain's report immediately after the flight though, Ambrose appears to have acknowledged the problems faced by the earlier American Catalina crews, sounding a warning for such flights in the future:

> Flights which cross large featureless areas and depend for their success on Astro-Navigation should only be taken, as this one was, in an emergency. Although we were successful in finding our objective, any small factor, such as a heavy patch of cloud—a rainstorm—thick haze or a mathematical mistake, could have destroyed a hard night's work and the alternative in our case was a further 1500 nautical miles flight and the job to be done all over again.

He also admitted that his decision to avoid the temptation to fly direct had saved the flight:

> I know now that, with the haze as thick as it turned out to be, had I done so, I would not have found the island. If I may stress anything, may I do so about the method that I used—I am convinced that it is the only safe way to attempt to find such a small objective.

The next unscheduled visit to the Cocos six months later would be the only time a Double Sunrise Catalina would come face to face with the enemy.

In February 1944 Tapp was asked to divert to the Cocos to collect a naval officer who had earlier been delivered there by warship. Tapp was not particularly happy with one aspect of his assignment, which would require him to arrive at the Cocos early in the morning and spend most of the day there, departing at dusk to cover the most dangerous Cocos–Colombo sector in darkness. Sitting at anchor at the Cocos Islands, the Catalina would be exposed to any Japanese air patrols.

Tapp duly arrived at the Cocos shortly after eight in the morning, where the locals assured him that the Japanese reconnaissance patrols, like those encountered by the Empire flying boat crews operating through Sumatra and Java earlier in the war, were so predictable you could set your calendar on the day they'd arrive overhead. Since the latest had been only two days previously, they were confident the next visit was still some days away. But this time around it would turn out the Japanese didn't keep to their normal schedule.

Tapp had finished breakfast and was walking back towards the jetty to check on the refuelling process when a Japanese 'Betty' bomber came around the corner of the island at around 1500 feet. Along with the locals with him Tapp dived for cover in a roadside gutter.

Much more exposed, however, was Rex Senior, stripped to the waist and standing on the Catalina's wing, supervising the refuelling and surrounded by four-gallon drums. Realising the only other aircraft anywhere in their vicinity would have to be Japanese, Senior and his second officer raced back along the wing and down to the tiny tender boat moored alongside the aircraft and scrambled aboard, realising their best chance was to get as far as possible from their Catalina. Then came the whistle of bombs falling and, thinking they would now be safer in the water, Senior tipped the dingy over, 'much to the chagrin of the second officer,' he would remember. But both bombs missed and the plane continued on its way, Senior surmising that the pilot was probably as surprised to see the Catalina as they were to see his 'Betty'.

There followed hours of tension while they unloaded everything moveable on the Catalina in case the Japanese returned in force, but once again the enemy demonstrated their strange behaviour in such circumstances. As well as their habit of operating to predictable patrol schedules, allowing the Allies some safety in movement, often they would not venture outside their assigned role, presumably in this case strictly a reconnaissance. There was also the possibility the 'Betty's' crew may simply have used the only two bombs they had. At dusk Tapp and his crew reloaded the Catalina and were relieved to leave the Cocos well behind them.

The only other emergency visit to the Cocos took place twelve months later when Frank Thomas's Catalina developed engine trouble. Again, as was often the case with the long Indian Ocean service, Thomas and his crew were presented with a difficult decision.

Thomas was well past the Cocos when the ignition on one engine began to falter, and although he had fifteen hours ahead of him he figured the aircraft might still be able to reach Ceylon even if the engine eventually had to be shut down. But he also had to take into account their chance of rescue on that stage of the flight would be limited. His unpleasant alternative, to land on the reef-strewn Cocos lagoon at night, was risky in the extreme, but he decided to chance it anyway and turned back.

Despite a wartime blackout in place, no navigation lights and radio silence, Thomas located the island and prepared to make his own lighting arrangements to set down by following a special technique Bill Crowther had used previously for emergency night landings. Heavy rain battered the Catalina as Thomas began his downwind run across the lagoon to allow his flight engineer Frank Maskiell to drop a series of flame flares from the rear blister. With the flares floating on the water, Thomas turned into the wind and executed what has subsequently been acknowledged as one of the most difficult of all Catalina landings. Two days later Captain Bert Ritchie flew in from Perth with a spare magneto and two engineers to work on the engine. That same Bert Ritchie would rise through the airline's operational ranks in the postwar years to eventually be appointed the airline's general manager.

Ironically, it would be Ritchie who would record one of the rare sightings of an enemy aircraft during the long Indian Ocean crossing. His aircraft was still five hours from Ceylon when dawn broke to reveal a Japanese flying boat. 'I think he was just as scared and anxious to get away as I was and as there was a bit of cloud about, we slipped into it and after about fifteen minutes he was never seen again.'

In the scheme of things, as the Japanese retreat forced them beyond reach of the Cocos, its sensitivity as part of a cone of silence in the middle of the Indian Ocean diminished, but it would go on to be an important transit point for Qantas postwar landplane services to Africa.

In between these excursions into the Cocos Islands, the Qantas operation was extended from Koggola to Karachi—a twelve-hour, 1400-mile flight—to help overcome a breakdown in the scheduling arrangement that was causing serious delays to the through service to the United Kingdom. Still pressed for both crews and aircraft due to the war effort, BOAC could reach no further than Karachi and the interim leg fell to an Indian airline connection, taking two days to connect Colombo and Karachi because of stopovers at Madras and Bombay. It must have struck the Qantas crews as a case of deja vu as it meant a return to a similar 1940 pattern when their Empire boats extended their Australia–Singapore sector on to Karachi.

By early 1944 Norm Roberts had overcome the Department of Civil Aviation's intransigence at Nedlands and the days of towing the aircraft backwards and forwards to the US base were over. His team now had their own building for servicing the aircraft and could remove an engine and send it to the RAAF's repair depot inland at Boulder for overhaul.

Although accommodation for the Qantas personnel was scattered throughout the city, few residents of Perth were aware of the role of these dark-coloured aircraft that operated only a few miles from the city centre. One commonly held belief was that they were heading off for missions to Papua New Guinea, and while such a misconception guaranteed the secrecy of the operation, for some it had a negative side.

Catalina crews were officially on the RAAF Reserve, but for security reasons they wore civilian clothes while off-duty, a requirement for which Rex Senior suffered several unpleasant consequences, once receiving a white feather neatly enclosed in an envelope. Then, while walking to work one morning through Kings Park, he stopped at a kiosk to buy cigarettes, only to be told by the woman behind the counter: 'Go and join up. There are no cigarettes for bludgers.'

At the other end of the route in Karachi, Senior would experience another incident which would baffle him for the rest of his life. Walking with one of his close friends navigator Dolf Nuske down a Karachi street, they were approached by a small Pakistani man who offered to tell their fortunes. For the equivalent of ten shillings the man produced what would turn out to be an almost textbook preview of Senior's life, but when Nuske held out his hand the man handed back his money with the comment: 'No tell, master.' Within two years, Nuske was dead, killed when his aircraft disappeared over the Indian Ocean.

In June 1944 the four-engine B-24 Liberator landplanes were delivered to Qantas and began to parallel the Catalinas on the route, now using Learmonth as their first Australian landfall. Not only were they able to carry five times the load of the Catalinas but slash ten hours off the flight time between Ceylon and Australia. With their entry on the route came another significant company development: the introduction of the 'Kangaroo Service', the result of a brainstorm between Hudson Fysh and Bill Crowther and a trademark which remains in the Qantas operations today.

Bearing a kangaroo emblem on the nose, the Liberators gradually began to supersede the Catalinas, which flew their final trips in July 1945. Soon after the Nedlands base was closed and the Western Operations

Division headquarters moved inland to Guildford. There would, however, be some lasting mementoes of this unique service. Every passenger carried received a coloured certificate denoting their membership of 'The Secret Order of the Double Sunrise' for experiencing the sunrise twice during their more than 24-hour flight.

Somewhat fittingly, and just by chance, Fysh, the man who had done most to carry the fight for the establishment of the service, became the holder of the Double Sunrise certificate for the longest of the Catalina flights—from Ceylon to Perth in thirty-one hours and fifteen minutes—on his way back from talks in London in August 1943.

Even after the war, Lester Brain would meet American airmen who found it hard to believe what the Qantas Catalinas had achieved, considering their own 2500-mile stretch between California and Honolulu the ultimate challenge.

Even with the coming of the jet age the Indian Ocean service stands as an incredible accomplishment, particularly when pitted against the very strict guidelines surrounding the operation of twin-engine aircraft over water, guidelines which existed well into the jet age. By the time they were withdrawn from service the Catalinas had crossed the Indian Ocean 271 times, experiencing only six in-flight engine shutdowns, a lasting tribute to the work of Roberts' men and the reliability of their engines.

Fysh would describe the Indian Ocean service as 'the most fascinating and romantic undertaking ever performed by Qantas'. Other aviation accolades would follow when the veil of secrecy was lifted after the war, although Fysh himself would repeatedly fail in his efforts to gain for them official recognition, despite pointing out the crews faced the same risks flying through enemy skies as any of their military counterparts. Had they been shot down and captured they would have suffered a similar fate. Frustrated, he created his own special company award, the 'Long-Range Operations Gold Star', which would later become known as 'The Crowther Cross', to be worn on the uniforms of those who took part.

Likewise, an attempt by Lew Ambrose to have the work of the Met service's Hogan and Grimes recognised by the Royal Meteorological Society in the United Kingdom also met with little success. When posted there as London manager in 1949 Ambrose approached the society, gaining the impression that perhaps Hogan and Grimes's war might have been too far away from the war in Europe. Instead he received an invitation to address the society about the service and, much to his embarrassment, was subsequently awarded a Society Fellowship. The two men he had admired so much received nothing.

As for the faithful Catalinas? Sadly, they were destined for a watery grave.

Due to the terms of Lend Lease under which any World War II aircraft emanating from the United States were forbidden from having any impact on the economy of the country to which they had been loaned at the end of hostilities, the four aircraft still in Perth were flown out to sea near Rottnest Island in November 1945, set with explosive charges and scuttled. Ironically, as if defying fate to the end, *Rigel Star* refused to submit to the explosive charges and wouldn't sink, forcing those charged with despatching her to fire five hundred rounds of .303 bullets before she caught alight and disappeared. The fifth Catalina, *Spica Star*, then at Rose Bay, was sunk off Sydney three months later.

As for the men who flew and serviced them, many would go on to stellar careers in Qantas and Australian aviation. In mid-1976 Bert Ritchie, now the airline's general manager, gathered them together for a reunion at Qantas head office in Sydney.

One of the speakers that night was Norm Roberts who, in his customary sardonic way, described the occasion as 'The Last Supper'. The passing of time would prove him right. In 1993 a small gathering of those who had taken part watched as a memorial was unveiled at Nedlands near where the launching ramp is now used by windsurfers.

Chapter 24

THE HOME FRONT

There's a commonly held belief that the Australia–United Kingdom connection via the Catalinas and the Liberators of the Double Sunrise service was the breakthrough that would lead to Qantas re-establishing itself as a major airline operator at war's end. While that's certainly true to a large extent, it would be the vast amount of war work the company undertook in support of the Allied air forces that would allow the airline to survive a period where most of its primary aircraft were either shot out of the sky or crashed in the service of the company or the RAAF.

Qantas's subsequent wartime work on the ground had its genesis in the threat of the war in Europe and Fysh's determination to establish his own facility to handle the overhaul of the Bristol Pegasus engines on his Empire flying boats. He was under no illusion as to what would happen if the war with Germany left him at the other end of the globe from the Imperial/BOAC facilities in the UK, telling the Department of Civil

Aviation's Edgar Johnston in late 1938: 'All this company requires is to be self-sufficient in the matter of engine overhaul, provision having already been made to maintain hulls and equipment.' Thus it was not simply the fact that he had signed an agreement to do so with his UK airline counterpart, but he had to face the added task of pressing the Australian government to provide the facilities he needed, particularly at Mascot.

It was a struggle, but soon Mascot was up and running, and although many of the facilities needed at Rose Bay were not yet in place, Brain had a clear vision of what Mascot could achieve, reporting to Fysh in August the following year that within a matter of months they would be capable of overhauling four engines each week. Running in parallel would be dismantling, maintenance and assembly of propellers in a building with provision for four months' supply of spare parts. Within days of Brain's letter arriving on Fysh's desk, Europe was at war.

But by the time of the Japanese attack on Pearl Harbor in December 1941, much of the rest of Australia was unprepared industrially to meet the demands to come. Fortunately for the Allies, a small group of exceptional men would take the lead in transforming peacetime economies into wartime ones. Each of the major participants had their own figureheads; in the United Kingdom's case it would be newspaper magnate Lord Beaverbrook, Churchill's appointee as minister for aircraft production, who took on the mammoth task of equipping the RAF with enough Spitfires, Hurricanes and other aircraft to win the Battle of Britain against overwhelming odds and form the basis for offensive missions over Europe.

In the United States, among others there was industrialist Henry J. Kaiser, who would mobilise the home front and produce a war machine unsurpassed in history, spreading his influence beyond his already well-established ship-building empire to encompass aircraft, vehicle and munitions production. Such was the driving force he created by tapping America's vast potential that a point would soon be reached where US dockyards would be capable of producing a Liberty ship in days rather than months.

Australia would see the emergence of South Australian industrialist Essington Lewis, his BHP background helping to establish Australia's aircraft and munition factories which, along with the Department of Aircraft Production (DAP) under Dan McVey, would handle the demands of US General George Kenney's 5th Air Force and the RAAF. Competition between Ivan Holyman's Australian National Airways (ANA), Ansett, Butler Air Transport and Guinea Airways for contracts under DAP was intense, particularly between Holyman's ANA and a Qantas which, even by the early stages of the war, had few aircraft of its own left. Holyman and ANA, however, with its widespread plant and domestic connection advantages, presented the greatest challenge.

Timewise however, the first, tentative Qantas steps into such war work had preceded the formation of the DAP by several years when Rose Bay undertook the conversion of its own two flying boats into armed versions for use by the RAAF in late 1939. No one involved at the time could foresee that by the latter stages of 1942 Arthur Baird would be reporting Rose Bay 'swamped with work' related to the RAAF, its own flying boats and the requirements of the US Air Force, along with Dutch marine aircraft that had survived the retreat through the Netherlands East Indies.

Beyond the shores of picturesque Rose Bay and Qantas facilities at Mascot and Archerfield, two other locations, Moorooka in Brisbane and Randwick in Sydney, would become essential to keeping the Allied air forces flying during the fight to stem the Japanese advance through the islands to Australia's north and position Douglas MacArthur's forces for the push back towards Japan.

As with Moorooka, Randwick was established by DAP for the overhaul of engines, with Qantas providing the expertise to oversee the work of three hundred workers ranging from former bricklayers to housewives, now playing their part in the war effort. Qantas works superintendent at

Randwick Ern Aldis would later recount with pride that although many of them came 'straight off the street' with only six weeks' training, they became part of a workforce Fysh would later describe as 'the star in his airline's overhaul crown'.

Nine different types of engines passed through the overhaul plant at Randwick, from the Empire flying boats' Bristols to the Pratt & Whitney engines used on Catalinas, with Randwick workers at one stage working a 56-hour week and reaching a peak overhaul output of sixty engines a month.

At Archerfield much of the initial engine work was on RAAF aircraft, but added pressure arrived in the form of the Wright Cyclones that powered the B-17 Flying Fortresses, soon streaming into Australia and operating out of north Queensland airfields on bombing missions into Papua New Guinea. The influx forced the DAP to create its Moorooka facility, like Randwick, under the supervision of Qantas.

Qantas engineers like Aldis, Jack Avery and Jan Aldous, acting in planning and supervisory roles, would become household names within the company after the war. Over them all was Dudley Wright, as assistant works manager the company's second-most senior engineer after the legendary Arthur Baird.

Such was the demand for expertise and the shortage of qualified people that promotions could come at a young age, occasionally at a personal price. When Jack Drinkall was appointed works foreman at Moorooka at twenty-one, he was so conscious of his youthful appearance among his workmates that he attempted to make himself look older by growing a moustache. According to engineering historian Bruce Leonard, it didn't work!

Although DAP provided most of the equipment at the workshops, the impact of the war on the supply of other essentials meant that engineers were often required to create their own special tooling. When complaints came in from Randwick's neighbours about the noise from engines under test, Ern Aldis designed his own muffler system by running a flexible tube from the engine exhaust into a 44-gallon drum lined with wool fibres.

Occasionally the bureaucratic eccentricities of war stood in the way. Desperately in need of an overhaul manual for the military's Wright Cyclone engines, Drinkall was told they were 'unavailable for civil use'. When he finally 'procured' one by devious means, he ripped the relevant pages out of it and distributed them to those on his overhaul line.

By contrast, it was often the generosity of the Americans to provide resources that impressed the Australians. Jan Aldous was showing a US general over the Liberator workshop at Archerfield when the American offered to overcome their obvious shortage of tools and other equipment. Next morning ten army trucks arrived outside the hangar and unloaded air compressors, a 240-volt generator, rivet guns and electric drills, all immediately boosting Aldous's production rate.

Along with the routine nature of engine overhaul came other essential works which had a direct bearing on the lives of those flying on the front line. Early in the New Guinea campaign, attacks by Japanese Zeros had revealed a fatal flaw in the US Air Force's B-24 Liberator bomber. Although the aircraft bristled with armaments, it had no forward gun turret and thus became vulnerable to head-on attacks by fighters. While those on the Liberator assembly lines in the United States quickly altered their design specifications for aircraft coming off the assembly line, supplies of tail turrets were rushed from the United States to Archerfield where Qantas removed the original nose structure and fitted a heavy machine-gun turret in its place.

The war work of Qantas would eventually involve most of the aircraft that would play central roles in the Allied victory, from the humble Tiger Moth and Avro Anson trainers, through the Liberators and Flying Fortresses to fighters like the Kittyhawk, the P-38 Lockheed Lightning and Airacobra, along with Marauder and Boston medium bombers and transport aircraft.

But heavy airframe maintenance and engine overhauls were not the only requirement necessary to keep aircraft flying during the war. Equally critical was the intricate workmanship involved in the maintenance of the calibrated aircraft instruments like gyroscopes, airspeed indicators and altimeters, so essential for taking their crews to the target and bringing them home.

Baird and Wright had started the company's instrument repair department in a tin shed adjacent to the Rose Bay base before the war and, as would later be the case with Aldis's improvised muffler apparatus, it owed its early reputation to that old adage that necessity is the mother of invention. An original operation that had seen vacuum requirements provided by a milking-machine pump soon blossomed after Japan entered the war into a sophisticated laboratory-like function in a converted bus depot in Double Bay, where watchmakers and jewellers brought their skills to the delicate instruments.

Getting the sensitive instruments back to the flight line without damaging them in transit was solved when George Roberts, one of the Longreach 'originals' and now running the instrument shop, placed them inside four-gallon Rheem water heater steel drums packed with horsehair in latex to absorb any shocks.

Roberts didn't stop there. When he ran short of the ball bearing races necessary for gyroscopes because stocks had to come from the United States, he set out to 'raid' the RAAF stores at Dubbo only to find as a civilian he wasn't allowed in. Then he discovered the RAAF commanding officer there was an old engineering buddy from Sydney who not only let Roberts loose on the ball bearing races but sent him back to Sydney with anything else Roberts could lay his hands on.

Roberts' instrument shop highlights another important aspect of Qantas wartime support operations: the employment of women. Along with the thirty employed by Roberts, many others contributed to the war effort at Rose Bay, Randwick, Archerfield and Moorooka. Despite joining an industry which prewar was strictly a man's world, the women were held in high regard for their hard work and dedication, although there would be some interesting aspects to their involvement.

Once, Aldis became increasingly mystified when he noticed some of his sixty female workers regularly disappearing into the women's locker rooms at Randwick. Finally working up the courage to confront them, he found they were shelling peas and peeling potatoes to save time preparing the evening meal at home. After mildly admonishing them for doing so on company time, he turned a blind eye to the practice for the rest of the war.

It would be another woman, however, who would be the catalyst for a workers' confrontation at Archerfield that would threaten the smooth working reputation of the base.

Connie Jordan came on the scene long before the world had ever heard of 'glass ceilings'. One of the most remarkable employees ever to grace a Qantas workshop, not only was she the first woman in Australia to hold a ground engineer's licence but she was a qualified pilot, had four musical degrees from London's Trinity College and taught ballet and ballroom dancing. Somehow she also found time to drive racing cars.

After several years with the Queensland Aero Club, Jordan joined Qantas in 1942, first stationed at Cloncurry and then Charleville, where she was the solitary female engineer for the Flying Doctor and Qantas services between Brisbane and Darwin. But it was when she arrived at Archerfield in 1942 as the only engineer qualified to sign out the company's Lockheed Lodestars that the trouble started. Most of the work on the Lodestars was being done at night so the aircraft could operate to Port Moresby during the day, but when the men learned a woman would be placed in charge they promptly walked off the job.

By the time Aldis and the union representative arrived on the scene, a large group of unhappy workers had gathered outside the hangar and the union man, standing on a ladder, launched into a fiery address to the assembled throng. 'I've never seen such a dastardly act done by anybody,' he opined, 'to put a team of able bodied men under the charge of a woman is unbelievable. I reckon it's probably the worst thing I have ever heard.'

By now Aldis and Harry Williams, who was responsible for the hangar team, could see days of workshop productivity flying out the window as the union man continued his harangue. But when he asked for any man who had a licence on the Lodestar to put up his hand, not only was there a dead silence but not a hand was raised. He continued to stare at the throng for a few more moments then, pointing to a Lodestar, continued:

> If not one of you men have enough brains to get a licence on this aircraft, you'd better go back to work for a woman and when one of you does get a licence, I'll make sure that man gets the job.

With that everyone went back to work.

Connie Jordan continued her career with Qantas at Rose Bay after the war, while still indulging in other aviation pursuits, including entering in the London to Christchurch air race in 1953. As the Japanese were pushed back through late 1943 and into 1944 and 1945 and the 5th Air Force moved further north to take the war to Japan, the Qantas support requirement, along with that by the other Australian airlines, began to diminish, but not before much praise would be heaped on their contribution. General Kenney himself would attribute much of the success of the New Guinea campaign to his air force's ability to deliver timely fighter support from Australia.

Another letter would arrive on Fysh's desk from one of Kenney's air group commanders, General Paul Prentiss, who Fysh had met in Port Moresby in the days of the Bully Beef Bombers. From his headquarters at Far East Air Service Command, now well beyond New Guinea, Prentiss wrote:

> This is a far cry from Ward's Strip—that was fun compared to this racket. I hope if you are up this way you will come in and see me and we will talk over old times.

> If the curtailment of work for the United States was based on excellency of work and general co-operation, your facilities would be among the last to be closed down. I want you to know how much we appreciate your whole hearted co-operation throughout this period.

All told, Qantas engineering repaired or overhauled 293 aircraft, 2814 engines and more than 24,000 instruments during the war, although George Roberts' own personal records put the number of instruments many thousands higher than that.

Chapter 25

THE END COMES

Through 1944 and into 1945, with the twin pincer movements of MacArthur's land forces and Admiral William 'Bull' Halsey's naval fleets now distantly engaged in the costly island-hopping advance on Japan, much of the Qantas focus would turn once again to the acquisition of aeroplanes to meet whatever aviation infrastructure Australia would be left with once the war ended.

Ironically, any remaining thoughts that may have centred around the use of the Empire flying boats would come to an end at Rose Bay in 1944. In January *Clifton* slammed into the water so hard during a night training landing that the aircraft was damaged beyond repair. In that instance only one member of the crew was slightly injured, but the airline was not so lucky eleven months later when *Coolangatta*, with Brain at the controls, suffered a drop in oil pressure immediately after take-off and stalled as it returned to land, killing one passenger and seriously injuring two others. Now only *Coriolanus* remained.

In the global sense, much of the debate about the future of civil aviation would take place against a background of a Britain crippled by war yet desperate to retain some semblance of influence against a resurgent United States with its own plans for postwar aviation dominance. In this context, for the British at least, Australia represented an important consideration, not only once again by geographically linking both ends of the prewar Empire but as a market for British aircraft. To Qantas's east the Pacific was threatening to became an 'American lake', with a well-equipped Pan American poised to enjoy the benefits of a nation which was ending the war in a dominant position.

Running parallel was the issue of whether air services in future should be run by free enterprise public companies or by government corporations, but whichever option was to prevail, Qantas was firm in its belief that any international services should be owned and fully controlled by Australia.

As McMaster, ever the pragmatist, put it bluntly to the board in late 1944:

> Australians cannot ignore the presence of outside competition and it is right there should be keen competition in order that the highest standards be maintained. Nevertheless Australia cannot allow her interests to be pushed aside, within her own rightful sphere of influence, by wealthy and powerful competition from neighbouring countries, good neighbours though they may be.

With the future structure of his airline and the equipment it would need uppermost in his mind, Fysh left for London in October 1944 to assess how BOAC and its government were approaching postwar planning. The journey itself gave him food for thought, cramped in an ageing Liberator for seventeen hours across the Indian Ocean and leading to the comment in his diary: 'Our two Libs are the world's oldest and worst Libs on the world's longest hop.'

Fysh found a London still under blackout conditions and German V1 rockets wreaking havoc across the countryside, one V2 landing just across the Thames from where he was staying. Neither did it take him long to deduce that BOAC was in even worse shape than his last visit and the aircraft prospects little better, leaving Qantas with little choice but to take on the Lancastrian, a civil version of the Lancaster bomber which at least offered better short-term prospects than the Avro York, an aircraft still under development and even more second-rate.

What he was really experiencing was the start of the end of the British aircraft manufacturing industry which, although having produced some of the most effective wartime bombers and fighters, had little chance of offering any challenge to an American industry now unassailable in production of such aircraft as the Douglas C-54, designed as a military transport but easily transformed into a modern civil airliner as the DC-4.

By the time Fysh returned home in January 1945 however, the die was cast as far as his airline's immediate postwar aircraft was concerned. Wedded to the 'Old Country', Qantas's Australia–London link would be with the Lancastrian, which offered passengers a 67-hour flight from London sitting inside a gutted fuselage in sideways facing seats, providing passengers with the choice of looking at the sky passing by its small windows on one side or staring at a blank fuselage wall on the other.

Promises were made that later Lancastrians would have windows on both sides of the fuselage but it was during a stopover in the United States on his way home that the seeds of his airline's next aircraft purchases were firmly planted in Fysh's mind. Invited by Lockheed for a flight in their pressurised Constellation, Fysh knew immediately where the future lay.

Within two years he would find himself in Prime Minister Ben Chifley's office to be told that despite the last-minute pleas of British Prime Minister Clement Attlee, his recommendation to buy the Constellation would be approved, signalling the beginning of a Qantas relationship with American aircraft for decades to come.

For Hudson Fysh himself, however, the transition from war to peace merely presented other challenges. There was little time to waste on reflections. Even before the Japanese had surrendered he was determined to ensure that standards of service would be maintained. Obviously concerned at signs of postwar 'complacency', in a three-page memorandum to his executives and senior staff in June 1945, he expressed his dismay that too many 'things are going wrong. Mostly small certainly but none the less careless and inefficient.' 'I seem to have the impression too, that we do not worry enough about the things that go wrong', although he took pains to suggest his comments were not in the spirit of criticism, but an effort to keep the airline 'moving in the right direction and maintaining its position of effective leadership.'

Acknowledging that there was much new work and the introduction of new and untrained staff there could be no excuses for complacency or 'second best'. Reaching for a nationalistic tone he wrote:

> The position of QEA makes the absolute demand of leadership. This is obvious. QEA are the chosen instrument of Australia's Civil Overseas Air Transport operations. We are in the category of such organisations as Broken Hill Proprietary, The Orient Company, or the Shell Company of Australia, much smaller in numbers and in business transactions, but just as fully representative of Australian National leadership and more in the public eye.

He called for the best services and operations, control and organisation and the 'best and smartest results'.

Warming to his theme, Fysh identified a lack of new ideas and in some cases a reluctance to change, challenging his staff to breathe life into the organisation with new ideas and innovation. The person who would succeed in Qantas would be 'the man with acceptable ideas who looks to the future'. He insisted that history had kept repeating that change was a fundamental condition of existence: 'We are however, not averse to accepting the new miracle of a 67-hour London/Sydney service. We must also not be loath to accept the detailed changes necessary in the running of it.'

In the meantime, the surrender of Japan in August 1945 and the echo of the last shots fading would bring a time for remembering.

Chapter 26

AMONG THOSE WHO SERVED

At the Australian War Memorial in Canberra a commemorative panel lists members of the RAAF Reserve who died during the Second World War. Of the eighteen names, twelve were crew members of Qantas Empire Airways.

Along with Campbell, Henderson and Little, who died when their Lodestar crashed shortly after take-off from Port Moresby in November 1943, the list contains the names of radio officer A.S. Patterson, purser W.G. Cruickshank and steward S.C. Elphick when Aub Koch's *Corio* was shot down off Koepang in 1942, and W.R. Bartley and J.J. Phillips, with Koch when his flying boat crashed into the sea off Port Moresby in April 1943. Also there is Bill Purton's crew Merv Bateman, Herbert Oates and Lionel Hogan when *Circe* went missing off Java in February 1942.

It would be seventy-two years before the mystery of the fate of the *Circe* was finally solved. While most believed, given the intense Japanese air activity around Java in late February 1942, that *Circe* had been shot down by fighters, there was nothing to prove this, a fact which would lead to years of protracted negotiations to resolve compensation issues surrounding the aircraft and those who had been lost.

Because no hard evidence pointed to enemy action, Purton and his crew were 'presumed dead' until after the war, while the US War Department, which had chartered the shuttles, the Australian government authorities and insurance companies argued for years over responsibilities for compensation. Eventually, it would be a tiny clue amid the mountain of correspondence involved in these exchanges that would lead a sharp-eyed historian to finally unravel the mystery of *Circe*.

Melbourne air traffic controller and president of the Civil Aviation Historical Society Phil Vabre had a passion for C Class Empire flying boats and had spent years researching them for a planned book on their relatively short but important history. In 2013, while reading through the *Circe* files, he came across a reference in the insurance company's papers that pointed to an excerpt from Japanese records held in the US War Department. It referred to a four-engine flying boat shot down on 28 February 1942 by a fighter operating out of Bali. 'If true, this was important information as the only four-engine flying boats in the area at the time were the Qantas Empires, and the only one lost in the air anywhere around that time was *Circe*,' Vabre would later write.

Aware that the Japanese government had been putting many of its war records online, he tracked down what appeared to be a valuable website but, unable to read Japanese, decided to post details about *Circe* on a web forum with a request for any information. His breakthrough came when noted historian and author of Japanese naval aviation studies Osamu Tagaya gave him the news he had hoped for.

Tagaya had followed Vabre's *Circe* details through the record books, first eliminating the operations from any Japanese aircraft carrier task force, until he reached what Vabre would describe as 'the smoking gun'.

On 28 February 1942, the Japanese Takao Air Group, operating from Bali's Denpasar airfield, had sent four of its twin-engine Mitsubishi G4M Betty bombers on individual patrols off southern Java. One of these aircraft, crewed by Flight Petty Officer First Class (FPO 1) Sadayoshi Yamamoto and FPO 1 Noboru Ashizawa, had sighted a four-engine flying boat around 250 miles from their base and shot it down.

Although the information jumped off the page at Vabre, he still had to prove that the Betty and *Circe* had been at the same place at the same time. Even allowing for navigational inaccuracies, the bearings noted by the Japanese crew certainly put them within range of the track that would have been flown by *Circe*. But, as Vabre explained:

> The final piece of the puzzle was to look at timings. This was trickier than it sounds as the various archival sources used a range of time-zone references, so everything had to be converted to a uniform reference.

Knowing *Circe*'s departure time and *Corinthian*'s ground speed, Vabre was able to calculate the time that *Circe* had arrived at the intercept location. *Corinthian*, only several minutes ahead, had obviously slipped past unnoticed by the Betty's crew. Probably taken by surprise, *Circe* would have had little chance against the faster, heavily armed Betty with its machine guns and twenty-millimetre cannon.

Following the loss of *Circe*, however, the saga of arguments over insurance liabilities in wartime was made even more complex by the unknown fate of an aircraft which, though under the control of the Australian Department of Civil Aviation, was actually under charter to the US War Department. Running parallel was an equally unfortunate tangle involving compensation for the widow of Purton's copilot Mervyn Bateman in a situation where the members of the crew could not be declared dead until years after the event. While Purton was officially a member of the RAAF Reserve, Bateman subsequently received a commission in the reserve as a flying officer, although bureaucratic arguments surrounding Mrs Bateman's eligibility for a war service pension went on for years, with Qantas supporting her in the meantime out of an insurance policy for its pilots.

Commemorative Panel 134, along with a plaque marking the sixty-fifth anniversary of the loss of Koch's *Corio*, have been the driving force behind the work of former Qantas flight service director Alan Kitchen, who has dedicated his post-Qantas retirement years to ensuring that Qantas staff who died in the line of duty are not forgotten. Much of Kitchen's passion and enthusiasm originate from his own participation among Qantas aircrew on the Qantas Boeing 707 charters that became known as Skippy Squadron, flying Australian troops to and from the war in Vietnam between 1965 and 1972. The 'Red Tail Rats', as the American air traffic controllers at Saigon airport christened them, flew more than three hundred missions into and out of the war zone, at times while fighting took place around them. Kitchen himself did six trips, an experience that set him on the path to remember Qantas's sacrifice in the Second World War.

In addition to the memorial panel, those who died are also listed on far-flung memorials throughout Australia and its near neighbours, Purton's crew at Ambon, others at Commonwealth war cemeteries at Port Moresby and Darwin. Another far more comprehensive honour roll exists at the Qantas Jet Base at Sydney's Mascot listing those who served, their names often carrying awards including the Air Force Cross, Distinguished Flying Cross, Distinguished Flying Medal and Distinguished Service Order.

A closer look at Qantas's wartime involvement, however, reveals some interesting facts about the paths some former and subsequent employees took during the war. Take John Charles Oram, for example.

Oram will be remembered as a flight steward operating on the Empire flying boats during the hectic retreat from Singapore and the Netherlands East Indies in the early months of the war. Part of Lew Ambrose's crew on the jetty at Broome and preparing to board *Corinna* when the Japanese Zeros swept in on 3 March 1942, he received high praise for operating the jetty's train to take the wounded ashore to hospital, only to find himself out of a job within months when the loss of its flying boats reduced Qantas's need for stewards.

Trained as a RAAF pilot under the Empire Air Training Scheme, Oram was posted to the Royal Air Force station at Wickenby in Lincolnshire. On a bombing raid shortly after the Normandy landings in 1944, Oram's Lancaster was hit and set on fire over the target and ditched in the sea with the loss of two of his crew. Oram was awarded the Distinguished Flying Cross. After a short break he was back in action again, completing a tour with the RAF No. 626 Squadron, leading to the award of a Bar to his previous honour in early 1945.

Former traffic clerk Tom Howes won a Distinguished Flying Cross for gallantry as a pilot officer in the Western Desert when the bomber in which he was a navigator was attacked and set alight by an enemy fighter, wounding the pilot and the wireless operator. After helping to pull the two men clear, Howes put out the fire that was spreading up the walls of the cabin, then found another fire in the aircraft's tail where the rear gunner, a man of eighty kilograms, had been wounded and his clothes now alight. Howes extinguished the flames, freed the gunner from his turret and administered morphine to ease the pain.

Flying officer Rodney Bainbrigge Archer, a former Darwin traffic officer, won his Distinguished Flying Cross in an attack on the German battleships *Gneisenau* and *Scharnhorst* off the Dutch coast after their daring escape through the English Channel and under the noses of the British in February 1942. Archer was killed three months later when his Beaufort bomber was shot down during an attack on the German battleship *Prinz Eugen* at Drontheim, Norway.

Others like Charles Raymond 'Bob' Gurney and Godfrey 'Goff' Hemsworth paid the ultimate price while flying on operations in the New Guinea theatre in 1942.

The story of those still flying with Qantas at the end of the war, and soon to be joined by scores of experienced wartime pilots, is a varied one.

Much to Fysh's regret, the remarkable Lester Brain, seeing a limited future with Qantas postwar, resigned to become general manager of newly created Trans-Australia Airlines (TAA) in 1946, then in 1955 was appointed managing director of de Havilland Aircraft. He died in June 1980 following a car accident six weeks earlier.

Both Bill Crowther, who flew the last flying boat out as Singapore fell and was one of the architects of the Indian Ocean service, and Lew Ambrose would fill senior management positions at Qantas until their retirement. In February 1985, on the fiftieth anniversary of his DH 86 landing on a circular playing field at Singapore's Seletar, Bill Crowther returned to Singapore to mark the occasion as a guest aboard a Boeing 747 flown by his son Graham. Amid all the pomp and ceremony of the occasion, Graham would later recount how local officials and the media appeared more interested in his father's experiences on that last flight out in early 1942 than much else scheduled to happen on that occasion!

That canny, fuel-saving Scot G.U. 'Scotty' Allan rejoined Qantas as London manager, then controller of technical development until retiring in 1961 as a deputy general manager and subsequently taking his extensive aviation experience further on the boards of Fiji Airways, Air Pacific, Polynesian Airlines and Malayan Airways.

Russell Tapp too remained with Qantas and had just taken up his post as manager in Ceylon when the Pacific war ended. Without hesitating he hitched a ride on a British Sunderland flying boat to Singapore and once established there sent a cable off to Sydney to tell them where he was, only to receive one back asking him what on earth he was doing there! When he told them he wanted to start the flying boat service again he was given approval to stay.

By now, with 18,000 hours in his logbook he had relinquished flying, and after a spell in Singapore served as manager in Hong Kong and Japan, line manager on the South African route and, finally, London manager until his retirement in 1958.

Bert Hussey flew his last aircraft, a Lancastrian, into Sydney in 1946 and retired the same year.

Eric Sims, who took part in the evacuation of Mt Hagen in DH 86s and narrowly avoided the Japanese attack on Broome, ferried the first of Qantas's Lockheed Constellations from the United States and supervised the training of the crews to fly them before retiring to become an examiner of airmen with the Department of Civil Aviation in 1954.

Steeped as he was in New Guinea's aviation history, it was hardly surprising that Orm Denny, who had planned the daring Mt Hagen rescue and led the Bully Beef Bombers into and out of the battlefronts at Buna and Gona, found himself back in New Guinea after the war to undertake the formidable task of returning air services to the territory. In the biggest farewell ever seen in Lae, staff flew in from all over New Guinea to farewell their popular regional director on his retirement in 1959. He later joined the Royal Flying Doctor Service's New South Wales division until retiring for a second time at age sixty-nine. He died in 1977.

Ron Adair, who flew General Gordon Bennett into Singapore from the Middle East shortly before it fell in 1942, retired from active flying in 1942 and later received an Order of the British Empire in 1955 for services to aviation. He died in Brisbane in June 1960.

John Connolly, who took part in the evacuations of Singapore, Rangoon and Java and wrote in such praise of the flying ability of Bill Purton in the days the Empires ran the gauntlet along the Sumatran coast, continued with Qantas after the war as a captain on Constellations.

As for Aub Koch, the man who showed remarkable courage and leadership to survive two crashes into the ocean, he joined Lester Brain at TAA and although according to his son John he would occasionally recount interesting stories from his past, he rarely spoke of the attack by the Japanese Zeros on *Corio*. Described by his son as a dignified man who was never heard to criticise anyone, he suspects, however, he had little affection for the Japanese.

All would be saddened by the death of Frank Thomas, who had first used that emergency estuary hideaway known as 'Thomas's Funkhole' in those last desperate days before the fall of Singapore, and in much easier times recounted his experience escorting the Spitfires bound for the defence of Darwin. Brain would later note that Thomas would often be the first to volunteer for a dangerous assignment and repeatedly requested release to join the RAAF or Atlantic ferry flights.

Thomas survived the war only to be lost with four other crewmen and five passengers when his Lancastrian disappeared over the Indian Ocean while flying between Colombo and the Cocos Islands in March 1946. The navigator on Thomas's aircraft was Dolf Nuske, whose fortune the Pakistani had refused to read in that Karachi street several years before. As if such a sign wasn't enough, Hudson Fysh's son John Fysh was on duty in Sydney that night when the cable came through from Perth saying that the Lancastrian had not reported in. Shortly before the cable arrived Nuske's wife rang saying she had a premonition. What happened aboard the Lancastrian would never be known but speculation centred around a crossover valve through which fuel could be transferred from one tank to another. For that reason smoking was strictly forbidden in case of a fuel leakage, although passengers were known to smoke in the lavatory.

Lew Ambrose too remained with Qantas after the war, and, flying another Lancastrian, took part in the unsuccessful search for Thomas's aircraft. Ambrose later became assistant operations manager under Bill Crowther and line manager for the Far East but appears to have found the daily peacetime head office interaction difficult to handle, never reluctant to share his often acerbic opinions of his colleagues with other staff, a habit which hardly endeared him to his peers. When asked what he intended to do on his retirement in 1967, his reply has since entered the Qantas lexicon:

> Aaah, I will return to my little memsahib in our home in Northbridge. My first project will be to build in my backyard a large strong cage. In it I will house all the savage beasts and birds of prey, together with all the poisonous snakes and spiders I can find, just to remind me of my days on the executive floor of Qantas House.

Rex Senior, who had flown on the Indian Ocean flights, been bombed by the Japanese at the Cocos and stood guard with a fire extinguisher as hundreds of litres of highly flammable fuel spewed past him after one of his Catalina's engines failed, left flying postwar to study medicine before establishing a practice in Robe, South Australia, which is still carried on by his son David. He died at Victor Harbour in January 2015.

Along with those at the sharp end of aircraft cockpits, most of those who had served as pursers, stewards, traffic officers and in engineering and support roles would remain in Qantas after the war. Men like Eric Kydd, Dave Thomson and Jim Lamb, who had managed to keep one step ahead of the Japanese through Java in 1942, would fill important roles in the engineering division, while instruments supremo George Roberts, one of the Qantas 'originals' from its formative Longreach days, became engineering equipment officer. Ever the sentimental optimist, Roberts, on learning *Coriolanus*, the last of the Empires, was to be scrapped, tried to buy it for a few dollars, intending to tow it up the Parramatta River and turn it into a garage on his block of land. His bid failed and the only trace remaining is one of its propellers, which Arthur Baird presented to the Rose Bay RSL Club.

For Postmaster General telegraphist Dave Campbell, the crash of his American DC-3 on the shores of Vansittart Bay after overflying Broome in early 1942 would be a life-changing experience, admitting years later to close friend Clive Troy: 'I worked out that if I was going to have to be in aeroplanes I'd learn to fly the bloody things myself.' True to his word, he joined the RAAF, gained his 'wings' and continued flying after the war, eventually becoming a senior captain with Ansett-Mandated Airlines in Papua New Guinea.

Attempts to trace what became of Mansfield and Company's redoubtable Malcolm Millar, who helped keep the Empire boats flying during the retreat through the Netherlands East Indies, or his colleague Frank Lane were unsuccessful, although Mansfield itself, via mergers with other shipping lines, continued on in Singapore postwar.

The end of the war would see significant changes in Qantas personnel as hundreds of aircrew and other servicemen and women returned home, gradually taking the roles of Crowther, Ambrose and others of the DH 86 and Empire flying boat era through the last of the piston-engined aircraft like the Constellation and on into the jet age.

Some, like R.F. 'Torchy' Uren, DFC, would come with exemplary war records. Uren had been a Beaufighter flight commander with No. 30 Squadron during the Battle of the Bismarck Sea and would go into newsreel history as Australian cine-cameraman Damien Parer filmed over his shoulder during the mast-height attack on Japanese ships.

Alan Wharton, DSO, DFC and Bar, would become director of flight operations and take the lead role in overseeing Qantas's incomparable safety record, but there would be many others, perhaps less known, who would take their wartime flying experience right through to the Boeing 747 era. Like Wharton, most had come from the fiery skies over Europe: Fred Phillips who did numerous sorties as a master bomber with the Pathfinders, and Merv Shipard who had thirteen confirmed 'kills' as a night fighter ace over Europe, the Western Desert and Malta. But while they and numerous wartime veterans flew the line as pilots, still others moved into varied positions throughout the company.

Ken 'Blue' Shepherd won his Distinguished Flying Cross as a navigator with Bomber Command's 460 Squadron, commanded by famous Australian bomber leader Hughie Edwards, VC, and was posted to Qantas offices in Japan, Papua New Guinea and Singapore before heading passenger reservations in Sydney. Another former navigator, Bill Lovell, flew with No. 455 Squadron, which had the rare experience of flying their Hampden bombers from England to Russia to help protect the vital Murmansk convoys.

Not only was it a hazardous flight to Russia in the first place, pushing the Hampdens to the very extreme range of their fuel, but once there, the Russians' paranoia took over. Afraid if they filled the Hampdens' tanks Lovell's people would fly back to England, the Russians provided only enough fuel to enable them to meet the incoming convoy, fulfil their protection role, and return to the airfield. Thus, on each mission crews faced the prospect that if they miscalculated their time over the convoy they would be forced to land in an icy sea, with probable fatal results. Lovell's decorated squadron commander on the Russian mission, Jack Davenport, would become one of Australia's foremost businessmen and later serve as deputy chairman of Qantas.

Many retained the dry, escapist humour of war. Lovell himself often delivered a light-hearted response to anyone who asked him about his thirty-three missions over Europe, explaining that while faulty eyesight may have ruined his chances of being a pilot, his crew nonetheless liked to fly with him as their navigator on bombing raids: 'They figured I was probably over the wrong target anyway!' Lovell would serve Qantas in management positions in New Zealand and Indonesia.

Bruce Otton also flew thirty missions over Germany in Halifax bombers at the tender age of nineteen and subsequently filled a personnel role in the Qantas operations division.

John Howell, who joined the operations planning branch in the fifties, served as navigator with the Royal Air Force and was awarded a DFC for achieving sixty night intruder missions over Germany in twin-engine Mosquitos. He retired as manager of procurement and supply, a role charged with negotiating the sale of Qantas' Boeing 707s.

Such veterans reshaped the Qantas structure after the war.

Others who left Qantas to serve in other arms of the military also returned, and perhaps one of these, E. 'Ben' Bennett-Bremner, is worthy of special mention.

When war broke out Bennett-Bremner, a former ABC journalist, was handling what in today's parlance would be media relations. Joining the army he was sent with the 2/2nd Battalion to Palestine and trained in desert warfare before relieving Australian units in Libya, then shipped back to Australia and within a matter of weeks into the New Guinea campaign.

Bennett-Bremner fought his way across the Kokoda Track as part of a machine-gun unit, almost making it to Buna until wounded in the leg. Close-range jungle fighting must have presented some problems for him as he'd smashed his glasses on board ship on the way to Port Moresby, leading to his wry comment in a letter home: 'I therefore became the range taker because I could see the target easier through the finder than with the naked eye.'

Back to his old role in Qantas as publicity officer after the war, in 1944 he found time to gather much of the still-fresh material into a book titled *Front-line Airline*, the first authoritative account of the airline at war. In the 1950s when Bennett-Bremner decided to venture out into his own public-relations company, Fysh had grave doubts it would work, suggesting it was too much of a risk but promising a job would always be open to him back at Qantas.

Fysh was right; the venture soon failed and 'Ben', as he was widely known, was back, destined to be involved in the airline's handling of the notorious Petrov Affair, when Evdokia Petrov, wife of the defecting third secretary of the Russian embassy in Canberra, was taken off a Qantas aircraft at Darwin while being escorted back to Russian by two armed diplomatic couriers.

Bennett-Bremner's seminal *Front-line Airline*, along with subsequent works by Fysh himself, would richly acknowledge those they would describe as 'The Toilers' at Qantas head office and throughout the mainland organisation, among them George Harman, Fysh's assistant general manager.

Born in England, Harman joined Qantas as organising secretary in Brisbane in 1930, his 'old country' attire of bowler hat and cane causing heads to turn in the outback as he took charge of the cash box and the ticket book while Fysh took Longreach locals on joyflights. During the most difficult days of Qantas's war, Harman repeatedly accepted enormous responsibility in running the company, particularly during the absences of Fysh on visits to London and to war zones, eventually to the point of a breakdown due to exhaustion.

Cedric Turner's finance division balanced the financial complexity of the airline's wartime charters with the Australian government and the Americans, arrangements which often changed on a daily basis. Along with providing invaluable financial advice during periods when the airline's very existence was at stake, Turner was destined to play an integral role in the postwar Qantas, succeeding Fysh as managing director when Fysh replaced an ailing Fergus McMaster as chairman.

Chapter 27

THE STRUGGLE FOR RECOGNITION

There is no denying that personnel flying and servicing unarmed Qantas aircraft through war zones during the Second World War were exposed to identical risk as those taken by the RAAF and other Allied organisations. In one important respect their risks were greater, something Fysh quickly realised at the very start of hostilities when he tried to have his flying boats armed to meet the threat of enemy fighters or bombers.

While the government was quick to assure him that this would not happen, Fysh nevertheless turned his mind to argue the case that the contribution of his crews to the war effort entitled them to similar honours and awards being handed out to the Mercantile Marine. Fysh saw no difference between those who sailed dangerous seas or flew above them.

His campaign began in the darkest days of mid-1942, initially with pleas to governments in both Canberra and Melbourne. When that achieved nothing he took the opportunity to raise it with Australia's representative in London, Stanley Bruce, and even BOAC's chairman, Lord Knollys, in the hope that Knollys could bring his own influence to bear.

As the war progressed McMaster too, his own contacts reaching to ministers and prime ministers, took up the challenge, detailing in a long submission to the minister for air, Arthur Drakeford, the campaigns which Qantas had been involved in from before the fall of Singapore, through the New Guinea campaign to the Double Sunrise service between Perth and Ceylon and beyond. Comprehensive lists were submitted of every person involved in Qantas operations in the war zones, from pilots to pursers, stewards, engineers and traffic officers.

Particularly revealing is a letter from McMaster to Drakeford in early 1944 referring to an army announcement that members of the Australian military who had been mentioned in despatches would be entitled to wear the award's emblem on their uniforms. More significant, though, McMaster argued, was a move to allow all servicemen to wear medals that indicated where they had served overseas, thus creating an unfair distinction with men who were compelled to serve in their home theatre. 'The above decisions have a direct bearing in regard to air crews operating Civil Aircraft to the forward areas, for in common with the members of RAAF mentioned, these civil air crews wished to be released for service and to serve in any theatre of the war, and were refused release and they had served in the forward areas, accepting the dangers and all that goes with front line air operations,' McMaster pointed out, adding that they were thus as entitled to any 'Pacific Medal' as anyone else.

Although Fysh at least managed to get commendations for some, including Brain, Crowther, Ambrose, Denny and Tapp, in the end his and McMaster's efforts were to no avail, a situation which many believed reflected poorly on the governments of the day.

In any appraisal of Qantas's formative years and on through the war, it is difficult to pay adequate tribute to the role played by McMaster as chairman. His support of Fysh through those troubled times and his perceptive grasp of the issues which would help lay the cornerstone for Qantas's future leaves one wondering what heights he could have achieved in contributing to the future of Australia itself had he decided to step beyond his role as a Queensland grazier and businessman.

Indeed there would be years of struggle ahead for an airline that ended the war with only one of its flying boats, *Coriolanus*, still functioning. Soon *Coriolanus* too would be destined for the scrap heap, signifying the beginning of the end of the flying boat era, a branch of aviation rapidly to be overtaken by the overwhelming thrust of the landplane, now benefiting from the existence of the scores of wartime airfields. Although less than eighteen months in existence, the flying boats had left an indelible footprint on the airline's colourful history.

Qantas' postwar years have been well documented, from transition to government ownership in 1947, to the fight to retain its role as Australia's sole international carrier, to breaking with its traditional British links to equip itself with the Lockheed Constellation, and on into the jet age. There would be more wars too: first the Malaya campaign then Korea, both of which would see Qantas play troop-support roles, then Vietnam, which would once again see the airline in the front line as it faced very real dangers operating into and out of war-torn Saigon.

Both McMaster and Fysh would received knighthoods, McMaster in 1941 and Fysh in 1953, but Fysh's final years at Qantas could hardly be described as enjoyable for him, marked by an at times difficult relationship between him as chairman and Cedric Turner as his chief executive and general manager. Replaced by former secretary of the Commonwealth Treasury Sir Roland Wilson, the first of a series of government-appointed public servants as the airline's chairmen, Fysh's retirement in 1966 left him bitterly disappointed at not being reappointed as chairman. Neither did he feel his Commonwealth pension fund of £14,450 was commensurate with those charged with running institutions of comparable size. Given his contribution since the airline's foundation, it is hard not to agree with him. When he set out to write his three-volume history of Qantas after his retirement, the airline provided him with an office and a typist in another building. Former director of Civil Aviation Don Anderson, when appointed Qantas chairman in 1973, was heard to express concern at Fysh's treatment and provided him with a consultancy.

Problems of a different nature confronted his co-founder Paul McGinness, who had left Qantas in 1922 and suffered a series of failures as he turned his hand to other pursuits, first with a banking venture in Victoria and later in an attempt at farming in Western Australia. In 1936 he tried unsuccessfully for a job at Qantas and was temporarily employed by the Department of Civil Aviation as caretaker of an airport in Tasmania. He served for a time with the RAAF in New Guinea and at Point Cook in Victoria during the war and, married for the second time, returned to Western Australia in 1951 to grow tobacco on a soldier settlement block near Albany. Suffering kidney and heart problems, he was admitted to hospital where he died of a heart attack in January 1952. Only the priest, his first wife and his daughter Pauline attended his burial in a Repatriation Department grave at Karrakatta in Perth. Fysh would never fail to acknowledge him as his 'co-founder' whenever Qantas's early days were mentioned, and arranged for Qantas to pay for and erect a memorial headstone on his old comrade's grave.

ACKNOWLEDGEMENTS

So many people helped with the work involved in this book that it is impossible to name them all and to attempt to do so would most likely lead to accidentally overlooking several who added much to the story. Their contributions were all the more important because nearly all of those who took part in these events are no longer with us and although some were given the opportunity to put their experiences down on tape or on paper, many of them left little beyond some fading black and white photos and sketchy diary notes.

That aside, the fact is this book could not have been written without the assistance of Phil Vabre, president of the Melbourne-based Civil Aviation Historical Society, who has spent years documenting the history of the Empire flying boats into a dossier that contains several hundred thousand words with the aim of producing a book of his own. Nothing I can say could adequately express my appreciation of his generosity. His extensive research, his attention to detail, his passion for the subject deserves that one day his own work will grace the coffee tables of anyone interested in this exciting era of aviation. Aviation historians such as Vabre ensure that history survives the changes in corporate culture that often lead to a diminishing interest in the past beyond what occasionally assists in publicising an anniversary or some such event that might add to a company's marketing value.

Sadly, what happens in between is often unrecorded and is at risk of being lost with the passage of time. Here, once again, Hudson Fysh is worthy of mention. During his long involvement with the airline he co-founded, Fysh's belief that Qantas was a unique organisation in Australia's development as a nation resulted in his insistence that photographs and records be taken of significant landmarks, thus ensuring they would be available for future reference. And due to the foresight of his son John, many of Hudson Fysh's own papers now reside in the Mitchell Library. I am also indebted to John Fysh for his often sage advice, along with his unique perspective not only of his father but of the Qantas of those days.

It was my good fortune to once again have the unstinting help of curator of the Qantas Heritage Collection David Crotty to whom I owe a great debt.

E. 'Ben' Bennett-Bremner's little known *Front-line Airline* published in 1944, proved an invaluable source. Bennett-Bremner's work, written at a time when the war was not yet over and its consequences still raw, allowed him access to a whole range of files, some of which, despite the best preservation efforts of those who followed him at Qantas, no longer exist. *Front-line Airline*'s appendices alone, providing details of operations, individual missions and who flew them, were of inestimable value and helped fill the gaps. Equally significant was Fysh's own personal account, *Qantas at War*. Published in 1968, it drew on his own recollections and diary notes and was invaluable in providing an understanding of the formidable challenges facing his airline in those desperate years.

Aub Koch's son John and many other descendants of those days were generous with their time and their willingness to share any memories and photographs, as was that determined band of historians, including Kevin Gomm and Dion Marinas, who have kept the important aspects of the Broome attack alive before they slipped from our grasp. To these and the scores of others who were so generous with their time, my sincere thanks. Also to former Qantas Flight Service Director Alan Kitchen for his knowledge of Qantas's wartime involvement.

From the outset, however, none of it would have seen the light of day without the enthusiasm of Rebecca Kaiser and her team at Allen & Unwin and their belief that the project was worthwhile. My thanks, too, to editor Simone Ford who somehow managed to translate the limited prose of an old aviation writer in a much more readable form.

Once again I benefited from the support of my family: wife Jose, who tolerated the wearying months as a distracted mind focused on events that took place so long ago; son Steven and daughters Suzanne and Frances, who not only assisted in the research but were a constant source of encouragement. My one wish is that grandson Benjamin will one day read about the courageous deeds of a remarkable group of men and women.

Appendix

QANTAS STAFF CASUALTIES

While serving with the company during World War II

Ambrose, L.R.	Captain	Injured
Bartley, W.R.	Purser	Missing
Bateman, M.W.	First Officer	Missing
Campbell, W.G.	Captain	Killed
Cruickshank, W.G.	Purser	Killed
Elphick, S.C.	Steward	Killed
Gibbs, W.J.	Purser	Injured
Henderson, J.R.F.	First Officer	Killed
Hogan, L.J.	Purser	Missing
Koch, A.A.	Captain	Injured
Little, K.G.	Traffic Clerk	Killed
Marshall, L.S.	First Officer	Killed
Martin, J.R.	First Officer	Injured
Martin, J.S.	Steward	Injured

Morris, J.	Traffic Clerk	Injured
Oates, H.G.A.	Radio Officer	Missing
Patterson, A.S.	Radio Officer	Killed
Phillips, T.J.	Radio Officer	Missing
Purton, W.B.	Acting Captain	Missing
Swaffield, C.H.C.	Captain	Killed
Tapp, R.B.	Captain	Injured

Killed while serving with the Armed Forces during World War II

Archer, R.B.	DFC	F/O	RAAF
Arkinson, W.E.		F/Sgt	RAAF
Doepel, J.		S/Pt	RAAF
Grimley, K.R.		S/Obs	RAAF
Gurney, C.R.	AFC	S/Ldr	RAAF
Hemsworth, G.E.	AFC	S/Ldr	RAAF
Horner, H.V.		F/Lt	RAAF
Johnson, J.		W/O	RAAF
Sharkey, R.B.		S/Obs	RAAF
Sloan, L.J.		P/O	RAAF

BIBLIOGRAPHY

Allan, G.U., & Shearman, E., *Scotty Allan: Australia's Flying Scotsman*, Clarion Press, Sydney, 1992

Bennett-Bremner, E., *Front-line Airline: The war story of Qantas Empire Airways Limited*, Angus & Robertson, Sydney, 1944

Byrnes, P., *Qantas by George!*, Watermark Press, Sydney, 2000

Fysh, H., *Qantas at War*, Angus & Robertson, Sydney, 1968

Gillison, D., *Royal Australian Air Force 1939–1942*, Australian War Memorial, Canberra, 1962

Gunn J., *Challenging Horizons: Qantas 1939*–1954, University of Queensland Press, St Lucia, 1987

Hunt, D., *Carriages to Catalinas: Captain Orm Denny, 1899–1977*, D. Hunt, The Gap, 1999

Jillett, L., *Moresby's Few: Being an account of the activities of No. 32 Squadron in New Guinea in 1942*, North Western Courier, Narrabri, 1945

Johnston, M., *Whispering Death*, Allen & Unwin, Sydney, 2011

Leonard, B., *A Tradition of Integrity: The story of Qantas engineering and maintenance*, UNSW Press, Sydney, 1994

Lewis, T., & Ingham, P., *Zero Hour in Broome*, Avonmore Books, Kent Town, 2010

Lock, C., *Finished with Engines: The story of Qantas' longhaul flight engineers 1941–2009*, Colin Lock, Sydney, 2013

Lockwood, D., *Australia's Pearl Harbour: Darwin, 1942*, Cassell Australia, Melbourne, 1966

Paull, R., *Retreat from Kokoda: The Australian campaign in New Guinea 1942*, William Heinemann Australia, Richmond, 1982

Penrose, H., *Wings Across the World: Pictorial history of British Airways*, Cassell, London, 1980

Prime, M.W., *Broome's One Day War: The story of the Japanese raid on Broome*, Shire of Broome [for Broome Historical Society], Broome, 1992

Robertson, J., *Australia at War 1939–1945*, Heinemann, Melbourne, 1981

Searle, R., *The Man Who Saved Smithy: Fighter pilot, pioneer aviator, hero: the life of Sir Gordon Taylor MC, GC*, Allen & Unwin, Sydney, 2015

Shaw, I.W., *The Ghosts of Roebuck Bay*, Pan Macmillan, Sydney, 2014

Sinclair, J., *Wings of Gold: How the aeroplane developed New Guinea*, Pacific Publications, Sydney, 1978

Vincent, D., *The RAAF Hudson Story*, Book 2, Vincent Aviation, Highbury, 2010

Other sources

Peter Malone, 'Spitfires Over Australia', www.spitfireassociation.com.au/spitfire-australia/

Interviews Lew Ambrose, Russell Tapp, Lester Brain held in the National Library of Australia

www.ozatwar.com

www.pacificwrecks.com

INDEX